Leadership for Change and School Reform

International perspectives

Edited by Kathryn A. Riley
and Karen Seashore Louis

London and New York

First published 2000 by RoutledgeFalmer
11 New Fetter Lane, London EC4P 4EE

Simultaneously published in the USA and Canada
by Routledge Falmer
29 West 35th Street, New York, NY 10001

RoutledgeFalmer is an imprint of the Taylor & Francis Group

© 2000 Kathryn A. Riley & Karen Seashore Louis

While the publishers have made every effort to contact the copyright
holders of previously published material in this volume, they would be
grateful to hear from any they were unable to contact.

Typeset in Galliard by Exe Valley Dataset Ltd, Exeter
Printed and bound in Great Britain by
T J International Ltd, Padstow, Cornwall

British Library Cataloguing in Publication Data
A catalogue record for this book is available
from the British Library

Library of Congress Cataloging in Publication Data

Riley, Kathryn A.
  Leadership for learning : international perspectives on leadership for change and school
reform / Kathryn A. Riley & Karen Seashore Louis.
    p. cm.
  Includes bibliographical references (p.)and index.
  ISBN 0-415-22792-5 -- ISBN 0-415-22793-3 (pbk.)
    1. Educational leadership. 2. Educational change. I. Louis, Karen Seashore. II. Title.

 LB2806 .R565 2000
 371.2--dc21

                                                         00-036886

ISBN 0–415–22792–5 (hbk)
ISBN 0–415–22793–3 (pbk)

Contents

Tables and figures

Tables

Figures

Contributors

John Bangs has worked for the National Union of Teachers since 1990, initially as Principal Officer with responsibility for Special Education and the National Curriculum, and more recently as Assistant Secretary, Education and Equal Opportunities. Before joining the NUT as an officer, he taught for nearly twenty years in Special and Secondary Schools in Tower Hamlets, London. Between 1986 and 1990 he was a Teacher Member representative on the Inner London Education Authority.

Kathryn M. Borman is Associate Director of the David C. Anchin Center and Professor of Anthropology at the University of South Florida. She has an ongoing interest in policy related to school reform and is currently working on a National Science Foundation project investigating the NSF's 'Urban Systemic Initiative' in four cities – Chicago, El Paso, Memphis and Miami. She is the author or editor of twenty books including, most recently, *Ethnic Diversity* in Communities and Schools (Ablex, 1998).

Brian J. Caldwell is Professor and Dean of Education at the University of Melbourne. He is co-author of several books that have helped guide educational reform in a number of countries, most notably the Falmer Press trilogy on self-managing schools with Jim Spinks: *The Self-Managing School* (1988), *Leading the Self-Managing School* (1992) and *Beyond the Self-Managing School* (1998). His international work includes presentations, projects and other professional assignments in Africa, the Arab States, East Asia, Europe, North America South-East Asia and the Pacific Rim, with several assignments for OECD, UNESCO, World Bank and the Asia Development Bank. He is a Fellow of the Australian College of Education and the Australian Council for Educational Administration. He was President of ACEA from 1990 to 1993 and was awarded its Gold Medal in 1994.

Jim Docking is an Associate Fellow at the Centre for Educational Management, the University of Surrey Roehampton, where he was previously Chair of the School of Education. Dr Docking was a member of the Roehampton team which carried out a comparative study on local education authorities and provision for children with Special Educational Needs, and is a member of the current Roehampton team on 'The role and effectiveness of the LEA', leading on data analysis. Jim has written extensively, particularly in the field of educational policy, managing classroom behaviour, exclusion from school and parental involvement in education. He is editor of *New Labour's Policies for Schools,* to be published by David Fulton in January 2000.

John Fitz is Reader in Education in the School of Social Sciences, Cardiff University. He has undertaken a number of funded projects in the analysis of education policy in the UK which include studies of the assisted places scheme, grant-maintained schools policy and school inspection. In addition, he has also co-directed research into training for multi-skilling in the UK and Germany and comparative research on the impact of assessment systems on teaching practices in the UK and the USA. His current research includes the study of the impact of educational markets on schools and an investigation of the National Grid for Learning.

Janet C. Fairman is a Research Associate at the Center for Educational Policy Analysis in New Jersey, at Rutgers University's Graduate School of Education. She recently completed her PhD in Educational Policy at Rutgers, focusing on middle-school mathematics teachers' beliefs about mathematics, national standards and assessment, and the influence of beliefs on classroom practice. She is currently conducting an evaluation of innovative, school-based programmes and school-community partnerships (such as school to career initiatives) in a low-income, urban district in New Jersey.

William A. Firestone is Professor of Educational Policy and Director of Research and Development at Rutgers Univesity's Graduate School of Education in New Brunswick, New Jersey. For the last twenty-five years he has been studying the effect of policy on teaching and how that effect is mediated by the actions of administrators. He is currently directing a study of the effects of New Jersey's state standards and assessments on mathematics and science teaching in elementary schools. He is also conducting a case study of a school–university collaborative.

Edward Glickman is an Associate Dean in the College of Education at the University of South Florida and Professor of Educational Administration. As a former superintendent, he is interested in leadership issues at all levels in the educational system.

Allyson Haag and **Judith Rosenberg** are graduate students in the Applied Anthropology programme at the University of South Florida. Both have carried out fieldwork at Celebration School and are interested in school culture change.

Alma Harris is Senior Lecturer in Education, University of Nottingham, and Co-Director of the Centre for Teacher and School Development. Her professional interests are in the area of educational management and teacher development. She has recently completed an evaluative project for the UK Department for Employment and Education. Publications include, *Teaching and Learning in the Effective School* (London Arena Press, 1998), *Creating the Conditions for Classroom Improvement* with D. Hopkins, M. West. M. Ainscow and J. Beresford (David Fulton Publishers, 1997).

David Hopkins is Professor of Education and Chair of the School of Education at the University of Nottingham. David is a long time consultant to the OECD on School Improvement and Teacher Quality and has consulted in some twenty countries on school development issues. He was involved in the evaluation of the DES 'School Teacher Appraisal Project', was Co-Director of the DES 'School Development Plans Project', and the ESRC 'Mapping the Process of Change in Schools' research project. David is currently Co-Director of the 'Improving the Quality of Education for All' (IQEA) collaborative school improvement network and is principal investigator on six other national and international research projects. He has published widely in the area of school improvement.

David Jackson has been the Headteacher at Sharnbrook Upper School and Community College, Bedfordshire for some ten years. Over that time, the school has almost doubled in size, and currently embraces a community with more that 1,500 students and 100-plus teachers. In recent years, he has held Visiting Scholar status at the School of Education, University of Cambridge, where he contributes regularly to teaching and research activities. He is currently working with Mel West on a study of Secondary Headship.

Doris Jantzi is Senior Research Officer in the Centre for Leadership Development at the Ontario Institute for Studies in Education of the University of Toronto. Her research interests include policy development, school improvement processes, and educational leadership.

Lisa Jones is doctoral student in Educational Policy and Administration at the University of Minnesota, and a research assistant at the Center for Applied Research and Educational Improvement. Her research focuses on issues of values in schools and higher education. Her current research is on conflict of interest and consulting among university faculty.

Kenneth Leithwood is Professor of Educational Administration and Director of the Centre for Leadership Development, Ontario Institute for Studies In Education, University of Toronto. His specialities are leadership, school improvement and organisational design. He has researched, published, and consulted widely in these areas. He is the senior editor of the *International Handbook of Educational Leadership and Administration* (Kluwer, 1996). His most recent books include *Changing Leadership for Changing Times* (Open University Press, in press) and *Organizational Learning In Schools* (Swets, 1999) co-edited with Karen Seashore Louis.

Karen Seashore Louis (co-editor) is currently Director of the Center for Applied Research and Educational Improvement and Professor of Educational Policy and Administration at the University of Minnesota. Her research and teaching interests focus on educational reform, knowledge use in schools and universities, and educational institutions as workplaces. Her research in K-12 education has focused on school improvement, educational reform and knowledge use in schools. Recent publications address the development of teachers' work in schools, the role of the district in school reform, urban education, comparative educational reform policies, the changing role of the principalship, and organisational learning.

John MacBeath is Professor and Director of the Quality in Education Centre, University of Strathclyde, Scotland. He has written and re-searched extensively in the areas of school evaluation and school improvement and is a member of the UK Government's Task Force on Standards. He is the editor of *Effective School Leadership, Responding to Change* (Chapman, 1998) and author of *Schools Speak for Themselves* (Routledge, 1998).

Angus MacDonald started teaching in 1969 in Glasgow. In 1972, he moved to a guidance post in Paisley and through senior management posts in Kilmarnock and Barrhead, to headship in Gourock High School, in 1986. He was later seconded for two years as Regional Management Training Consultant and since 1996 has been Head of Service at Inverclyde.

Lejf Moos is from the Royal Danish School of Educational Studies where he is Associate Professor and Director of the Research Centre for School Leadership, School Development and School Evaluation (CLUE). He has researched in many areas of leadership and was a major contributor to *Effective School Leadership, Responding to Change* edited by John MacBeath (Chapman, 1998). He is interested in school development and school evaluation and has published widely, athough mostly in Danish.

Kathryn Riley (co-editor) is Professor and Director of the Centre for Educational Management at the University of Surrey Roehampton, and Knowledge Co-ordinator of the World Bank's 'Effective Schools and Teachers' Thematic Group. She has researched and written on issues of leadership, management and organisational change. She has published widely and her most recent book, *Whose School is it Anyway?* (Falmer

Press, 1998), has been acclaimed as a lively and challenging book. Other publications include *Quality and Equality: Promoting Opportunities in Schools* (Cassell, 1994) and *Measuring Quality: Education Indicators, United Kingdom and International Perspectives*, which she co-authored with the late Desmond Nuttall (Falmer Press, 1994).

David Rowles is Principal Researcher at the Centre for Educational Management, the University of Surrey Roehampton. Before joining Roehampton, he was Senior Inspector of Schools in the London Borough of Merton, where he concentrated on management issues and professional development. His most recent areas of work have focused on Ofsted inspection, and on the impact of teacher appraisal. David leads the fieldwork of the Roehampton team on 'the role and effectiveness of the LEA'.

Pat Seppanen received her EdD from the Harvard Graduate School of Education. Since completing her degree she has specialised in evaluating educational and community programmes. Her current research focuses on interagency collaboration, systems change, systems accountability and use of performance indicators, and educational reform policies. She is a Research Associate and Co-Director of the Center for Applied Research and Educational Improvement at the University of Minnesota.

Mark Smiley is Professor of Education at the University of Illinois, Chicago. He received his PhD from Vanderbilt University. His research and teaching interests focus on educational organisations and leadership; the teaching profession; teacher professional development; schools as organisations and work redesign; co-ordinated children's services. school reform and organisational change, particularly in urban settings. He is currently directing the evaluation of the Annenberg Initiative in Chicago.

Mel West is Professor of Educational Leadership University of Manchester, He was previously Director of the 'Improving the Quality of Education for All (IQEA) Project', University of Cambridge. He has been involved in school improvement initiatives in several countries, and has worked directly with school leaders on school development issues in a range of cultural contexts. His research interests centre around school management and improvement issues, and he is currently engaged in a series of projects looking at the influence of ICT on school management and classroom practices.

Preface

The issue of leadership for change and improvement is now high on the research and policy agendas of many countries. With some inevitability, thinking about leadership has focused on school leaders – who they are and how they exercise their leadership. Governments and practitioners alike continue to assume that leadership – and in particular the individual leadership of the headteacher or school principal – provides a powerful explanation for variations in educational reform initiatives. Whilst school leadership is important, so too is that of other groups and organisations which have a strong relationship with schools and an interest in the reform agenda. For the purposes of this book, we have conceptualised leadership not as a role-based function assigned to, or acquired by, a person in an organisation, who uses his or her power to influence the actions of others, but as a network of relationships among people, structures and cultures (both within, and across organisational boundaries).

In this challenging and timely book we bring together leading educational researchers and educators from Australia, Denmark, Canada, England, Scotland, the US and Wales to comment on leadership in the round: an expanded view of leadership which is augmented by fresh insights into the nature of school change. Contributors develop the concept of leadership from a relational perspective and by so doing, expand our appreciation of the many additional sources of leadership provided to schools, and offered within schools. Their invaluable insights also serve to illuminate the influence of global and international trends on leadership, and enable us understand the particular ways in which leadership is bound in local and national context and rooted in learning: adult learning, as well as student learning.

In writing this book, we see our task as providing an intellectual diet, rather than an expansive treatment of the subject of leadership. The analysis presented here has a contemporary resonance, illuminating emerging issues which will shape the future of education, challenging the notion that change can be managed in a linear and uncomplicated way. We hope that the chapters in this book, which highlight new theories and new actors in the school improvement process, will set the stage for a generation of research that emphasises international perspectives and emerging areas of investigation.

KATHRYN A. RILEY and
KAREN SEASHORE LOUIS

1 Introduction

Relational leadership for change

Karen Seashore Louis and Kathryn A. Riley

Leadership and change: the research traditions

In the context of educational leadership studies, the purpose of this book is to be on the one hand *heretical* by espousing perspectives that have been minimally addressed in the existing literature, and on the other hand, *integrative*, because we aspire to bring together perspectives that are potentially compatible, if not currently combined. We begin, therefore, with an exploration of some of the research traditions which underpin thinking about leadership and change before outlining the ways in which the book is structured to tackle some of the questions which are central to our understanding of leadership for learning and change.

In recent decades, research on leadership and change has emphasised the predictive and the normative. Both in Europe, and in the English-speaking countries, most research in the field could be classified as falling into one of two bins: 'school improvement' and 'school effectiveness'. The former examined policy and practice levers that could explain why change happens in some contexts but not in others; the latter focused on the development of better information about the nature of schools that performed better on standardised or national tests. For the most part, neither has focused intensively on issues of leadership, except to include examinations of the headteachers or school principals as a factor in more effective schools,[1] or to examine the ways in which their actions and behaviour can affect the course of an improvement process.[2]

In its early inception, the school effective literature was seen as a welcome challenge to the social pathology of failure, demonstrating as it did that schools could make a difference. However, a number of problems emerged. According to critics, research findings became interpreted as 'laws of science' that could be applied to all teachers and schools and analysis failed to distinguish sufficiently between the 'effective' school and the 'good' school. (Gammage 1985, Riley and MacBeath 1998).

Notions of what constitutes a 'good' school are bound in culture and context and, as Harold Silver has argued, they change over time:

> Good schools have been ones (in the past) which have trained girls to be good wives and mothers, or which trained boys to serve the commercial ethic of the Empire. 'Good' has been an infinitely adaptable epithet, used of schools of many kinds, by interested parties of many kinds.
>
> (Silver 1994: 6)

Not only do constructions change over time but they also vary among stakeholders. Parents, teachers, school principals and national, state and local governments may not share the same priorities about what makes a good school – or school leader (Riley 1998a). Differences in perception surface at times of crisis in a school's history (Riley 1998b), or when major innovation is planned (as is described vividly in the case of Celebration School, Chapter 11).

The research literature has also focused on the role of leadership in managing the change process (Huberman and Miles 1984; Firestone and Wilson 1985), which foreshadows some of the topics raised in this book. In particular, role structures, values, interactions and collaboration in schools were found to be related to change (or lack thereof) (Little 1982; Rossman, Corbett and Firestone 1985). The ability of qualitative, smaller-scale studies to locate factors – especially leadership factors- that seemed to influence the outcomes of change encouraged a focus on how to manage better, a change process that inevitably takes place in rather chaotic, unpredictable and often non-rational contexts (Louis and Miles 1990). This focus is, perhaps, most recognised in the syntheses developed by Fullan and his colleagues (Fullan and Stiegelbauer 1991; Fullan 1993). The leadership emphasis in this work is often exclusively on the role of the formal school leader. Louis and Miles (1990), for example, focused on the role of the principal as an orchestrator of an open-ended process, while Leithwood and Steinbach (1995) discussed the school principal as an 'expert problem-solver'.

Influenced by the results of early studies of effective schools (Brookover 1979; Rutter 1982), the 'effective schools movement' has moved into high gear and has taken another perspective on leadership and change. The recent trend has been to look for characteristics of schools and classrooms that add to the performance of all students, and there is a great deal of evidence that the formal school leader is an important factor, at least in English-speaking countries (Stringfield and Teddlie 1991; Mortimer *et al.* 1988).[3] Stringfield (1995) has argued that more attention needs to be paid to school-based interventions that use effective schools research, arguing that 'high reliability' (vigilance on the part of leaders in maintaining the organizational features that obtain successful achievement outcomes) outweighs other considerations in school improvement.

Although priorities and perspectives may vary, contemporary authors agree with the need for a synthesis of school effectiveness research with school improvement research (Reynolds *et al.* 1996). Studies of 'situated leadership' in qualitative research, which focus on what specific leaders do to promote change, evoke questions about generaliseability. In contrast, the treatment of leadership in the recent school effectiveness research is limited in its capacity to measure how leadership behaviours influence the school's culture, wider environment and/or the instructional practices that could improve student learning. In other words, while the school improvement research has generated a list of normative behaviours for school leaders, the effective schools research is largely silent on the issue of 'how to get there' – the process by which less effective schools may become more effective.

An additional gap in the leadership and change literature is at the level of analysis. While Leithwood and Steinbach (op. cit.) have investigated 'expert problem-solving' at both the school and the education agency/district level, most research has concentrated on the school itself, with the neighbour-hood, community, local education agency/district professional associations and national policy viewed largely as 'context'. Most school effectiveness and school improvement research has focused only on the school as the unit of analysis and has tended to ignore the role of leadership outside the formal role responsibilities of the designated school leader. Even research that expands the view of influence tends to examine 'teacher empowerment' within an individual school (Marks and Louis 1997). The school focus is not surprising, given the consensus of an international study team that 'the school is the unit of change' (Van velzen *et al.* 1986) – a view which has often been interpreted as an exclusive emphasis on the functioning of the school as an autonomous organisation.

Emerging theories

Our critique of the dominant research streams is not intended to be dismissive. We know far more at the turn of this century about how school leaders may affect the development and achievement of pupils than we did a few decades ago. The research on leadership has also suggested some new and promising directions to be explored. But while our brief review demonstrates that school improvement has been well studied over the past decades, our knowledge base is never sufficient to keep pace with current demands. That change is a recurring and festering problem is reflected by titles like Sarason's (1990) *The Predictable Failure of Educational Reform*, and Cuban's (1990) 'Reforming again, again, and again'. Research has taught us that the problem of change is much deeper than the adoption of new innovations. It also includes:

Implementation: Was the innovation ever really implemented?
Fidelity: Once implemented, did the innovation maintain its integrity and purpose?
Impact: Have students been positively and significantly affected?

Institutionalization: Did the innovation become integrated into the school's mission and organization?
Maintenance: Did successful programmes continue to exist?
Replication: Was it possible to transfer the innovation from one school context to another?

Out of all of these dimensions, one of the most perplexing continues to be how to make changes in the 'substantive core of teaching and learning' – what it is that teachers actually do in their classrooms (Tyack and Cuban 1995; Elmore 1995). There is a great deal of 'school improvement' activity that is ultimately unconnected to any improvement in student learning. As Newmann and Associates (1996) point out, it is easy for instructional techniques that are potentially intellectually stimulating, like cooperative learning or student portfolios, to be implemented in ways that promote only lower level thinking.

Change management and school improvement

In exploring why change has been and continues to be perceived as an unsteady course for school organisations, we have highlighted a number of issues related to school improvement that have important implications both for research and practice. Louis, Toole and Hargreaves (1999) identify a number of problems that persist in the study of change, and that provide a context for this volume. Paraphrased to focus on the intersection of leadership and change, these are:

• What are the changes that potential leaders in school improvement seek in schools?
• How do potential leaders know if improvement has occurred?
• How do potential leaders decide 'how to get there' and what their role should be?
• How do potential leaders manage a highly turbulent political and social environment in which change must be enacted?
• How do potential leaders manage the effects of a turbulent environment on the dynamics of an individual school – the locus of change?

Looking over these problems, it is not surprising that we *hear challenges to the notion that change* can be 'managed' by focusing resources. Planned change approaches are criticised for their confidence in a linear improvement process and the 'manageability' of organisations (Louis 1994). Mintzberg (1994) described *The Rise and the Fall of Strategic Planning*; Beer, Eisenstat and Spector (1990) formulated the problem as 'Why change programs don't produce change'. Based on their research, Morgan and Zohar (1997) asserted that an individual's direct leverage over work results – and by extension a school's ability to influence a change process and outcomes – is very limited. Along the same theme, one popular 'solution' to increased organisational productivity – Total Quality Management – was shown to fail for 70 per cent of those who implemented it (Beer *et al.*, op. cit.), and some companies identified by Peters and Waterman (1982) as excellent, appeared to be in trouble after a three-year follow-up (Easterby-Smith 1990). The *wicked* nature of the problems, environments and solutions involved in school improvement *requires* a new and more generative conceptualisations of both the 'change problem' and of school improvement paradigms.

But there are alternative paradigms for school change which integrate under-researched components of the change process (Voogt, Lagerweij and Louis, 1999). School development, according to these authors, is the result of three influences:

*   *Planned efforts* (from within and from outside) to bring about educational and organisational changes.
*   *Autonomous developmental processes* (organisational life-cycles) that cover natural processes such as the ageing and replacement of staff, cultural changes in response to internal and external evolution, and changes in technology or other core components of organisational functioning.
*   *Major anomalies, and minor unanticipated events*, both positive and negative, that must be factored into the organisational learning process. These might include unanticipated deaths or departures of key people, radical changes in environmental characteristics or policies over a short period of time, or newsworthy events such as fires.

Taken together, the three incorporate both the small proportion of improvement outcomes that can be directly affected by deliberate efforts to improve, and the much larger proportion that is not directly subject to planned intervention.

What is surprising in studies of school change is the lack of powerful empirical evidence for the unplanned components of the development process, and the role of actors other than the designated leader in change. Too often, analyses of organisational change examine planned or strategic efforts, while noting only in passing that unplanned change is also important (Daft and Huber 1987). More '*unplanned*' organisational learning is also considered increasingly as an additional 'tool' to create more effective organisations (see, for example, Smylie, Lazarus and Brownlee-Conyers 1996), although we know little about when or how '*unplanned*' but productive change occurs. Insufficient attention is paid to the indirect effects of 'normal crises' on school functioning, although there are many case studies that testify to its impacts on learning and development (see, for example, Rollow and Bryk 1995; Louis and Miles 1990). Even less research emphasis is placed on the developmental life-cycles of school (see Sarason (1972), on new organisations, and Tichy (1981) on the relationship between autonomous development cycles and planned change).

Actors on the leadership stage

The role of 'external actors' – including business groups, teacher associations, local education authorities and actors at the state and national level –is rarely mentioned in the comparative, international writing on school change.[4] This omission is particularly unfortunate given the anecdotal evidence that groups that are outside the formal hierarchical authority structure have increasing influence at the school level in many, if not most countries. This book explores the contribution of some of these groups.

In general, the intersection between the school improvement and the education leadership literature is limited and is, in our view, excessively occupied with a 'consensus model' for organisational change. To give one example, proposals for 'transformational leadership' in business and educational settings focus largely on significant shifts in goals, strategies and culture in which organisations have a unitary culture. *Yet,* we also know that educational organisations, like other sectors, have multiple professional groups and cultures. When we think of schools, the cultures and resultant issues often focus on differences between administrators and teachers, or between the school and the parent/community constituency. But many of the key issues are ignored when we take a school-focused perspective – for example, the relationship of business communities and labour unions to local school change efforts.

We have divided the core contributions to the book into three main parts. In each of these parts, contributors tackle questions that are central to our broader understanding of leadership and change and which enable us to explore the complexities.

Part 1: Perspectives on leadership: leadership and change within schools

Contributions focus here on the ways in which national context shapes leadership and the contribution which school leadership can make to organisational learning and change. A unifying theme is: 'Leadership for Effective Learning' and a range of pressing questions emerge:

*   How can leaders create intelligent, thinking schools? How can they develop their own self-knowledge? (John MacBeath with Angus MacDonald, Chapter 2)
*   How can leadership and leaning be linked together, and how can leadership be extended to embrace teachers and students? (Mel West, David Jackson, Alma Harris and David Hopkins, Chapter 3)
*   If leadership is distributed, what impact does principal and teacher leadership have on student engagement? (Kenneth Leithwood and Doris Jantzi, Chapter 4)
*   How can school leaders support and sustain teachers in meeting the pro-

fessional challenges created by the knowledge society? (Brian Caldwell, Chapter 5)

- How does national context shape the ways in which leadership is viewed and exercised at the school level? (Lejf Moos, Chapter 6)

Part 2: The capacity of local systems to respond to educational reform and change and rethink their local leadership role

The dynamics of agencies and actors at the intermediary system level is an under-explored and troublesome area. Inevitably, a focus on systems throws up issues of power and politics, as intermediary levels of governance have to draw their authority from national or state governments, and their legitimacy from schools themselves. The immediate questions are about boundaries, goals and expectations:

- What are the characteristics of effective intermediary authorities (local education authorities and school districts), and what are the ways in which they contribute to the local leadership climate? (Kathryn Riley, Jim Docking and David Rowles, Chapter 7)
- What are the boundaries of authority which affect the capacity of agencies and actors to lead and govern? (John Fitz, William Firestone and Janet Fairman, Chapter 8)

Part 3: The leadership stage: new actors, new roles

In this part contributors focus on the many organisations and actors which seek to shape the direction of education: teacher unions and business, as well as exploring the tensions which emerge when different actors compete for the lead roles. Teacher unions, both in Europe and North America, have typically been viewed as defenders of the status quo, rather than as agents of educational reform. In many countries, businesses are taking a more proactive role in education: a development welcomed by some but viewed with caution by others. The business in question here is that of the Disney Corporation which took a lead role in creating Celebration School. The questions which emerge from contributors' examination of the role of these organisations are central to the management of change:

- What is the role of teacher unions and professional organisations in educational reform and change? (John Bangs, Chapter 9)
- If they become engaged in the reform agenda, how successful are they? (Karen Seashore Louis, Patricia Seppanen, Mark Smylie and Lisa Jones, Chapter 10)

- Do the various communities – business, teacher, parental and community – hold different constructions of what makes a good school? When views differ, how are they mediated? (Kathryn Borman with Edward Glickman and Allyson Haag, Chapter 11)

In the concluding chapter (12), we present a range of conceptual themes which have emerged from these contributions and draw attention to the many and disparate voices on the leadership stage. We hope you find the book informative and challenging.

Notes

1 For example, the 'principal as an instructional leader' has been a variable in many examinations of effective schools. See, for example, Stringfield and Teddlie 1991; Southworth 1995.
2 A recent summary of this research is in Murphy and Louis 1994.
3 The evidence from other countries is more mixed, but we tend to view this as a problem of direct translation of survey items that evoke different responses in different cultures.
4 We refer here to empirical literature. There are, of course, many exceptions.

References

Beer, M., Eisenstat, R. and Spector, B. (1990). 'Why change programs don't produce change', *Harvard Business Review* 68(6): 158–9.

Brookover, W. (1979) *School Social Systems and Student Achievement: Schools Can Make a Difference,* New York: Praeger.

Cuban, L. (1990) 'Reforming again, again, and again', *Educational Researcher* 19(1): 3–13.

Daft, R. and Huber, G. (1987) 'How organizations learn', in N. DiTomaso and S. Bacharach (eds), *Research in Sociology of Organizations,* vol. 5, Greenwich: JAI Press.

Easterby-Smith, M. (1990) 'Creating a learning organization', *Personnel Review* 19(5): 24–8.

Elmore, R.F. (1995) 'Structural reform and educational practice', *Educational Researcher* 24(9): 23–6.

Firestone, W. and Wilson, D. (1985) 'Using bureaucratic and cultural linkages to improve instruction'. *Educational Administration Quarterly* 21: 7–30.

Fullan, M. (1993) *Change Forces,* London: Falmer Press.

Fullan, M.G. and Stiegelbauer, S. (1991) *The New Meaning of Educational Change,* New York: Teachers College Press.

Gammage, P. (1985) *What is a Good School?,* University of Nottingham: National Association for Primary Education.

Huberman, M. and Miles, M.B. (1984). *Innovation Up Close: How School Improvement Works,* New York: Plenum Press.

Leithwood, K. and Steinbach, R. (1995) *Expert Problem Solving: Evidence of School and District Leaders,* Albany, NY: SUNY Press.

Little, J.W. (1982) 'Norms of collegiality and experimentation: workplace conditions of school success', *American Educational Research Journal* 19(3): 325–40.

Louis, K.S. (1994) 'Beyond managed change: Rethinking how schools improve'. *School Effectiveness and School Improvement* 5(1): 2–24.

Louis, K.S. and Miles, M.B (1990). *Improving the Urban High School: What Works and Why*, New York: Teachers College Press.

Louis, K.S., Toole, J. and Hargreaves, A. (1999) 'Rethinking school improvement', in J. Murphy and K.S. Louis (eds) Handbook of Research as Social Administration, San Francisco: Jossey Bass, pp.251-276.

Marks, H.M. and Louis, K.S. (1997) 'Does teacher empowerment affect the class-room? The implications of teacher empowerment for instruction practice and student academic performance', *Educational Evaluation and Policy Analysis* 19(3): 245–75.

Mintzberg, H. (1994) *The Rise and the Fall of Strategic Planning*, New York, London, etc.: Prentice-Hall.

Mortimer, P., Sammons, P., Stoll, L., Lewis, D. and Ecob, R. (1988) *School Matters: The Junior Years*, Wells: Open Books.

Morgan, G. and Zohar, A. (1997) 'Het 15–procent-principe: Geef uw werk een hefboomeffect', *Holland Management Review* 53, Amsterdam: Bonaventura.

Murphy, J. and Louis, K.S. (1994) *Reshaping the Principalship: Insights from Transformational Reform Efforts*, Thousand Oaks, CA: Corwin Press.

Newmann, F.M. and Associates (1996) *Authentic Achievement: Restructuring Schools for Intellectual Quality*, San Francisco: Jossey-Bass.

Peters, T.J. and Waterman, R.H. (1982) *In Search of Excellence: Lessons from America's Best Run Companies*, New York: Harper & Row.

Reynolds, D., Bollen, R., Creemers, B.P.M., Hopkins, D., Stoll, L. and Lagerweij, N.A.J. (1996) *Making Good Schools: Linking School Effectiveness and School Improvement*, London, New York: Routledge.

Riley, K.A. (1998a) 'Creating the leadership climate', *International Journal of Leadership in Education*, (2): 137–53.

—— (1998b) *Whose School is it Anyway?*, London: Falmer Press.

Riley, K.A. and MacBeath, J. (1998) 'Effective leaders and effective schools', in J. MacBeath (ed.) *Effective School Leadership: Responding to Change*, London: Paul Chapman.

Rollow, S. and Bryk, A. (1995) 'Catalyzing professional community in a school reform left behind', in K.S. Louis and S. Kruse (eds) *Professionalism and Community: Perspectives on Reforming Urban Schools*, Thousand Oaks, CA: Corwin.

Rossman, G, Corbett, H. and Firestone, W. (1985) *A Study of Professional Cultures in Improving High Schools*, Philadelphia: Research for Better Schools.

Rutter, M, Maughan, B., Mortimore, P., Ouston, J. with Smith, A. (1982) *Fifteen Thousand Hours: Secondary Schools and their Effects on Children*, Cambridge, MA: Harvard University Press.

Sarason, S.B. (1972) *The Creation of Settings and Future Societies*, San Francisco: Brookline Books.

—— (1990) *The Predictable Failure of Educational Reform: Can We Change Course Before It's Too Late?*, San Francisco: Jossey-Bass.

Silver, H. (1994) *Good Schools, Effective Schools*, London: Cassell.

Smylie, M., Lazarus, V. and Brownlee-Conyers, J. (1996) 'Instructional outcomes of school-based participative decision making', *Educational Evaluation and Policy Analysis* 18(3): 181–98.

Southworth, G.W. (1995) *Looking into Primary Headship: A Research Based Interpretation*, London: Falmer Press.

Stringfield, S. (1995) 'Attempting to enhance students learning through innovative programs: the case for schools evolving into high reliability organizations'. *School Effectiveness and School Improvement* 6(1): 67–96.

Stringfield, S. and Teddlie, C. (1991) 'Observers as predictors of schools: multiyear outlier status on achievement tests', *The Elementary School Journal* 91: 358–76.

Tichy, N. (1981) *Managing Strategic Change*, New York: Wiley.

Tyack, D. and Cuban, L. (1995) *Tinkering Toward Utopia: A Century of Public School Reform*, Cambridge, MA: Harvard University Press.

Van Velzen, W.G.,, Miles, M.B., Ekholm, M. and Robin, D. (1985) *Making School Improvement Work*, Leuven/Amersfoort: ACCO.

Voogt, J., Lagerweiji, N. and Louis, K.S. (1998) 'School development and organisational learning', in K. Leithwood and K.S. Louis (eds) Organasational Learning in Schools, Lisser, Netherlands: Swets & Zeitlinger, pp.237-260.

Part 1

Perspectives on leadership

Leadership and change
within schools

2 Four dilemmas, three heresies and a matrix[1]

John MacBeath with Angus MacDonald

'The world cries out for firm leadership'. So ran the headline in the British newspaper the *Daily Mail* of 31 August, 1998. There was, it reported, a simultaneous crisis of leadership in Russian and in the US, evoking images of a rudderless world adrift in the ether. In the following month British newspapers carried headlines such as 'Headteachers to go back to school', signalling the government's plan to retool school heads with the skills required of leadership for the new Millennium. There is a widely shared belief that robust leadership will not only save the world and restore our nations but also improve our schools.

In this view, leadership tends to be equated with heroic individuals who possess the skills to turn things round. It is a belief that has been reinforced by case stories of school principals and headteachers rescuing doomed schools, injecting a renewed self belief through their own personal vision and ambition. There is enough evidence from these individual cases, and from the research literature, to substantiate the belief that effective schools need strong leaders, but then again, that view may need a closer scrutiny. Our own three-year study suggests that solutions may not come that simply.

Our study 'Effective leadership in a time of change' (Kruchov, MacBeath and Riley 1998) involved four countries and grew from a common interest in England, Scotland, Denmark and Australia in the role of the headteacher (principal, or 'school leader' in Denmark) in leading or facilitating school improvement. The four countries of the study were brought together by a shared concern to find answers to questions such as these: faced with the growing tensions of management and leadership, how do school leaders, reconcile the conflicting demands on them? Are some better at it than others? If so, what might be their secret and where have they learned it? Is a measure of 'effectiveness' in leadership the ability to resolve those differing expectations? To what extent does it mean understanding, shaping and exceeding the expectations of key stakeholders – teachers, students, parents? How do school leaders realise their own personal vision of what a 'good' school should be? How does 'leadership' become a shared responsibility in and beyond the individual school?

We were also interested in the permanence and transferability of leadership qualities. Did effective leadership travel across cultures? Did the skills of leadership travel within cultures or between one school and another? What lessons could we learn from such a study that would benefit people in post, or those following a career path in preparation for leadership?

We did not wish, however, to conduct a traditional research study in which school leaders and their schools were simply objects of the research. We wanted them to be involved as participants and partners in an exploratory journey. We saw the sharing between practitioners and researchers, and the networking across countries, as a potentially rich source of understanding and professional growth for them, as well as for us.

In some important respects the project design we arrived at was new to us all, and one from which we hoped we would all learn as we went along. We wanted the project to be collaborative, responsive and evolving. We used a range of methodologies – individual and joint interviews (with leaders, parents, school board members, pupils), card-sort activities, school visits and conferences/workshops. We met as a whole group (forty school leaders and seven researchers) three times over the life of the project, to share findings as they emerged and shape the next stages of enquiry. As these conference workshops were held in Scotland, Denmark and England this also gave us opportunities to visit one another's schools, to give each other feedback as critical friends and to test our developing hypotheses against day-to-day practice. Of themselves, these visits provided many challenges to our ideas not only on leadership but on more deeply held cultural values.

We were to discover in the early phases of the project that our research model, in itself, presented a challenge to the participating school leaders. In their experience, researchers did the hard work, analysed and interpreted and then presented their findings. Instead, we were asking them to engage with us in analysis and interpretation, asking them to help us make meaning out of data whose origins lay in quite different historical and cultural contexts. Frustrations and anxieties had at times to be worked through patiently and with an optimism that something of both theoretical and practical value would emerge at the other end.

Involvement in the research project presented a challenge to participating school staff, not primarily in terms of their thinking and beliefs about research but because there were priorities to be weighed and tensions to be resolved. The project required some investment of emotional energy and a certain amount of time out of school. There were cost-benefits to be weighed, which some school leaders found more difficult than others. This was in itself rich data and helped us understand what was to become a central theme of the research – the dilemmas of leadership.

Through conferences, workshops and school visits, as well as individual interviews, we identified a range of dilemmas faced by school leaders. Some were common to the four countries of the study, others were uniquely a product of a particular culture, or political economy. We saw the sharing and analysis of these dilemmas as an important part of the process, although we did find resistance to sharing with some of the participants because of the private and worrying nature of the tensions which they faced. That reluctance to speak about those tensions was further evidence of their real and deeply-felt nature.

The following are just a few of the dilemmas identified through the study, but they are ones which illustrate the specificity of the context whilst, at the same time, raising questions of general principle – strategic and ethical.

Dilemma number one: commercialisation

With devolution of management to individual school site, school leaders in all our countries found themselves having to be much more astute financial managers. They had not only to balance the books but in doing so to generate income and, however much against the grain of their values and political affiliation, seek sponsorship from private sector companies. In the United Kingdom and Australia such sponsorship is increasingly common. From the company viewpoint the company gains wider exposure for their products in an increasingly competitive marketplace, and schools, with their ready-made captive youth market, are an obvious target. An Australian headteacher describes his dilemma:

> I have been approached by a large national company which wishes to place screen saver messages about its products on all of our computers. We are a large secondary school and we have over a hundred computers available for student use. The company markets itself directly to adolescents and its screen saver message advertises its products directly to computer users whenever they are not actively working on tasks of their own. There is a considerable license fee payable to the school if I agree. We are always in need of extra funds, yet I am uncomfortable with the idea that students would be exposed to single product advertising in a manner which tacitly seems to endorse those products.
>
> (Dempster and Mahony 1998, 130)

Dilemma number two: school performance

During the late 1980s and early 1990s there was a shift in policy focus from measuring inputs to measuring outcomes: an approach which drew on methodology and indicators from school effectiveness research. 'Outcomes' equated with attainment on test and examinations and aggregated measures of student achievement became critical yardsticks by which government, parents and the wider public were encouraged to make judgements about the performance, quality and standards of schools. This public focus on school performance has created dilemmas for headteachers. One English headteacher expressed his dilemma in these terms:

We know that we lose quite a number of good local students to other schools in the city because their parents see our results in the League Table – results which, because of our student base, place us in the bottom third of the list. The Council wants to set aside some money from this year's budget to offer ten students from our local primary schools a substantial bursary to attend this school. The money would be taken from the little we have at our discretion and I am troubled by the 'gung-ho' manner in which Council members are discussing a decision which they say will lift our standards.

Dilemma number three: teacher performance

The formal appraisal of staff by headteachers is increasingly a matter of policy, but nonetheless a contested and fraught notion. Teaching remains in many countries a 'closed door' issue, both in a conceptual and literal sense. There is a deeply held view that teachers are professionals who should carry out their work unsupervised. It such a climate it can be difficult for a school leader to gain a first-hand view of the practice of their teachers. This is seen at its most acute in Denmark where there has been no precedent for external evaluation of schools, nor of 'interference' in the classroom by anyone else, leader or not. The classroom is the teacher's professional domain. New legislation, however, requires the school leader to take a more interventionist role than in the past. A Danish school leader describes this as follows:

> There is an ethical issue in going into classrooms to find out what is going on and whether it is good enough and making teachers insecure by having them feel that I am spying on them. I'm not sure what position I should adopt.

The emphasis on achievement and competition among schools has also exposed weaker teachers and put pressures on school leaders to deal with underachieving and ineffective teachers. For some, this has given a mandate for intervention but not necessarily relieved the burden of responsibility for doing something. Complaints about teachers also come from another direction. School leaders find themselves having to respond to letters, phone calls or impromptu visits from aggrieved parents. Such complaints have to be dealt with quickly but with regard to 'due process', that is formal pro-cedures, which if not properly followed could lead to legal action supported by teacher unions and associations.

One of the few options open, and one not unknown to companies in the private sector, is to turn up the heat and make life increasingly uncomfort-able for the individual in question. For headteachers this was the 'Catch 22' situation and they found themselves caught between the ethics of treating people badly and the ethics of allowing children's education to suffer.

Difficulties are compounded when the issues are not clear-cut but lie in that shadowy domain of professional competence. As one Scottish headteacher commented:

> We've got a teacher who gets constant complaints from parents and students. We've given him a lot of professional development and gone through all the business of setting targets etc. He has met some of them but not others so it still isn't clear cut. Should I now make his life a misery to get rid of him?

Dilemma number four: the unspoken issues

There are many problems whose origins do not lie within schools but when they come to light within the school context are meat and drink to a sensationalist press and a source of immense disquiet to parents. Sex, Aids and drug education are perennially controversial but the threat of an exposé in local or national newspapers may tempt headteachers into prevarication and cover up. An English headteacher describes that dilemma:

> I dare not admit publicly that we've got a drugs problem in the school in case it damages our reputation. This would mean that we would lose pupils and therefore funding. Yet, if I don't admit it we can't undertake a concerted effort with the parents and support services to tackle it properly. Neither do I want to permanently exclude the offending students as other schools have done, even though I know that would improve our reputation.

The examples given here capture the spirit of the dilemmas headteachers encounter in different countries. In their discussions with us, headteachers reported that they often felt alone, cast in the role of arbiter or mediator, relying on personal values and professional ethics to find a morally defensible decision. Such a role runs against the tide of collaborative approaches to leadership and the sharing of power in decision-making which, as has been argued (Dempster and Mahony 1998), are ethical issues in their own right.

Dilemmas involve people, resources and power and, more often than not, all three are implicated in particular courses of action chosen. If Giddens's (1984) definition of power is accepted as the exercise of control over people and resources, then it is clear that ethical decision-making is about the school leader's use of power. This goes a long way towards explaining why the model of leadership employed by the principal is so critical in the way a school is run and critical in the resolution of competing demands.

These four dilemmas, and many more, provided a basis for exploring some general principles of leadership. A number of principles emerged out of a joint activity which we called 'principles for principals'. These focused on children, staff and external relations.

Children

- children come first
- children have a right to a good education and to be safe
- their health and welfare are priorities

Staff

- decisions about staff should be consistent and based on clear criteria
- staff ought not to have to carry colleagues
- it is the head's responsibility to deal with staffing situations
- one ought not be manipulative
- staff have a right and a duty to be involved in improving quality
- the head has a right and a duty to know what is going on

External relations

- do as you would be done by in relation to other schools
- heads should recognise their wider responsibility to the community
- heads should recognise the external context and lobby or galvanise political support if necessary

Such principles need rigorous scrutiny. They also have to be tested in practical circumstances if they are to be more than a bland set of pieties to which even ruthless, autocratic and morally reprehensible heads might readily subscribe. The devil lies in the detail, first in how consistently principles such as these can be applied in resolving real life dilemmas; second, in defining what is meant by such terms as a 'good education', 'health' and 'welfare' for children. Such issues mark the continuation of debates which, in our view, are necessary in the professional development of heads.

Discussions arising from these workshops also gave rise to a number of what might be called 'heresies' since they do not fit neatly into competencies frameworks and checklists of effectiveness in leadership. The following are three heresies which arose during the project, as well from a wider biographical and research literature.

The first heresy – break the rules

The school leaders in our study found it increasingly difficult to stay within the strict boundaries of national or local guidelines. They were expected to be creative problem-solvers, in respect of financial management, and in their relationships with those to whom they were accountable at central office and government. Hampden-Turner and Trompenaars argue that leaders must constantly seek the creative exceptions to the rules:

> The integrity of an enterprise, its value to stakeholders, must depend on how well universalism (rules of wide generality) is reconciled with particularism (special exceptions).
>
> (Hampden-Turner and Trompenaars 1993: 7)

It was in the particularism that leaders in our study faced their dilemmas, testing the universal rules and often finding that a new principle had to be forged. The danger of universalism is a constant quest for the right answer, the exemplary set of rules, the perfect plan. Remember Passchendale and the perfect plan which sent twenty thousand allied soldiers to their deaths in a matter of minutes, warn Hampden-Turner and Trompenaars. It was a plan designed by generals far from the front line. Churchill's biographer, Andrew Roberts (1995), comments in the following terms on Churchill's leadership qualities that 'He was a young man in a hurry who always broke the rules. It was a secret behind his greatness'.

There were numerous examples from our study of school leaders who succeeded only because they bent and broke the rules. One example from a Scottish headteacher concerned the appointment of a new teacher. She knew this young man, an enthusiastic recent graduate, would inject new life into her school but there were no vacancies in the department for which he was qualified. She appointed him as a learning support teacher then once in the school found opportunities for him to teach history, with the strong warning, 'Don't tell anybody you haven't got a qualification'.

'It is better to ask for forgiveness than for permission' is a maxim to which that headteacher subscribed. In the last decade of the 1990s the political climate has given a licence for such deviance to school leaders who would, in previous times, been more scrupulous rule observers. In the post-Thatcher years, local education authorities, particularly in England, have played a diminished role in overseeing schools, so leaving more space for headteachers to approach the rules with flexibility and creativity because, as they saw it, it was the only way to survive in a competitive climate. During the 1990s their political masters had exemplified creative rule-breaking on a grand scale and with such impunity that it became a key issue around which the 1997 General Election was fought.

While English headteachers were the quickest to admit to being 'political' and sometimes manipulative in order to achieve their goals, the Danish schools leaders were least comfortable with this role and found it difficult to conceive of themselves as political operators. This was as much a product of different historical traditions and conceptions of leadership as it was of contemporary politics. The Danes do not have a literature or public celebration of charismatic and heroic figures such as Arnold of Rugby, Sanderson of Oundle or A. S. Neill, all of whom were larger than their schools. Neill, who had a profound influence on generations of teachers in many countries throughout the world, was the most spectacular of rule breakers in both school philosophy and practice.

The second heresy – the true leader is an excellent follower

The historical legacy which sees heroic individuals as synonymous with their schools has, in Britain at least, led to the place called school being seen by headteachers as 'theirs' and as bearing their imprint. It is commonplace for heads to refer to 'my school' and 'my staff' and although in some cases this may be no more than a conventional shorthand, for others it is a literal expression of how they see themselves in relation to the school.

In our study, many headteachers in their first post experienced a pressure to assert their authority from the outset. Like the new classroom teacher, they followed the counsel to start tough and relax later because it cannot work the other way round. To expose yourself immediately as having a lot to learn is as risky a business for an untried head as for a noviciate class teacher. New heads and new teachers recognise that they are on trial and they know that a successful trial is one in which you convince the jury on their grounds, and play skilfully to their expectations and preconceptions.

School leaders also bring to the role their own conceptions of leadership, shaped by conventional notions which place the leader is 'in front' or 'on top'. One of the first exercises in the four-country study was to ask school leaders to depict themselves and their role using coloured markers and large sheets of poster paper. Some portrayed themselves standing at the top of a pyramid or ascending a steep hill pulling staff behind them. One head-teacher had created such an image and had then obliterated it with a cross, drawing himself at the centre of a complex web and writing beside it 'in the thick of things' (MacBeath, Riley and Kruchov 1998).

Leaders are in the thick of the action, agrees Ken Leithwood (1992). Leaders lead not from the apex of the pyramid but from the centre of the web of human relationships, says Joe Murphy (1994). David Hopkins (1992) offers a further metaphor and suggests that good schools are sailed rather than driven. They are steered from the stern, tacking and changing with a reading of wind and current. Peter Senge has a similar conceptualis-ation:

> In a learning organisation leaders may start by pursuing their own vision, but as they listen carefully to others' visions they begin to see that their own personal vision is part of something larger. This does not diminish any leader's sense of responsibility for the vision – if anything it deepens it.
>
> (Senge 1990: 352)

We found that as school leaders became more secure in their role, it became easier for them to extend the boundaries of their comfort zone. They were able to explore other ways of developing the vision and of establishing their authority. 'Seek first to understand before seeking to be understood' is Covey's fifth of seven hallmarks of highly effective people. It is, as he claims, an extremely powerful process. It is disarming both to the speaker and to the listener and can effect a paradigm shift. It can, of course, be used as a powerful technique in the repertoire of psychological tricks, yet another useful management technique. It may well work, in a pragmatic sense and even in a professional sense, but it will ultimately fail in a moral sense if it is not 'congruent', that is if it not aligned with a genuine desire to learn and to grow as a person and as a leader. Following the lead of others, suggests Covey (1994), requires self-assurance of the highest quality.

In our own study, pupils, parents and teachers were agreed on one thing – the primary quality of 'good' headteachers was the ability to listen. Richard Paul describes (1997) it like this:

> A passionate drive for clarity, fair-mindedness, a fervour for getting to the bottom of things, for listening sympathetically to opposing points of view, a compelling drive to seek out evidence, a devotion to truth as against self-interest.

The third heresy – good leaders behave like grown-ups

This seems hardly a heretical proposition yet leadership is so often associated with larger-than-life characters that quiet unobtrusive 'followership' goes unrecognised. Does 'heroic leadership' serve primarily to fulfil the needs of the individual rather than the organisation? Is it designed to create dependence or independence?

From psychological and biographical evidence it could be argued that many 'great' leaders had a deep need to engender the dependency of others. Howard Gardner's (1996) biographies of leaders reveal unfulfilled childhood needs and adult years spent compensating for the missed opportunities of childhood. The psychologist Eric Erikson (1965) postulates seven stages to be worked through from infancy to maturity and, following his argument, many of those who aspire to lead others have never successfully made it through the egocentric phase or successfully come to terms with the expectations of their parents. In the language of transactional analysis (Berne 1964) this is the ' child-in-the-adult' coming to the fore, demanding to be the centre of attention, needing to be reassured of one's own power and status.

Ostrander and Schroeder (1996) describe an adult trying to exorcise the parent-in-the-adult by repeating just before sleep the affirmation that she was a good and capable person. She awoke one morning to hear an internal voice saying, 'Forget all that, you are really a shit'. Those powerful voices and images that come to us during or at the edge of sleep, are often puzzling and disquieting because they are not under our conscious control. They seem to have a life of their own, drawn up from the internalised memory bank of childhood experience. Such voices are quite typically authority figures, a parent or a teacher, a shadowy figure off stage but still trying to direct or stage manage.

One biographer of Margaret Thatcher describes her leadership style as having been shaped by her early childhood: unable to put her father in his place nor give her mother hers. Webster writes:

. . . shifting of attention away from her mother is characteristic of Mrs Thatcher's treatment of her. Beatrice remains a shadowy figure, her qualities seldom named, much less praised, her existence merged into and superseded by the figure of Alfred. . . . There is no inheritance claimed from Beatrice, and could scarcely be one, since she is presented as a figure without identity, a part of 'Daddy' without any apparent capacity for independent thought or action.

(Webster 1990: 7)

A substantial body of work on the exercise of authority (Adorno *et al.* 1950) reveals a frightening tendency for mature adults to submit to the authority of others who are perceived as having status. The corollary to this is the 'authoritarian personality', the grasping of opportunities to exploit human frailty in order to impose control over perceived subordinates. Are these inborn characteristics or are they learned in early childhood and reinforced in the school years? Models of leadership presented to us in our school years may play their part in giving shape to those personality traits. Perhaps there are opportunities to break into that self-perpetuating cycle by exposing children and young people to alternative exemplars of leadership?

How then can headteachers behave like grown ups? Thomas Sergiovanni (1992) describes five different ways in which headteachers may derive their authority. He calls these bureaucratic, psychological, technical-rational, professional and moral:

Bureaucratic authority is hierarchical and in bureaucracies hierarchy equals expertise. Those at the top know more than those at the bottom. They set standards which teachers have to reach. They enforce these through the 'expect and inspect' strategy and there is in-service when teachers fall short. Accountability is from bottom to top.

Psychological authority is the appliance of management wisdom. It is underpinned by working at human relations, by congeniality, by recognising people's needs and encouraging and rewarding them. The strategy is 'expect and reward'. The reward culture is an implicit statement of accountability from bottom to top.

Technical-rational authority is grounded in research, in evidence and in science. Knowing the research, being aware of good and best practice, being able to defend the position allows the head and senior management to provide the right kind of in-service support which provides teachers with the skills that have been identified by experts. Accountability is implicity and explicitly from bottom to top.

Professional authority is where there are collective and agreed norms which are translated by teachers into professional standards. Professional knowledge is created in use, by teachers working together and sharing knowledge. Teachers recognise their mutual responsibilities to one another and hold one another accountable. They require little monitoring from the top.

Moral authority derives from the explicit shared values of a community. These are not necessarily 'professional' values but those which hold a community together and which, of themselves, guide actions and accountability. What people do is driven not by what is rewarded, or by what works, nor by self-interest. It is led by what is right and in the interests of the whole school.

Whether or not these can ever be neat discrete types, and whether or not we go along with Sergiovanni's typologies, there are valuable insights to be gained from thinking about a school culture in relation to these. Perhaps the most valuable of all, and the one most congruent to the findings from our study, is that authority need not be located in the person of the leader but can be 'out there' in between and among people. If this can be achieved its force is much stronger. It is mutually reinforcing. In the absence of that shared authority the psychological tricks of management come not of their own and management is seen as sustaining the motivation, reinforcing through reward – or, where such mechanisms fail, reverting to a simple command structure.

The sociologist Emile Durkheim famously said that where mores are sufficient law is unnecessary, and where mores are insufficient, law is unenforceable. It is a fundamental law of teaching, observed frequently in the breach, that to lead by command is inimical to learning. It is short term, pragmatic at best, and carries with it a singular and indelible message about authority. For the teacher who has succeeded in establishing a shared set of mores, the test is to leave the classroom in the expectation that at whatever time she returns the class will be on task, working, cooperatively or individually. An equivalent test of effective leadership is what happens when the headteacher or the whole senior management are out of the school.

Where there is professional and moral authority in a school the headteacher is freed to be a follower and a learner. Where there is professional and moral authority it is much easier to accept disagreement and conflict. People can only argue when there is ground for agreement. The improving school is one in which these differences are not simply respected but engaged with in a genuine search for meaning.

Leaders in our study found themselves caught between pragmatism, expedience and self-interest, on the one hand, and ethical principles and personal integrity, on the other. There is a fine line separating these two sets of behaviour. Lessened effectiveness may be the price paid for integrity, while 'selflessness' may prove to be a dangerous and self-indulgent excess in many contexts.

And a matrix

One of the participating headteachers in our project, Gus MacDonald, wrestled with these ethical dilemmas and heresies. He wrote his own reflections on his attempts to reconcile these tensions in the day-to-day practice of a large comprehensive school in the once thriving shipbuilding conurbation of the Clyde. He concludes (MacDonald 1998: note 2):

> It would be an unremarkable statement to say that leaders in schools, as in other situations and organisations, rely upon their knowledge in making judgements and decisions. The difference between good and successful leaders and those who are less so may depend, in part at least, upon their awareness of the state of their knowledge. The following small grid, the title 'The MacDonald Management Metacognition Matrix', would be altogether too grandiose, may help to illustrate the point made above. In the grid, the horizontal axis refers to the leader's state of knowledge in relation to any situation or decision, while the vertical axis refers to his or her awareness of that state of knowledge.

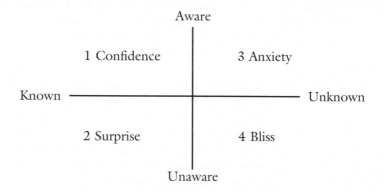

It is surely good leadership and good management to be as knowledgeable as possible about any decision or situation. The greater the degree of certainty, and the more one is aware of that, the greater is the confidence with which leadership can be delivered. The first quadrant, then, is labelled *Confidence;* this is the state of mind where the leader is aware that his or her knowledge is sound and sufficient enough to form the necessary judgement, or make the necessary decisions. Those looking at leadership from the outside often take the common-sense view that this is how decisions are made. The leader waits until he or she is aware that they have sufficient knowledge and then decides. Those involved in leadership know that only very seldom are they allowed this luxury and that to seek this state before making a decision would, in practice, be the paralysis of leadership. Most often, decisions and judgements have to be made in very different conditions.

Leaders quite often make decisions and judgements in the condition of *Surprise*; this is an ability much admired and valued by others. In this condition, the leaders surprise themselves. It occurs where a new situation has arisen and the leader is surprised to find himself or herself reacting with a sense of sureness of touch, of knowing just what to do and then doing it. It is as though the leader was unaware of what s/he knew until the situation itself demanded the response and s/he found it already formed. It may be to do with unarticulated knowledge, or it may be to do with the ability to see through the detail of the situation to the fundamental issues, and then to apply the relevant principles to it to produce a resolution. Whatever it is, it is much prized by others because it conveys a sense of ability to 'think on one's feet', or of a very profound depth of experience. It inspires confidence and trust. For this reason, the wise leader will keep his or her sense of surprise well hidden and s/he will look exactly as s/he had been aware of this knowledge all along. In practice, this quadrant is indistinguishable from the first quadrant. Perhaps this is why it is so seldom acknowledged.

The third quadrant is that of *Anxiety,* the condition in which leaders feel that most decisions and judgements are made. Most situations will not permit a leader the time to find out about all the things about which s/he does not know. The shrewd leader will, of course, reduce the uncertainty as far possible; beyond that, the leader will consult (to try to gain more information, but also to spread ownership of the 'fall-out' if things go wrong), develop fall-back positions and stage his or her commitment to the decision so that there is some flexibility to respond as more information emerges. Inevitably, the degree of uncertainty creates anxiety, and the more the leader is aware of what s/he does not know, the greater the anxiety will be. This condition can also lead to paralysis of leadership, because it can of course affect the individual to a major degree. This is why leadership requires real courage.

One of the most difficult tasks is to sustain both flexibility of response and the belief in the outcome that inspired the decision in the first place, during the gap between the commitment to the decision and the realisation of the outcome itself. Anything that goes wrong within this time gap, however unconnected it may seem to be, tends to be linked to the original decision, especially if it was contentious. The leader must uphold and defend the decision, while bearing in mind the possibility that the connection might, in truth, be there.

The fourth quadrant, *Bliss,* is the most interesting one because this is the condition in which all decisions and judgements are truly made. Awareness of lack of knowledge is *Anxiety;* lack of awareness of lack of knowledge is *Bliss.* The trouble, however, with being unaware of what we need to know, and do not know, is that we lack both prompt and motive to make us find out. As leaders – as human beings – we are always in this situation; we can never be sure that we are aware of all that we need to know, whether we actually know it or not. If this were a Mediaeval Management Matrix, this quadrant would be clearly marked 'Terra Incognito' and 'Here be Monsters' for this is truly unknown territory and monsters do lurk here – the monstrously unlucky, the monstrously unlikely and the monstrously unfair – and they can take any form. Every leader carries this 'Terra Incognita' into every situation, however familiar, or new, it may appear. This condition is so all-pervading and permanent that we cease to recognise it and we operate in practice often as though it does not exist. Perhaps this is necessary or else leadership would really be paralysed; except that good leadership allows for the unexpected.

The good leader will look more widely and think harder about possible consequences of any decision, but probably there is only one set of activities available to leaders to help them map at least some of the 'Terra Incognita' we know must be there and to identify the monsters that might lurk within. This is one reason for the importance of consultation and the bringing of different views, sets of knowledge and experiences to bear on an issue or problem as a leadership activity.

It is, however, not the only one. There is always an element of consent involved in leadership. Our managers are appointed by due process, but we choose to invest our trust, belief and confidence in our leaders. Consultation is the means by which this consent is maintained. Our loss of trust in our leaders is often the reason for its withdrawal. It is hard for someone who knows something as a simple matter of fact to appreciate that her or his leader does not know it, harder still for that person to appreciate that the leader is not aware that s/he does not know it, and completely impossible to understand why s/he was not asked. Consultation is, therefore, an essential leadership activity and it is an interesting question indeed to consider why, even when entered into with goodwill on all sides, it so often goes awry.

It is, however, in the moment of crisis, the time of emergency, that the heroic qualities of the leader as an individual are most needed, most visible and most appreciated. This is the point at which consultation procedures are seen to be both inappropriate and burdensome and our hero moves swiftly and single-handedly to meet and resolve the crisis that has arisen. In fact, of course, what really happens is rather different. In a time of crisis, the school leader is much more likely to indulge in a swift piece of selective consultation. The choice of individuals consulted will be governed by speed of availability, as well as by ability to contribute. The leader will generally have some strategy as to how to proceed forming in his or her mind and this will 'bounced off' the chosen group, taking other ideas and strategies into account.

At this stage, an entirely different strategy for dealing with the crisis could emerge. If appropriate, the staff will be informed of what has happened, the need for speed of reaction will be explained and staff will be told how matters will be dealt with and what they should do. Once the immediate crisis has passed, the school leader will then set in motion a process of inclusive consultation, debriefing staff, checking on the effect of the decisions made and making adjustments where appropriate. Finally, once matters have been fully resolved, staff will be informed and the situation will be returned to normal. It is a most curious contradiction that it is in serious situations of this kind (which affect the whole organisation) that staff most expect to be kept fully informed, and yet the leader of the school or organisation is most perceived to be acting alone. Perhaps it is the very high profile the leader must take, combined with the fact that the 'normal' processes of consultation do not happen in the expected order, that leads to these apparently contradictory views.

School leadership is very much more than the passive acceptance of staff that they must do as the headteacher says simply because the individual concerned has been appointed to that position. A school leader, at any level in the organisation, has won the trust, belief and confidence of staff to a significant degree and these are assets which the staff has given to the leader. Where there is merely passive acceptance, these assets are withheld and where there is perceived betrayal, disappointment or loss of confidence, these assets can be withdrawn. Consultation is the main means by which the leader in a school, or any organisation, maintains the consent of staff to the trusteeship of these assets, as well as the main means by which the leader reduces and maps the 'Terra Incognita' which s/he carried into any and every situation. The conclusion must therefore be to emphasise the importance of consultation, even where the last word for school managers is 'meta-cognition'.

In conclusion

We concluded from our study overall that one of the essential elements of effectiveness in educational leadership was the kind of metacognition exemplified by Angus MacDonald. On its own it will not necessarily make him or her an effective leader, since the ability to think about one's situation, as MacDonald himself points out, is also attended by the danger of paralysis. And, as we know from many people in positions of power, ignorance is often bliss, and serependipity often accompanies the unstudied or even the 'wrong' decision. We have also argued that intuition, antennae, 'vibes', 'reading the context' are inherent skills of effective leadership but that these are not just gut instincts. They arise from an emotional and social intelligence linked to a well-rehearsed cognitive databank of principles and experiential lessons internalised.

That is why in our conclusion to the study we come down so firmly on the questions of context, rather than leadership as some universal product or recipe. When deregulation has been pursued, when decision-making has been localised, when safety-nets and supports have been withdrawn, when policy parameters dictate particular courses of action, all of these circumstances add to the specificity and complexity of the climate in which decisions must be made at school level. The challenge lies on at least two fronts: first, articulating the professional values that underpin the school leader's role; and second, developing consistent approaches to the complex ethical dilemmas of everyday school life.

Our study did little more than scratch the surface of the range of dilemmas which confront principals or headteachers. As well as those described in this chapter, there are also issues of student selection, streaming, exclusion, ineffective and incompetent teachers, hiring and firing of teachers with an eye to economics and the teacher age profile, short-term contracts and continuity of employment, income generation, self-evaluation and inspection, to name but a few. There is a substantial knowledge base about the management of this terrain which is not always easily accessible. It can be found in part in research literature, in part in management manuals, in part through contacts with other headteachers, as a researcher in one's own school and with the support of critical friends.

Without this kind of personal research and the accompanying theoretical development much of the experience that heads gain from working through their ethical dilemmas will be lost to colleagues who might benefit from it. Under new public sector management, the tensions between the different goals for schooling are becoming increasingly irreconcilable On the one hand there are those who are pushing schools to operate like businesses and to pursue the educational equivalent of profit maximisation. On the other hand, schools are ultimately concerned with the development of students who are not only employable, but also autonomous, responsible, moral individuals who are effective members of society (Association of Teachers of English of Nova Scotia 1996).

Heads who are able to model moral leadership in the way they run their schools are more likely, in our view, to concentrate on the ultimate goal of schooling, even though they may be constantly under pressure to do otherwise.

Notes

1 This chapter is a distillation of some of the themes from a four country research project 'Effective Leadership in a Time of Change'. The project involved eleven researchers from those four countries. These were Chresten Kruchov, Lejf Moos and Johnny Thomassen from Danmarks Laerhojskole, Copenhagen (The Royal Danish School of Educational Studies); Kathryn Riley and Pat Mahony from Roehampton Institute London, England; Joan Forrest, John MacBeath and Jenny Reeves from QIE, University of Strathclyde, Scotland, Neil Dempster (Griffith University, Queensland and Lloyd Logan (University of Queensland). Angus MacDonald participated in the project as a headteacher.

2 This section has been adapted from MacDonald 1998: 166–71.

References

Association of Teachers of English (1996) *A Shared Vision: A Report on Education Business Partnerships*, Halifax: Nova Scotia Teachers' Union.

Berne, E. (1964) *Games People Play*, New York: Grove Press.

Bohm, D. (1983) *Wholeness and the Implicate Order*, New York: Ark.

Covey, S. (1994) *The Seven Habits of Highly Effective People* (revised edition), New York: Simon and Schuster.

Dempster, N. and Mahony, P. (1998) 'Ethical challenges in school leadership', in *Effective School Leadership: Responding to Change*, London: Paul Chapman.

Erikson, E. (1965) *Childhood and Society*, Harmondsworth: Penguin.

Gardner, H. (1996) *Leading Minds: An Anatomy of Leadership*, London: Harper Collins.

Giddens, A. (1984) *The Constitution of Society*, Cambridge: Polity Press,.

Hampden-Turner, C. and Trompenaars, L. (1993) *The Seven Cultures of Capitalism*, New York: Doubleday.

Hopkins, D. (1992) 'Changing school culture through development planning', in S. Riddell and S. Brown (eds) *School Effectiveness Research: Its Messages for School Improvement*, Edinburgh: HMSO.

Kruchov, C., MacBeath, J. and Riley, K. (1998) 'Introduction' in, J. MacBeath (ed.) *Effective School Leadership : Responding to Change*, London: Paul Chapman.

Leithwood, K. A. (1992) 'The move towards transformational leadership', *Educational Leadership*, 49 (5): 8–12.

MacBeath, J., Riley, K.A. and Kruchov, C. (1998) *Images of Leadership*, Scotland: QIE, University of Strathclyde.

Macdonald, A. (1998) 'Postscript'. in J. MacBeath (ed.) *Effective School Leadership: Responding to Change*, London: Paul Chapman.

Murphy, J. (1994) 'Transformational change and the evolving role of the principal', in J. Murphy and K. Seashore Louis (eds) *Reshaping the Principalship: Insights from Transformational Reform Efforts*, Newbury Park: Corwin.

Ostrander, S. and Schroeder, L. (1996) *Superlearning 2000*, New York: Dell.

Paul, R. (1997) 'Dialogical thinking: critical thought essential to the acquisition of ritual knowledge and passions', University of Glasgow: unpublished seminar paper.

Roberts, A. (1994) *Eminent Churchillians*, London: Weidenfeld and Nicolson.

Senge, P. (1990) *The Fifth Discipline: The Art and Practice of the Learning Organisation*, New York: Doubleday.

Sergiovanni, T. J. (1992) *Moral Leadership: Getting to the Heart of School Improvement*, San Francisco: Jossey-Bass.

Webster, W. (1990) *Not a Man to Match Her*, London: The Women's Press.

3 Learning through leadership, leadership through learning
Leadership for sustained school improvement

Mel West, David Jackson, Alma Harris and David Hopkins

In this chapter we reflect on the British and international contexts for leadership studies, examining the centrality of leadership and the dominant models emerging from effectiveness studies (transactional leadership) and school improvement research (transformational leadership). We present an alternative view of leadership (post-transformational leadership), which has emerged from our work with consistently improving schools within the Improving the Quality of Education for All (IQEA) Project, and present some propositions and paradoxes drawn from our work with, and research in, those schools. These, we believe, offer a more dynamic *set of* insights into leadership for sustained school improvement than those which currently dominate the literature and practice in the training of school leaders.

At the core of this chapter are a number of emerging assumptions about leadership for school improvement. These have evolved from our ten-year experience of working on school improvement projects with schools in a variety of geographical locations within the United Kingdom; from our ongoing research; and from our much more detailed work with a small selection of the most successful of these schools within what we have called the Moving Schools Project (West *et al.* 1997). Our views about leadership and learning are thus well grounded – and are consistent, we believe, with the emerging pictures about successful leadership of school improvement elsewhere in the world.

The context

One of the fundamental areas of agreement between researchers who have investigated educational change concerns the powerful impact of head-teachers on processes related to school effectiveness and school improvement. Research findings from a variety of countries and school systems draw similar conclusions about the importance of the headteacher in school development and change processes (e.g. Van Velzen *et al.* 1985; Diagram and Macpherson 1987; Myers; Hopkins *et al.* 1994; Ainscow *et al.* 1994;

Stoll and Fink 1996). This research identifies consistently that those schools which have demonstrated the capacity to improve themselves, tend to be led by headteachers who have made a significant contribution to the effectiveness of their staff. Whatever else is disputed about this complex area of activity known as school improvement, the centrality of leadership in the achievement of school level change remains unequivocal.

This should not surprise us – it is now more than twenty years since leadership was identified as one of the key components of 'good schools' by Her Majesty's Inspectorate of Schools in England. HMI stated that *without exception, the most important single factor in the success of these schools is the quality of the leadership of the head* (DES 1977: 36). Since that time, the changes imposed upon the UK education system have expanded radically the role and responsibilities of the headteacher. In particular, the local management of schools has resulted in the headteacher becoming a manager of systems and budgets as well as a leader of colleagues. In addition, the increasingly competitive environment in which schools operate has placed a much greater emphasis upon the need to raise standards and to improve school outcomes.

One of the major growth areas of the burgeoning management development field has been headteacher training. While much of this training has been narrowly focused and competency driven, it has nonetheless, re-inforced the centrality of the head's role in leading school development and improvement. This broadening of interest in, and understanding of, the head's leadership role parallels the pattern of development of leadership theory generally. For example, there has been an increasing emphasis upon the links between leader behaviour and the 'culture' of the school (Hopkins *et al.* 1994; Sergiovanni 1994 Murphy and Louis, 1994).

In the UK the adoption of local management of schools has come from a belief in the relationship between decentralisation and enhanced school effectiveness. In particular, the shift towards the self-management of schools has been premised upon the assumption that management decisions are more likely to be effective if they are located within the institution. This emphasis upon 'self-management' has been welcomed by many head-teachers, primarily because of the possibility it offers for increased control over policies and resources and expanded scope for leadership.

What starts as freedom to move around budget items and resources, to alter and to develop new priorities, inevitably brings with it new staff management issues. Indeed, it may well be that it is not the technical skills of financial or resource management that we have to assimilate, but the rather more complex interpersonal skills needed to create support for new priorities amongst the staff group. It is here, in the exercise of interpersonal skills in times of difficulty, as well as times of growth, that the leadership qualities of the headteacher will be tested. It may be that the current emphasis within headteacher training focuses too much on the technical competencies of management, and not enough on the personal and interpersonal qualities that are likely to be needed as schools take increased responsibility for improving themselves.

Similarly, this focus on the relationship between leaders and work groups and the ways in which the leader can develop and harness the relationship has been reflected in the development of leadership theory generally – it is not a 'school' issue as such. Murphy (1991) suggests that thinking about leadership falls into a number of phases – building towards the current interest in the links between leader behaviour and organisational culture. We believe that these phases can be broadly clarified as follows:

- Initial interest in the personal qualities and characteristics of 'successful' leaders which result in *personality* or *trait* theories of leadership.
- Increasing focus on what it is that leaders actually do – are there some behaviours and approaches which are consistently associated with successful leadership? Such inquiries support the development of *behavioural* theories of leadership.
- Growing awareness that task-related and people-centred behaviours may be interpreted quite differently by different groups and in different contexts, prompting explanation of how the particular context might best be accounted for within a general theory, and resulting in a variety of *situational* approaches to leadership.
- Most recently, emphasis on the links between leadership style and the culture of the organisation – a movement away from the notion of leadership as *transformational*, having the potential to alter the cultural context in which people work.

It is this last phase that has had most influence on the debate about leadership in education over the past decade – with the (so-called) 'trans-actional' and 'transformation' approaches being explored in some detail and in a number of countries. Inevitably, there seems to be a preoccupation with 'transactional' models in systems where strong central control has been retained, while in those systems where de-centralisation has been most evident, considerable interest in 'transformational' models has emerged. It is worth briefly contrasting these two 'stereotypes' of the leadership role.

In the more stable system, where maintenance has a higher priority than development, and the headteacher is seen as playing a major role in protect-ing and promoting the interests of the system, a transactional approach is frequently found. In such an approach, the emphasis will tend to be on the management of the school's systems and structures, on creating efficiency and effectiveness, and on achieving prescribed outcomes. The role of the transactional leader is to focus upon the key purposes of the organisation and to assist people to recognise what needs to be done in order to reach the desired outcomes. When the parameters for success are well defined, transactional leaders can be very effective. They may even be effective in bringing about certain kinds of organisational change – those where the parameters are very clearly identified, where conformity rather than creativity is valued, and where it is hoped to retain organisational structures and relationships despite changing (say) education content or method. Transactional leadership approaches, therefore, seem best suited to static school systems and communities.

It has been widely argued that complex and dynamic changes, such as the 'cultural' changes that are required for sustained school improvement, are less likely to occur as a result of transactional leadership (Stoll and Fink 1996, Beare *et al.* 1989). A model of leadership more congruent with the requirement of cultural change is that of transformational leadership. This style of leadership focuses on the people involved and their relationships, and requires an approach that seeks to transform feelings, attitudes and beliefs. Transformational leaders not only manage structure, but they purposefully seek to impact upon the culture of the school in order to change it. It has been argued that cultural transformation and all the associated complexities that surround school-based change are at the heart of school improvement. Consequently, both theoretically and conceptually, transformational leadership would appear to be consistent with a desire to bring about school improvement, rather than simply 'change' the school.

Of course, while the centrality of leadership in this school improvement process is indisputable, there is an issue over who the 'leaders' are in the interest of improvement efforts. There is a growing research literature that points towards the importance of leadership at all levels within the organisation. For example, the leadership role of what might be termed 'middle managers' has been identified as important, for example, in explaining differential school effectiveness (Sammons *et al.* 1996; Harris *et al.* 1995). Similarly, there are increasing calls for and acceptance of a leadership role for teachers in the context of their own areas of direct responsibility. Yet there is some research evidence that suggests that there is an ever-growing divide between 'leaders' and 'followers' as a result of the changes arising from the self-governance of schools (Wallace and Hall 1994). The strong managerialist culture apparent in some schools has reinforced the separateness of the senior management team and has claimed leadership as an activity for the few, rather than the many.

In our own work with schools committed to continuous improvement we have found that such schools feel restricted by this formulation of leadership as a function of hierarchy and are moving beyond it. Instead, these schools develop both leadership and 'followership' as broadly based functions within the culture of the school.

We have noted elsewhere (Hopkins *et al.* 1994) that a school that looks to the headteacher as the single source of direction and inspiration is severely constrained in its development capacity. Yet school structures often reinforce this rather limited view, imposing a hierarchy of roles over the real distribution of knowledge and skills. Our work with schools leads us to conclude that a more dynamic and decentralised approach to leadership is most often associated with school improvement. In practice, this means that headteachers give others real authority and help them to develop to be able to use this authority wisely. This means relinquishing the idea of structure as control, and viewing structure as the vehicle for empowering others. But it is not easy to surrender control. Even when goals are agreed, it is not always easy to trust others to use their own knowledge and skills to bring change about. Yet trust is essential to support the leadership climate. The transformational approach is grounded in trust:

> Trust is the essential link between leader and led, vital to people's job, status functions and loyalty, vital to fellowship. It is doubly important when organisations are reaching rapid improvement, which requires exceptional effort and competence, and doubly so again in organisations like schools that offer few motivators.
>
> (Evans 1998: 183)

This is a powerful call for much greater attention to relationships and to the articulation of values within the headteachers' conceptualisation of the leadership role – but is this echoed in findings of the various research studies that have asked what makes an effective school? What picture of the headteacher emerges from such studies, and what does it tell us about school leaders?

School leadership – the picture emerging from effectiveness studies and school improvement literature

There is no shortage of publications extolling the need for effective leadership in schools and colleges (see, for example, Caldwell and Spinks 1992; Crawford *et al.* 1997; Grace 1995). There is, however, some divergence of opinion concerning the nature of effective leadership. Research into school effectiveness and school improvement has contributed to an evolving concept of leadership, with particular emphasis upon the leadership of the headteacher. While both traditions agree upon the importance of leadership, they tend to view it from different theoretical positions.

School effectiveness research tends to emphasise the importance of structure in organisational development and change. It has taken little account of the different management levels within the school, or of the process factors which contribute to the effectiveness of individual schools or departments. In direct contrast, the school improvement research tradition has been concerned largely with process factors, seeing these as the keys to organisational development and change.

There are some generalisations one can make about the nature of the school effectiveness research tradition. In the first place, its proponents have a concern about what they regard as 'effectiveness'. They have taken for granted, in Scott's (1987) terms, that schools are rational, goal-orientated systems, that the goals are clear and agreed, that they relate to pupil or student achievement, and that those achievements should be measurable. Effectiveness can be assessed by comparing the levels of achievement in these measurable attainment targets in order to identify in which schools pupils are achieving more, and in which less. (Such approaches imply that the issue of educational goal-definition – what schools are for – is resolved, or at least not within the scope of the research.)

A second key characteristic of school effectiveness research has been its attempt to link the quality of performance with particular characteristics in the school. A wide range of school characteristics have been identified and correlational analysis has been undertaken that links particular characteristics with higher pupil performance. Sammons *et al.* (1995) proposed eleven characteristics which research suggests can be associated with effective schooling. This list of effectiveness factors embraces school-wide and classroom-focused concerns, with a strong focus on leadership, unity, order and high expectations.

In considering the school as an organisation, these studies focus on the technical core, the structure that supports it, and the leadership provided for staff. The values and principles that support decision-making, and the ways in which leadership shapes the relationship between the members of the school, receive less attention. In an earlier study, Mortimore and colleagues (1988), for example, identified purposeful leadership of the headteacher as one of the key factors in school effectiveness in British junior schools:

> Purposeful leadership occurred where the headteacher understood the needs of the school and was involved actively in the school work,
>
> (pp. 250–1)

But beyond identifying the leader as someone who was a resource provider and a visible presence, little attention was paid to what 'purposeful' leaders actually do that makes the difference.

It is our view that a major limitation of effectiveness studies is that they have tended to focus attention upon a top-down model of leadership and have not looked at within school interactions, or processes in any depth. Much of the school effectiveness research has neglected leadership at other layers within the organisation, construing leadership as the presence of the headteacher and the senior management team. However, the most recent school effectiveness findings have pointed towards the importance of leadership at other layers within the organisation, particularly the middle management level (Harris *et al.* 1995; Sammons *et al.* 1996; Harris 1998).

In general, the effectiveness research has rarely been detailed enough to provide information on what is needed to improve schools, except by implication. The lack of a dynamic definition of leadership has meant that the practical application of much of the effectiveness research base has been limited to a series of exhortations about school development and improvement, rather than offering a basis for action. Because the school effectiveness movement is strongly normative in orientation, it interprets leadership primarily in transactional terms. It is here that the leadership model adopted by school effectiveness researchers is in our view vulnerable, insofar that it is restricted by an overly rational view of organisational change and development.

In contrast to this position, school improvement researchers have tended to emphasise the norms and values which shape individual and collective action at the school level. In the school improvement literature the unit of analysis tends to be conceptualised as the whole school as an organic and dynamic culture. There is an increasing recognition of the importance of the different layers within the organisation, e.g. the importance of acknowledging that the school is often a hierarchical and bureaucratic system. A key assumption within the school improvement literature is that school improvement strategies can lead to 'cultural' change in schools through modifications to their internal conditions, using leaderships to eliminate the restrictions of bureaucracy and promote a more collegial structure.

Within school improvement it is often proposed that cultural change (which supports new teacher collaborations, new teaching and learning processes that, in turn, lead to enhanced outcomes for students) needs to be a central focus of leadership studies. The types of school cultures most supportive of school improvement efforts appear to be those that are collaborative, have high expectations for both students and staff, that exhibit a consensus on values, that support a secure environment and those which encourage *all* teachers to assume leadership roles appropriate to their experience. In summary, the role of leadership in school improvement is to bring about *cultural* change by altering the processes which occur within the structure and not necessarily to affect the structure itself.

This suggests that transformational leadership, rather than transactional leadership, is the leadership style offering the best prospect for school improvement. Such leadership arises when 'leaders are more concerned about gaining overall co-operation and energetic participation from organisation members than they are getting particular tasks performed' (Mitchell and Tucker 1992: 32). This model of leadership is more consistent with school improvement because it places the emphasis upon processes and interaction. In such a model, effective leaders exhibit a feel for the process of cultural change and model their expectations through example, rather than instruction.

The argument we have putting forward in this chapter so far, is that, in general terms, leadership is conceived in relation to the transactional model in school effectiveness research, and in relation to a transformational leadership approach within school improvement studies. However, in our view neither of these approaches captures the dynamic nature of leadership in those schools that are able to sustain development. Models and conceptualisations of leadership within the two research traditions have contributed to an understanding of leadership at a theoretical level but they have provided little guidance concerning the ways in which leaders act to bring about sustained school improvement. Consequently, what is needed is a leadership model that synthesises existing approaches while providing sufficient scope to capture how leaders encourage and manage school improvement in action. In the next section we describe the leadership approach of headteachers we have observed in schools with which we have worked and where there has been a formal commitment to bringing about school improvement over a number of years.

The background to IQEA

The *Improving the Quality of Education for All* (IQEA) project was established some ten years ago. Initially developed at the University of Cambridge, it is now based both in Cambridge and at the University of Nottingham. To date, over 100 schools have been involved in the IQEA network. The project is grounded in the belief that schools are most likely to strengthen their ability to provide enhanced outcomes for all students when they adopt ways of working which are consistent both with their own aspirations as a school community and with the current reform agenda. In so doing, it is our belief that such approaches will also provide a context for teacher learning, too – about pedagogy and about leading school development.

At the outset of IQEA (see Hopkins *et al.* 1994, 1996), we attempted to outline our own vision of school improvement by articulating a set of principles that provided us with a philosophical and practical starting point. These principles were offered to schools as the basis for collaboration in the IQEA project. In short, we were inviting the schools to identify and to work on their own projects, but to do so in a way which embodied a set of core values about school improvement which have within them significant implications for the way in which leadership is conceptualised within the school. The five principles underpinning the IQEA project are:

- School Improvement is a process that focuses on enhancing the quality of students' learning.
- The vision of the school should be one which embraces all members of the school community, as both learners and contributors.
- The school will seek to develop structures and create conditions which encourage collaboration and lead to the empowerment of individuals and groups.
- The school will seek to promote the view that enquiry, and the monitoring and evaluation of quality is a responsibility which all members of staff share.
- The school will see in external pressures for change important opportunities to secure its internal priorities.

These principles have stood the test of time within the project and still inform our work. Inevitably, and rightly, though, we have deepened our own learning and understanding of them through our collaborations with the schools involved.

One of the richest sources of insight evolving from our work with those schools that have most successfully sustained their school improvement endeavours has been in the domain of leadership. We have seen 'transformational' leadership approaches create considerable movement in some contexts, which has then foundered, either when key personnel have moved on, or because the leadership behaviours required at the outset of the project became increasingly less relevant to the schools' subsequent growth states (Hopkins *et al.* 1997). However, in a few of our schools, and in particular those we studied within the *Moving Schools Project,* we found headteachers and others who were grappling with the complexities of leadership for school improvement; who were studying leadership in context; who were wrestling with the structural and cultural shifts implicit in our school improvement model; and who were engaging with the enquiry process as a means of studying and learning about leadership as well as about teaching and learning issues. What has emerged in these schools is a dispersed leadership model which is both opportunistic and 'intrapreneurial' in seeking ways in which to encourage and provide support for a broadly based leadership approach. There are a few schools in which, through the openness to questioning of fundamental assumptions to which collaborative enquiry gives rise, a new paradigm of leadership seems to have emerged. From these actively improving school contexts we would draw three conclusions:

• School leaders in these schools develop expanded repertoires of leadership.
• Such schools offer a context for the development of new understandings about leadership style.
• In such schools collaborative enquiry provides the opportunity for teachers to study, to learn about and to share leadership.

The sorts of changes that we have observed in these schools involves a different, dispersed and more diffuse style of leadership. In its most highly developed form, we have observed 'shared influence' settings which developed leadership which is intuitive, confident, self-effacing, empathetic, risk-taking, trusting and visionary. These are not the skills readily developed on headteacher training courses, nor do they sit neatly with the competency-based skills training currently being promoted in England by the Teacher Training Agency. Indeed, these are characteristics not readily found in one individual. They are characteristics not so much of the leader, but of leadership.

In the remainder of this section, drawn in part from writings in the field and in part from our own experience with schools, we will set out some of the implications of such approaches for school improvement efforts. We have structured our thoughts and findings under the following headings. (1) multi-level leadership built around values; (2) empowerment and active democracy; (3) learning as a source of leadership; (4) learning and leadership paradoxes.

(1) *Multi-level leadership built around values*

As has been observed earlier, the school effectiveness literature propagates a view of leadership centred around strong headteachers with a clear instrumental vision for the school. They tend to have dynamic or forceful personal qualities and a high instructional focus. School improvement writers have, meanwhile, built up transformational leadership models of practice from settings in which school leaders have, by definition, 'transformed' their schools. There are two particular flaws to this latter approach. On the one hand, transformational characteristics are, in our experience, unsustainable over the long haul. Second, as Donahue (1993: 299) has pointed out, 'the plain fact is that there simply are not enough good principals to go around'.

In contrast, the model we are proposing offers a more sustainable and attractive conceptualisation of leadership for a profession which, by the nature of the personnel it recruits, has the potential for leadership widely spread amongst organisational members. It is also our experience that, if this potential is to be realised, then it will have to be grounded in a commitment to learn and develop that inhabits the structures of the school as well as the classroom – it is likely that the school will conceive and act differently from the traditional explanations of leadership and structure. Our view of leadership, then, is not hierarchical, but federal (Handy 1990). It is a view which is both tight and loose; tight on values, but loose on freedom to act, opportunity to experiment and authority to question historical assumptions. It is this tightness on values, and its focusing of purposes, which in our experience is the critical precursor to the sort of dispersed leadership model we are advocating.

As long ago as 1976, Weick portrayed schools as loosely coupled systems. The unpredictable trail of causality and the comparative privacy of classroom practice render schools unusually loosely connected as organisations. Weick proposed that they should become tight in ways other than visible accountabilities – through consensus on values. This concept is an important one, because it is values, not vision, that gives the start point. Our experience in the *Moving Schools Project* amongst our IQEA schools is that vision emerges collaboratively from collective enquiry. The evolution of vision becomes a saga which makes meaning of the improvement journey as it evolves, whilst leadership articulates, enacts, reaffirms and actively supports transformational learning values. But the vision itself derives from the exploration of opportunities in the twin contexts of a 'value set' and on a physical/ educational environment.

It follows that leadership in the schools that we have studied is not perceived as being inextricably linked to status or experience. It is available to all because it stems from individual initiative, informed by common purposes. It is 'taken' as well as 'given'. In this way, coaching and mentoring have become important leadership qualities, designed to support individuals but also to expand leadership capacity. This process in the most highly developed schools sees also the evolution of shared understandings about leadership through school development work – as schools research their own practice; generate their own knowledge.

There is now a good deal of evidence from studies elsewhere that is compatible with this view of a learnt leadership capacity, most particularly in the literature on learning organisations (Louis and Leithwood 1998). Here, leaders are stimulators (who get things started); they are storytellers (to encourage dialogue and add understanding); they are 'networkers' and 'copers'; they are problem-scavengers, too (Louis 1994). They tend to have a wider social repertoire than has been customary in hierarchically conceived educational settings, so as to encourage openness and to maintain relationships whilst wrestling with ambiguity. They will be improvisational and comfortable with spontaneity (Joyce *et al.* 1993; Joyce et al. 1999). They will care, deeply, about teachers, about students and about education. They will be less personally ambitious (perhaps a long time in post?) and instead will be remorseless about improvement. In such settings, leadership provides a context for adult learning focusing on 'helping staff to confront, make sense of and interpret the emerging circumstances' of the school (Louis 1994: 6).

The TQWL study (*Teacher Quality of Work Life* – Rosenblum, Louis and Rossmiller 1994) is in some ways compatible with our own IQEA work, and here, too, interesting images of leadership in action have emerged. Effective school leaders were viewed as facilitators; they delegated and empowered ('made teachers invent solutions to problems'). They were not efficient (but were proactive; they hung around; they knew what was going on and had an open door; they encouraged drop-in). They modelled risk taking (including addressing problems and dealing with cynicism). They emphasised caring for students (a view of teachers as teaching kids as well as subjects). They actively used knowledge and ideas (and were seen to respect educational knowledge). They provided leadership around *values* (staff saw their schools as values-orientated).

This theme of 'values leadership' (which appears in one of our concluding propositions) is so crucial to our view of leadership for sustained school improvement that it warrants a slightly more detailed explanation. It involves building up a consensus around higher order values that members of the school community can relate to and believe in. It involves moving from what Brighouse (1991) has called the lowest common denominator of school aims to the highest common aspirations stemming from shared values and beliefs. It requires us to articulate these beliefs and hold actions accountable to them – by those leading at all levels. It includes openness and an acceptance of alternative interpretations of the organisation. It also involves making school an explicitly human environment, fun both to work in and to learn in. In our own work, we have observed that the opportunity for leadership (and learning to lead) in a values-orientated and supportive context has been a major driving force for school improvement activities.

It will be evident that in the IQEA schools that we are describing, leadership is not invested in hierarchical status, but experience is valued and structural characteristics (mixed-aged teams, cross-institutional collaboration, etc.) encourage all actors to be drawn in and valued for their contributions. Such structural arrangements provide the context within which the leadership capacity for school improvement is expanded and leadership characteristics are naturally learnt.

(2) *Empowerment and active democracy*

The concept of multi-level leadership outlined above is descriptive of an organisational culture involving emancipation through collaborative learning. It implies active participation at all levels, which we are choosing to call 'active democracy' (all participants; rather than 'representative democracy' – unelected leaders in hierarchical roles). Such a formulation both requires and provides pervasive staff development systems. Some of the more advanced IQEA schools are evolving such systems located around the mutual learning and the opportunities for growth inherent within collaborative processes. Through the partnership with university staff and its access to knowledge sources, this is combined with learning drawn from outside the school to support enquiry processes, to assist understandings about leadership and the implementation of change and so on. This, in itself, expands leadership capacity.

From our work we would suggest that neither age nor experience is a dominant factor in the ability to learn, nor attitudes or enthusiasm for collaborative approaches. Our own findings are compatible with those of Louis *et al.* (1994) and Joyce *et al.* (1993), in that collaborative work has been found to increase the involvement, engagement and affiliation across all staff. Both professional potential and human need are satisfied – as is the moral purpose that is often rendered dormant by the stultifying constraints of traditional hierarchical school structures. Teachers are motivated through seeing their professional skills valued, and by being offered opportunities to share with and lead others; by having their capacities continually expanded – and by feeling that their school is making a difference to the lives of young people. Despite our agnosticism about age and experience, it may well be that such contexts, where leadership is both learned and shared, are more likely to engage the mid-to-late career teachers whom Huberman (1993: 247) found tended to retreat from school level issues into 'cultivating their own gardens within their classrooms'.

Clearly, top-down direction and institutional hierarchies are antithetical to democracy in action. Multiple partnerships, with shifting leadership, offer a more appropriate set of structural norms. They have also proved to be more likely to impact upon student learning.

It is worth mentioning in this context that we are beginning to see in one or two of our schools a further 'post-transformational' leadership dimension emerging. As teachers' expectations of students increase, it is not only in the domain of academic achievement, but also with regard to students' capacities to share actively in the democratic process itself – to research their own environments and to become active participants in school improvement. Indeed, in one of the schools studied within the *Moving Schools Project,* students are involved as sources for perspectives on change, as co-researchers and enquirers, and as active participants in the implementation of improvement activities (Jackson *et al.* 1998).

As Fielding (1997) has pointed out, there are a small but growing number of instances from both sides of the Atlantic that suggest the potential and power of a transformative approach involving students. Within a number of our IQEA schools we are seeing students involved in staff task groups looking at various aspects of the school's development agenda. The work of Suzanne SooHoo (1993) and Patricia Campbell (Campbell *et al.* 1994) in America, and Jean Rudduck (1996) in the United Kingdom are other examples where deep student involvement in institutional evaluation and enquiry have been explored. In the *Students as Researchers Project* at Sharnbrook Upper School (one of the IQEA schools), students are active evaluators, knowledge-producers, democratic participants and their potential to support school improvement is valued. They are also entrusted with understandings about the values that bind leadership within the school and – and this is particularly relevant to our present discussion – they become both actors who help to develop values and transmitters of those values to other students. In other words, they add further to the leadership density within the school.

(3) *Learning to study learning*

Schools have often been described as learning systems. Transformational learning involves the creation of socially (mutually) constructed interpretations of facts and knowledge (data) which either enters the organisation from the outside or is generated from within the school. The literature on school improvement is articulate on two themes which have relevance here, but have perhaps been under-conceptualised. The first relates to professional development. Whilst arguing strongly for professional development processes to support school improvement, we are generally less clear about how this operates within improving schools – the way in which teachers within the school learn together, expand their capacities and their personal masteries. A second issue consistently referred to in the school improvement literature is the development of the schools 'capacity' for improvement – where capacity is often quite narrowly conceived. These theories are, in fact, inter-related.

Three components that we would consider to be crucially important to capacity development are: the generation of contextual knowledge through enquiry; the utilisation of that knowledge to challenge organisational development dysfunctionalities; and the transfer and utilisation of knowledge to develop leadership capacity. It is worth developing this theme. Schools cannot (unlike other organisations) easily engage in massive personnel and leadership change to effect improvement. Schools which wish to develop have to do so from where they are and with what resources – financial and personnel – they have.

Fortunately, schools are also well placed to develop their professional, human and intellectual capital because they recruit adults motivated by learning who also, for the most part, wish to 'make a difference' for young people (Fullan 1993). Regrettably, though, many schools with which we have worked are structured in ways that are antithetical to teacher learning and in which shared learning is not culturally embedded. It is both ironic and disappointing that the creative potential and the goodwill of teachers can be frustrated by patterns of organisation that owe more to control than development.

However, this is not always the case – in some of the schools with which we are working structure is seen as something that should derive from, rather than determine purposes. And within that structure, the teacher is nurtured as the most vital and renewable resource. Our work with IQEA schools leads us to support Wohletter's (1994: 273) findings. His team found that, in twelve actively re-structuring and improving schools, the schools distinguished themselves by:

> Intense interest in professional development, [which] was viewed as an ongoing process for every teacher in the school, as well as for the principal . . . such schools worked to build the capacity of the entire staff to help manage the school . . . and to develop a common knowledge base among all members.

We are not, of course, talking here about traditionally conceived in-service or professional development activity; what we are observing is new and different types of professional knowledge acquisition – including the development of relevant understandings about leadership.

In concluding this section, and to illuminate the argument, it may be of help to give an example from one school of the way in which leadership understandings have evolved from the shared study of 'leadership in action'. In this particular school, which has been in our IQEA project for seven years, there has been a deliberate policy to involve the wider staff group in leading the school's development. Membership of the 'cadre' group, responsible for the coordination of the project within the school (see Hopkins *et al.* 1994, Hopkins *et al.* 1996), has deliberately been rotated to give different members of staff the opportunity to manage the project. Indeed, the term 'project' in itself shorthand for an interlocking series of initiatives which have a common focus – improving teaching and learning in the school – but a broad base across departments and groups. Over the years, the school has refined its arrangements for co-ordinating these efforts, and currently distinguishes between IQEA Project Leaders, who overview development, and Enquiry Partnership leaders, who take responsibility for particular developments. At any one time, a group of two or three staff will be acting as Project Leaders, and as many as ten Enquiry Partnerships may exist, each comprised of between three and five members of staff.

For each of these leadership roles the school has evolved descriptions of leadership activities. These are open, shared and refined each year by participants as they are tested out against their own experience of leadership in action. After seven years, there are few members of staff left who have not contributed to this process, many having experience of both roles. A brief summary of the roles is set out in the following table:

Table 3.1 A summary of leadership roles

Project leaders' role	*Partnership leaders' role*
Plan the programme	Co-ordinate the partnership
Ensure meetings are well planned	Manage workloads and timescales
Problem-solving for the school improvement cadre group.	Maintain morale (review successes; focus on achievements) – keep the focus manageable
Connect with the wider knowledge-base (and be knowledgeable!)	Ensure relevance and integrity of research
Manage the external support:	Anticipate need and seek appropriate support
– universities	
– networks with other schools	Generate dialogue within and beyond the partnership
Generate dense communication systems.	Network into other school systems; keep staff informed
Facilitate implementation	Involve relevant others, as appropriate.
Conjure resources:	
– money	Help to interpret data and to generate recommendations.
– time	
– creative ideas.	Share with, learn from and support partnership leaders – within and outside IQEA sessions
Be a source of:	
– professional development support	
– vision for the endeavour	Engage with implementation issues
– theoretical and practical knowledge	Make it work for your partnership and for the school
– optimism and joy	
– humility!	

It is our contention, and this would be strongly supported by the school, that involvement in these roles constitutes a major vehicle for leadership development within the school.

(4) *Leadership and learning – some paradoxes*

This final section explores briefly some of the paradoxes which have emerged in our work with schools. The first relates to leadership longevity, and in particular the 'shelf-life' of the headteacher or school principal. Accepted wisdom – with which we would be in general agreement – appears to be that a period of time between 5 and 8 years is an appropriate term for head-teachers. Michael Rutter's (1979) pioneering School Effectiveness study in Great Britain suggested that around 5 years was an appropriate term. Recent government announcements in Britain about fixed-term contracts for headteachers talk in terms of 7 or 8 years. The paradoxical finding from our research appears to be that, whilst this may be true for many school contexts, those schools exhibiting the characteristics that we have described above appear to achieve that state with continuity of leadership – the same headteacher, but with evolving or changing styles and repertoires.

The second paradox relates to what we might term 'professional unlearning'. Of course, schools engaged in sustained improvement activities have to learn new ways of working – as professional learners, as teachers and as leaders. But we cannot simply add new ways of working; we have also to find ways to unlearn the old ones, too. In the CO-NECT Project (Goldberg and Richards 1996: 83), the work is described as 'slanted as much towards becoming an unlearning organisation as it is to becoming a learning one'. Subtraction is as important as addition (perhaps, in some settings, more important). The creation of fluid leadership patterns involves the unlearning and relearning of relationships and allegiances as organisational fluidity and alternative collaborations become the norm. As schools evolve and change, so different characteristics of the leadership repertoire are required. We have to unlearn, too, some of the assumptions that led to historical customs, rituals and practices. Unless unhelpful, irrelevant, redundant or contextually incongruent practices are shed – inappropriate leadership practices most of all – overload and conflict are inevitable.

The third paradox emerging from our work with schools is one that has been documented elsewhere. Schools adopting the IQEA approach to school improvement seek to create multiple learning opportunities and to embrace more dispersed leadership arrangements. Hierarchies dissolve, and with them are shed outmoded concepts such as the link between status and experience, and the notion of subordinates – an incompatible notion within professional organisations. Other values replace respect for position. Sergiovanni (1994: 223) writes about the new skill of 'followership'. As new leadership oppor-tunities are created, so those who previously led must learn the skills of followership: 'professional and moral authority are substitutes for leadership that cast principals and teachers together into roles as followers of shared values – a shared followership'. School leaders, as well as other staff, have to learn that collaboration requires that they allow 'position' to be determined by the tasks at hand. The 'leader' can play an important role here – but it will not always be easy to accept that following appropriately is better than leading habitually. Post-transformational leadership requires that all staff learn the skills of mentor, peer-coach, adviser, helper, carer, learner – and follower, too.

Conclusion: some propositions

In this chapter we have argued that sustained school improvement requires a rather different conception of leadership from those described in the contemporary literature. We have suggested limitations to both trans-actional and transformational leadership models as a means of providing leadership for the long haul in school improvement. In the previous sections we have also attempted to provide some understanding of what post-transformational leadership might look like in both principle and practice – and have given examples from the schools with which we work.

In concluding, we have set out nine propositions which, together, seem to encapsulate some of the key themes we have raised in this chapter and provide the parameters for what we term 'post-transformational leadership'. It seems to us that this is the conceptualisation of leadership most appro-priate to long-term improvement endeavours in schools.

Proposition 1
The focus for leadership in actively improving schools is the creation and expansion of improvement capacity – a complex blend of structural and cultural development combined with an evolving contextual and theoretical knowledge-base. Such capacity change – culture, structure and knowledge – supports continuous organisational and professional renewal.

Proposition 2
Schools seeking to develop dispersed leadership models will move from the lowest common denominator of shared aims to the highest common factor of shared values and beliefs.

Proposition 3
Leadership in actively improving schools will challenge the system path-ologies, organisational dysfunctionalities and other barriers to school development that have historically inhibited school improvement work.

Proposition 4
In actively improving schools, the focus is less upon the characteristics of 'the leader' than upon creating shared contexts for adult learning about leadership. School leaders develop leadership capacity.

Proposition 5
School leaders in continuously developing schools give away leadership and coach others to be successful.

Proposition 6
Actively improving schools will have reconceptualised the nature and delivery systems for adult professional learning – both as a vehicle for pedagogic learning and as a means of generating leadership density.

Proposition 7
Leadership in continuously improving schools not only expands, but changes over time. Leadership repertoires and styles will evolve as the school's own cycle of development evolves.

Proposition 8
Post-transformational leadership operates significantly in the domains of induction and coaching, cultural transmission and values articulation.

Proposition 9
In schools with a highly developed improvement capacity, not only do staff at a variety of levels take on leadership and cultural transmission roles, but so do students. Students are seen as a significant voice, as co-leaders in the school improvement efforts, as well as the prime focus for school improvement activity.

References

Ainscow, M., Hopkins, D., Southworth, G. and West, M. (1994). *Creating the Conditions for School Improvement,* London: David Fulton.

Beare, H, Caldwell, B.J. and Millikan, R.H. (1989) *Creating an Excellent School,* London: Routledge.

Brighouse, T. (1991) *What Makes A Good School?,* Stafford Network Educational Press.

Caldwell, B. and Spinks, J.M. (1992) *Leading the Self-Managing School,* Lewes: Falmer Press.

Campbell, P., Edgar, S. and Halstead, A. (1994) *Students as Evaluators,* in 'Phi Detta Kappan, vol.76, no.2, October.

Crawford, M., Kydd, L. and Riches, C. (eds) (1997) *Leadership and Teams in Educational Management,* Buckingham: Open University Press.

Dalin, P., with Rolff, H, G and Kleekamp, B (1993) *Changing the School Culture,* London: Cassell.

DES (1997) *Ten Good Schools,* London: Department of Education and Science.

Donahoe, T. (1993) *Finding the Way: Structure, Time and Culture in School Improvement,* 'Phi Delta Kappan', vol.75, pp. 298–305.

Duignan, P and Macpherson, R (1987), 'The Educative Leadership Project', in *Educational Management and Administration* 15: 49–62.

Evans, R. (1998) *The Human Side of School Change,* San Francisco: Jossey Bass.

Fielding, M (1997) 'Beyond school effectiveness and school improvement: lighting the slow fuse of possibility', *The Curriculum Journal* 8(1): 7–27.

Fullan. M, (1992) *Successful School Improvement,* Buckingham: Open University Press.

—— (1993) *Change Forces: Probing the depths of educational reform,* London: Falmer Press.

Goldberg, B. and Richards, J. (1996) 'The Co-NECT design for school change', in Stringfield, S. and Ross, S.M. (eds) *Bold Plans for School Restructuring: The New American Schools' Designs,* New Jersey: LEA Associates.

Grace, G. (1995) *School Leadership: Beyond Educational Management,* London: Falmer Press.

Handy, C. (1990) *The Age of Unreason,* Boston, MA: Harvard Business School.

Harris, A., Jamieson, I. M. and Russ, J. (1995) 'A study of "effective" departments in secondary schools', *School Organisations* 15 (3).

Harris, A. (1998) 'Differential departmental performance,' *Journal of Education Management and Administration* 27 (3), Summer.

Hopkins, D., Ainscow, M. and West, M. (1994) *School Improvement in an Era of Change,* London: Cassell.

Hopkins, D. West, M. and Ainscow, M. (1996) *Improving the Quality of Education for All,* London: David Fulton.

Hopkins, D. Harris, A. and Jackson, D. (1997) 'Understanding the school's, capacity for development: growth states and strategies', *School Leadership and Management* 17 (3): 401–11.

Huberman, M. (1993) *The Lives of Teachers,* New York: Teachers College Press.

Jackson, D., Raymond L., Wetherill, E. and Fielding, M. (1998) 'Students as partners in the school improvement process: students as researchers', paper presented at the ICSEI Conference, Manchester, Jan. 1998.

Joyce, B., Calhoun, E. and Hopkins, D. (1999) *The New Structure of School Improvement,* Buckingham: Open University Press.

Joyce, B., Wolf, J. And Calhoun, E. (1993) *The Self Renewing School,* Alexandria, VA: Association for Supervision and Curriculum Development.

Louis, K.S., Marks, H.M. and Druse, S. (1994) 'Teachers' Professional community in restructuring schools', paper prepared for the American Educational Research Association, New Orleans, April 1994.

Louis, K.S. (1994) 'Beyond "Managed Change". Re-thinking how schools improve', in *School Effectiveness and School Improvement* 5 (1): 2–24.

Louis, K.S. and Leithwood, K. (1998) *Learning Organisations,* Lisse: Swets and Zeitlinger.

Mitchell, D.E. and Tucker, S. (1992) 'Leadership as a way of thinking', *Educational Leadership,* February.

Mortimore, P. (1998) School Matters: *The Junior Years,* Wells: Open Books.

Murphy, J. (1991) *Restructuring Schools; Capturing and Assessing the Phenomen on,* New York: Teachers College Press.

Murphy, J. and Louis, K. A. (1994) *Reshaping the Principalship Insights from Transformational Reform Efforts,* Thousand Oaks, CA: Corwin Press.

Myers, K. (ed.) (1995) *Schools Make a Difference Project,* London: Falmer Press.

Reynolds, D., Hopkins, D. and Stoll, L. (1993) 'Linking school effectiveness knowledge and school improvement practice towards a synergy, *School Effectiveness and School Improvement* 4 (1): 37–58.

Rosenblum, S., Louise, K.S. and Rossmiller, R. (1994) School leadership and teacher quality of work life', in Rossmiller, R. Murphy, J. and Louise, K.S. (eds) *Reshaping the Principalship: Lesson from Restructuring Schools*, Newbury Park: Corwin Press.

Rudduck, J., Chaplain, R. and Wallace, G. (1996) *School Improvement: What Can Pupils tell Us?*, London: David Fulton.

Rutter, M., Maugham, B., Mortimore, P. and Ouston, J. (1979) *Fifteen Thousand Hours*, Wells: Open Books.

Sammons, P. (1996) 'Complexities in the judgement of school effectiveness', *Educational Research and Evaluation* 2(2): 113–49.

Sammons, P., Hillman, J. and Mortimore, P. (1995) *Key Characteristics of Effective Schools: A Review of School Effectiveness Research*, London: Institute of Education/OFSTED.

Scott, W.R. (1987) Organisations: *Rational, National and Open Systems*, Englewood Cliffs: Prentice-Hall.

Sergiovanni, T.J. (1994) *Building Community in Schools*, San Francisco: Jossey-Bass.

SooHoo, S. (1993) 'Students as partners in research and restructuring schools', *The Educational Forum* 57: 386–93.

Stoll, L. and Fink, D. (1996) *Changing Our Schools: Linking School Effectiveness and School Improvement*, Buckingham: Open University Press.

Smyth, J. (ed.) (1989) *Critical Perspectives on Education Leadership*, Lewes: Falmer Press.

Van Velzen, W., Miles M., Eckolm, M. *et al.* (1995) *Making School Improvement Work*, Leuven, Belgium: ACCO (Academic Publishing Company).

Wallace, M. (1994) *Planning for Change in Turbulent Times: The Case of a Multiracial Primary School*, London: Cassell.

Wallace, M. and Hall, V. (1994) *Inside the SMT: Teamwork in Secondary School Management*, London: Paul Chapman.

Weick, K. (1976) 'Educational organisations as loosely coupled systems', *Administrative Science Quarterly*, 21(I): 1–19.

West, M., Ainscow, M. and Hopkins D. (1997) 'Tracking the moving school: challenging assumptions, increasing understanding of how school improvement is brought about,' paper presented at the European Education Research Association Annual Conference, Frankfurt.

Wohltetter, P., Smyer, R. and Mohrmam, S.A. (1994) 'New boundaries for school-based management: the high involvement model', in *Educational Evaluation and Policy Analysis* 16: 268–76.

4 The effects of different sources of leadership on student engagement in school

Kenneth Leithwood and Doris Jantzi

Leadership may be offered by many different people in a school, and may also arise from non-personal sources. The study described in this chapter examined the relative effects on student engagement of school leadership provided by principals, teachers, and those in other roles. Also examined were the effects of 'total leadership'. Data for the study were survey responses from a total of 2,727 teachers and 9,025 students in 110 elementary and secondary schools in one large Ontario school district.

The study

This study was prompted by the results of a review of literature on principal effects reported by Hallinger and Heck in 1996 (Hallinger and Heck 1996a, b). Hallinger and Heck discovered that the common professional and public assumption of large principal leadership effects on school outcomes, an assumption accounting for the key role assumed by school reform initiatives, was not warranted. Instead, their analyses suggested that principal effects were small and usually required exceptionally sophisticated research designs to detect. Results of this review demonstrated that most principal leadership effects on students were indirect, leading to the recommendation that more attention be given to school conditions through which such leadership influence flowed.

Results also suggested that future research measure the moderating influence on leadership of key context variables such as the socio-economic status of the school population. In addition, Hallinger and Heck's analyses found that in almost all of their forty principal effects studies, student achievement, mostly basic math and language scores on standardised achievement tests, was used as the dependent variable. While an obviously important, and some would say 'preeminent' set of outcomes, they are by no means the only important outcomes for which schools are accountable. Evidence available at present, however, sheds little light on the consequences for leadership of important, non-achievement student outcomes, and whether the avenues of leadership influence differ depending on type of student outcome.

Finally, the Hallinger and Heck reviews stimulated us to consider just how narrowly school leadership is usually conceived. Research on school leadership is heavily oriented to the principalship. And if, as Hallinger and Heck claimed, there are only approximately forty acceptable, empirical studies of principal leadership spread over a 15 year period, it is safe to assume that the effects of other sources of school leadership are greatly understudied.

Arising from these issues identified in the Hallinger and Heck (1996 a, b) analysis, this study addressed three questions. What is the relative influence on the school, as a whole, of the leadership offered by those in different roles? How much of the variation in school conditions and student outcomes is accounted for by teacher as compared with principal leadership? Does the total amount of leadership exercised in a school account for significant variation in school conditions and student outcomes?

In the framework used to guide our study, leadership is assumed to directly affect students, as well as school and classroom conditions, and both sets of conditions directly and indirectly affect student engagement with school. The effects of leadership, as well as school and classroom conditions, are moderated by family educational culture, which also has a direct effect on student engagement with school. This section summarises research relevant to each element of our framework, indicating how that research influenced our approach to each of the three research questions.

Leadership

The effects of two different conceptions of leadership were examined, including role-specific leadership and leadership conceived of as an organisation-wide phenomenon.

Role-specific leadership

The two most frequently examined sources of school leadership are principals and teachers. While substantial literatures have developed about each (touched on below), there is almost no evidence available concerning their relative effects. As a consequence, we know little about such critical matters as how these two sources of influence interact in schools, how they might work synergistically to add value to the school, or what would be the most cost-effective distribution of scarce leadership development resources.

The independent literatures concerning principal and teacher leadership are primarily concerned with the forms and effects of such leadership. About the forms of principal leadership, there is a considerable body of literature. For example, a recent review of literature (Leithwood and Duke, in press) was able to locate a total of 121 articles addressing forms of primarily principal leadership in just four prominent educational administration journals within the past decade alone. These articles described twenty distinct forms of leadership which the reviewers further classified into six generic leadership approaches. Distinguished by their basic foci, key assumptions, and nature and locus of leadership power, these approaches included instructional, transformational, moral, participative, managerial, and contingent leadership. Notwithstanding this considerable attention to forms of principal leadership, as well as the influence typically attributed to some of these forms by qualitative studies (e.g. Hannay and Ross 1997), quantitative evidence about principal leadership effects remains surprisingly tentative (Hallinger and Heck 1996a).

Teacher leadership may be either formal or informal in nature. Lead teacher, master teacher, department head, union representative, member of the school's governance council, mentor – these are among the many designations associated with formal teacher leadership roles. Teachers assuming these roles are expected to carry out a wide range of functions: representing the school in district-level decision-making (Fullan 1993); stimulating the professional growth of colleagues (Wasley 1991); being an advocate for teachers' work (Bascia 1997); and improving the school's decision-making processes (Malen, Ogawa and Kranz 1990). Those appointed to formal leadership roles are also sometimes expected to induct new teachers into the school, and to influence positively, the willingness and capacity of other teachers to implement change in the school (Fullan and Hargreaves 1991; Whitaker 1995).

Empirical evidence concerning the actual effects of either formal or informal teacher leadership are limited in quantity and report mixed results. For example, many of the more ambitious initiatives establishing formal teacher leadership roles through the creation of career ladders have been abandoned (Hart 1995). And Hannay and Denby's (1994) study of department heads found that they were not very effective as facilitators of change largely due to their lack of knowledge and skill in effective change strategies. On the other hand, Duke, Showers and Imber (1980) found that increased participation of teachers in school decision-making resulted in a more democratic school. Increased professional learning for the teacher leader also has been reported as an effect of assuming such a role (Wasley 1991; Lieberman, Saxl and Miles 1988).

The concept of leadership does not take on different meanings when qualified by the term teacher or principal: it entails the exercise of influence over the beliefs, actions, and values of others (Hart 1995). What may be different is how that influence is exercised and to what end. In a traditional school, for example, those in formal administrative roles have greater access than teachers to positional power in their attempts to influence classroom practice, whereas teachers may have greater access to the power that flows from technical expertise about teaching and learning. Traditionally, as well, teachers and administrators often attempt to exercise leadership in relation to quite different aspects of the school's functioning, although teachers often report a strong interest in expanding their spheres of influence (Taylor and Bogotch 1994; Reavis and Griffith 1993). These are reasons for expecting different effects from principal and teacher leaders, exercised through different conditions in the school.

Leadership as an organisation-wide phenomenon (total leadership)

The idea that leadership is not confined to those in formal managerial or leadership roles is at least 60 years old (Pounder, Ogawa and Adams 1995; Barnard 1968). Recent interest in distributed leadership has been promoted by 'substitutes for leadership' theory (e.g. Kerr 1978), and institutional theory which argues that leadership is an organisation-wide phenomenon (Ogawa and Bossert 1995; Pounder, Ogawa and Adams 1995). Organisational restructuring initiatives have stimulated enquiry about distributed conceptions of leadership, also, as flatter, team-based, more organic structures began to be favoured over hierarchical structure (Banner and Gagné 1995), a trend that swept through educational organizations in the form of site-based management (Murphy and Beck 1995). And teacher leadership in the form of mentoring, career ladders, and greater participation in school decision-making, as discussed above, has become one of the central pillars in recent school reform initiatives (Hart 1995), further stimulating interest in non-managerial, distributed forms of leadership.

While support for the idea of distributed leadership is widespread, empirical evidence concerning its nature and effects in any organisational context remains extremely thin (Bryman 1996). To illustrate, Ogawa and Bossert (1995), in arguing for the promise of an institutional approach to research on leadership, fail to cite a single empirical study in their consideration of implications for such research. A decade after the idea of substitutes for leadership was first published, Jermier and Kerr (1997) observe that 'we do not have much research on the processes through which the substitutes themselves exert their effects'. Similarly, the literatures on site-based management, shared decision-making, and teacher leadership offer skimpy insights about the effects of those distributed forms of leadership about which they are centrally concerned (Leithwood and Menzies 1998; Conley 1993; Little 1995).

When leadership is viewed as an organisation-wide phenomenon, it has many potential sources, in addition to teachers and principals. Parents and students are other obvious sources, for example, as are those non-personal, organisation qualities identified in the 'substitutes for leadership' literature such as task clarity and certainty, intrinsic sources of teacher rewards, formalisation of the curriculum (Pitner 1986), state regulation of instruction, and teacher peer groups (Firestone 1996). A largely unexplored expectation that arises from viewing leadership as an organisation-wide phenomenon is that the total amount of leadership from all sources in the school may account for significant variation in school effects (Bryman 1996: 284). But we are unaware of empirical tests of this implication in school contexts. Our study provided one such test limited, however, to a focus on personal sources of leadership only.

School and classroom conditions mediating leader effects

As Hallinger and Heck (1996a) note:

> principal leadership that makes a difference is aimed toward influencing internal school processes that are directly linked to student learning. These internal processes range from school policies and norms (e.g., academic expectations, school mission, student opportunity to learn, instructional organization, academic learning time) to the practices of teachers.
>
> (1996a: 38)

Because the largest proportion of principal effects on students are mediated by conditions or characteristics of the school, a significant challenge for leadership research is to identify those alterable conditions known to have direct effects on students, and to enquire about the nature and strength of the relationship between them and leadership. Hallinger and Heck (1996) found evidence of only one mediating variable, school goals, consistently interacting with principal leadership. One reason for such limited results may be insufficient importance attributed by researchers to their choices of mediating variables. Leadership typically is 'abstracted from the organizational processes of which it is a part [rather than being viewed] as a special kind of organizing activity' (Hosking and Morley 1988: 92–3).

Mediating school conditions included in this study were selected from a wide-ranging reviews of theoretical and empirical literature concerning classroom, school and district effects (Leithwood and Aitken 1995). Results of this review were sorted into seven categories reflecting elements often associated with the design of formal organisation (Galbraith 1977; Daft 1988; Banner and Gagné 1995).

Mission and goals

These are what members of the school understand to be both the explicit and implicit purposes and directions for the school. Evidence suggests that such purposes contribute to school effectiveness, to the extent that members are aware of them, and to the extent they are perceived to be clear, meaningful, useful, current, congruent with district directions, and to reflect important educational values. This variable bears close similarity to what Stringfield and Slavin (1992) refer to as 'meaningful goals' and what Reynolds *et al.* (1996) label 'shared vision and goals'.

Culture

This variable consists of the norms, values, beliefs and assumptions that shape school members' decisions and practices. The contribution of culture to school effectiveness depends on the content of these norms, values, beliefs and assumptions (e.g. student centered). It also depends on the extent to which they are shared, and whether they foster collaborative work. This variable shares elements of Reynolds *et al.* (1996) 'learning environment' and the 'consensus and cooperative planning' to which Scheerens (1997), and Creemers and Reetzig (1996) refer.

School planning

The explicit means used for deciding on mission and goals and on the actions to be taken for their accomplishment is the meaning of this variable. Planning processes contribute to school effectiveness to the extent that they bring together local needs and district goals into a shared school vision (Mortimore 1993; Hargreaves and Hopkins 1991).

Instructional services

These are interventions by teachers with students aimed at stimulating students' learning. Practices associated with this variable include, for example, instructional planning, the consideration of learning principles, clarification of appropriate instructional goals, decisions about curricular content, selection of instructional strategies, and the uses of instructional time. A large literature supports the important contribution to school effectiveness of these and closely related variables (Reynolds *et al.* 1996; Creemers and Reetzig 1996) and suggests that classroom-level variables are a much more powerful source of achievement variation than are school-level variables (e.g. Bosker *et al.* 1990).

Structure and organisation

This variable is defined by the nature of the relationships established among people and groups in the school and between the school and its external constituents. Such relationships contribute to school effectiveness, evidence suggests, when they support the purposes of the curriculum, and the requirements for instruction. Structure and organisation also contribute to school effectiveness when they facilitate staffs' work, professional learning, and opportunities for collaboration. This variable includes elements of what Reynolds *et al.* (1996) include in 'shared vision and goals', as well as in school ethos or 'learning environment'.

Information collection and decision-making

The nature and quality of information collected for decision-making in the school and the ways in which members of the school use that information and are involved in decisions also influences school outcomes. Schools benefit when information for decision-making is systematically collected, varied, and widely available to most school members for decisions. This variable is reflected in the importance attached to 'monitoring student progress' (Reynolds *et al.* 1996; Mortimore 1993) although it extends considerably beyond this focus.

Policies and procedures

Guidelines for decision-making and action in the school is the meaning of this variable. These guidelines contribute to school effectiveness when they are student oriented, encourage continuous professional growth among staff, and encourage the allocation of resources to school priorities without stifling individual initiative. Evidence for the importance of this variable can be found in the concept of 'high expectations', 'consistency' and 'control' (Mortimore 1993; Creemers 1994).

Student engagement with school

The non-standard measure of student outcomes chosen as the dependent measure in this study, student engagement with school, was conceptualised, after the work of Jeremy Finn (1989), as having both behavioural and affective components. Extent of students' participation in school activities, both inside and outside of the classroom, is the behavioural component. The affective component is the extent to which students identify with school and feel they belong, an internal state found to mediate a wide range of achievement and behavioural outcomes among students. As it was defined and measured in this study, student engagement is quite similar to the 'social cohesion' variable used by Oxley (1997) as a dependent measure for her test of the effects of community-like school qualities on students.

Student engagement was chosen as the outcome measure for several reasons. Expanding our understanding of leadership effects beyond basic math and language achievement was one of the reasons. The second reason was that it measures, directly and indirectly, educationally significant variables. For example, for many students, dropping out of school is the final step in a long process of gradual disengagement and reduced participation in the formal curriculum of the school, as well as in the school's co-curriculum and more informal social life. Reversing such disengagement is a necessary requirement for achieving the ambitious outcomes advocated by most current school reform initiatives. Variation in schools' retention rates are likely to be predicted well from estimates of student participation and identification (Finn 1989). Second, some factors giving rise to students becoming at risk are to be found very early in the child's pre-school and school experiences. Patterns of student participation and identification are sensitive to the consequences of these factors as early as the primary grades.

Change in a student's participation and identification is a reliable symptom of problems which should be redressed as early as possible (Lloyd 1978). Finally, at least a modest amount of evidence suggests that student engagement is a reliable predictor of variation in such typical student outcomes as social studies, math, and language achievement (Finn and Cox 1992; Dukelow 1993).

Family educational culture

In this study, family educational culture was used in place of more commonly used socio-economic status (SES) measures to represent contributions to student outcomes from home and family sources. Historically, SES has been the most powerful predictor of student success at school (e.g. Coleman *et al.* 1966; Bridge, Judd and Moock 1979). And it also has been shown to influence the form of leadership exercised by principals (Hallinger, Bickman and Davis, in press). But SES is a crude proxy, masking a host of family interactions which have powerful educational consequences. These interactions vary widely across families, often without much relation to family income, for example.

The content of family educational culture includes the assumptions, norms, values and beliefs held by the family about intellectual work, in general, school work in particular, and the conditions which foster both. Six literature reviews were used as the sources of seven dimensions of either the family's educational culture or resulting behaviours and conditions demonstrably related to school success (Bloom 1984; Walberg 1984; Scott-Jones 1984; Finn 1989; Rumberger 1983, 1987). Taken as a whole, these dimensions represent what Walberg (1984) referred to as the 'alterable curriculum of the home'. This curriculum, twice as predictive of academic learning as SES according to Walberg's analysis, includes:

- Family work habits: students benefit from a home environment which includes a reasonable degree of routine, emphasis on regularity in the use of space and time, priority given to school work over other activities, and adult models of a positive attitude toward learning.
- Academic guidance and support: student growth is fostered by the quality and availability of parental discussion, help and encouragement in relation to school work and by the provision of conditions which support such school work (e.g. study aids).
- Stimulation: aside from school work, students benefit from a home environment which provides opportunities to explore ideas, events and the larger environment. These opportunities may arise, for example, during meal conversations, in response to news events, as part of family travel and the like.
- Language development: student growth is assisted by opportunities in the home for developing correct and effective use of language and by

speaking the language of school instruction in the home. Especially among young children, cognitive development is assisted when adult language is relatively elaborated and when messages are made explicit and context-free.

- Academic and occupational aspirations and expectations: school achievement and school completion are strongly related to parents' aspirations and expectations. Such aspirations and expectations have their most positive effect when they are both realistic and high for the individual child, and when they manifest themselves in specific standards for school achievement established with the child.
- Providing adequate health and nutritional conditions: ensuring a balanced diet and adequate sleep are minimum conditions to be fostered by the family.
- Physical setting: it is important to provide personal space for students which is sheltered from excessive social stimulation. Excessive noise also has been linked to reading disorders, impaired auditory discrimination and poor performance on visual search tasks.

Research methods

Data about leadership, school conditions, student engagement, and family educational culture were collected through surveys in one large school district in a Canadian province. One survey collected data from teachers on school conditions and leadership, the other collected evidence from students on their engagement with school and their family's educational culture. The district, serving a population of approximately 58,500 urban, suburban, and rural students, employed a total of 4,456 teachers, and 201 principals and vice principals in 100 elementary and 16 secondary schools. Results of the survey were analysed using several forms of multivariate statistics. For a more detailed, technical description of research methods, see Leithwood and Jantzi (1998). In sum:

- Descriptive statistics (means, standard deviations) were calculated for responses to items measuring each variable and the reliabilities of the scales formed by those items were calculated (Appendix, Table 1).
- A factor analysis was conducted on all items measuring the mediating variables. Results suggest that these items loaded on two factors – classroom and school (Appendix, Table 2).
- Separate regression analyses were computed to estimate the proportion of variation in each mediating variable explained by principal and by teacher leadership (Appendix, Table 3).
- Path analyses (LISREL) were conducted to estimate total direct and indirect effects of three forms of leadership on student engagement (Appendix, Table 4).

Principal and teacher leadership

Results of the study provided evidence of principal and teacher leadership effects considered separately, as well as the relative effects of these two sources of leadership. One finding was that the effects on student engagement of both sources of leadership are substantially moderated by family educational culture. This moderating effect is especially strong for teacher leadership. A plausible implication of these findings is that high levels of student engagement reduce teachers' perceived needs for teacher (or principal) leadership. Student engagement could be conceived of as a substitute for leadership (Howell 1997), as well as a student outcome.

A second important finding was that neither source of leadership, principal or teacher, had statistically significant effects on student engagement, at least when family educational culture was included in the analyses. Two quite different interpretations of these results are possible. The most obvious interpretation is that student engagement in school is not affected in any important way by school leadership, an interpretation fundamentally in contradiction with the assumptions of most school professionals, normative assertions about the role of leadership in schools (e.g. Hudson 1997; Foster 1989), and the results of most school effectiveness studies (e.g. Mortimore 1993). This might be termed the 'romance of leadership' interpretation, after Meindl's (1995) argument that leadership is a convenient, phenomenologically legitimate social construction which, nonetheless, masks a complex, multi-sourced bundle of influences on organisational outcomes.

A second interpretation of these results, after Hallinger and Heck (1996b), cautions against dismissing, as not meaningful, the admittedly small effects of principal and teacher leadership on student engagement. The relationships between these two sources of leadership and school conditions are moderately strong, explaining 66 per cent of the variation in school conditions, a proportion that does not change by adding family educational culture to the analyses. Their total effects on student engagement are just as strong as the total effects of school conditions and stronger than classroom conditions.

To put this interpretation in a broader context, recent reviews of empirical research on school effectiveness suggest that educational factors for which data are available explain, in total, something less than 20 per cent of the variation in student cognitive outcomes (very little evidence is available concerning such non-cognitive outcomes as the one used in this study). Reynolds *et al.* (1996) suggest 8–12 per cent for research carried out in the United Kingdom, while Creemers and Reetzig suggest 10–20 per cent for studies carried out 'in the Western Hemisphere . . . after correction for student intake measures such as aptitude or social class . . .' (1996: 203). Variation within this range from study to study may be explained by, for example, school size, type of student outcome serving as the dependent measure, nature of students, and department and subject matter differences.

While these relatively small amounts of explained variation are now considered to be both meaningful, and practically significant, a school is not a single variable. It is an aggregate of variables – the so-called correlates of effective schools, or the school and classroom conditions used as mediating variables in this study. Some of these variables most likely contribute more strongly than others to school's effects, although they have yet to be unpacked empirically, except for distinguishing between classroom and school-level factors (Creemers and Reetzig 1996; Scheerens 1997). Efforts to do the unpacking, however, realistically begin with very modest amounts of variation to be explained, especially if it is assumed (reasonably) that at least a handful of factors contribute to explained variation. This was Ogawa and Hart's (1985) argument in claiming importance for their finding that principal leadership explained 2–8 per cent of the variation in student performance. Under such circumstances, knowing the relative explanatory power of a variable will be at least as interesting as knowing the total amount of variation it explains.

Finally, the results suggest that teacher leadership effects far outweigh principal leadership effects before taking into account the moderating effects of family educational culture. When this variable is taken into account, teacher leadership effects are reduced considerably, but remain at least as strong as principal leader effects. More teacher leadership has been advocated over the past decade for several reasons but without much evidence that it has the potential its advocates claim. Evidence from this study is similar to Heller and Firestone's (1995) conclusion that principal leadership does not stand out as a critical part of the change process.

Results of our study further suggest that the effects of both principal and teacher leadership are mediated by most of the same school and classroom conditions. Only in relation to mission, culture, and structure and organisation were there differences of any consequence in the amount of variation explained by each source of leadership. Principal leadership explained more variation in mission and culture, whereas teacher leadership explained more variation in structure and organisation. On the basis of this evidence, it seems that teacher and principal leadership exert largely the same amount of influence on many of the same features of schools and classrooms. This challenges the wisdom of current policies governing the allocation of leadership development resources within many districts and provinces/states. Disproportionate amounts of these resources are allocated to the development of leadership capacities of those aspiring to, or already in, the principalship. Redistributing these resources more equally among those in teacher and administrator roles would appear to be more appropriate.

Total leadership

While principals and teachers are obviously important sources of leadership in schools, there are longstanding and compelling reasons to inquire about other role-related and non-person sources of leadership (Barnard 1968; Bryman 1996; Jermier and Kerr 1997). Conceiving of leadership as something that may be widely distributed throughout the school in persons, as well as in elements of the school's design, raises the largely unexamined possibility that the greater the total amount of leadership exercised, the better off is the organisation (e.g. department heads, headteachers, committees, principals).

The aggregated influence of seven role-related sources of leadership was used to construct a measure of total school leadership in our study. This measure was then used in an effort to examine the total direct and indirect effects on student engagement. Results indicated that total leadership had non-significant, negative effects on student engagement. It also had significant, positive, but much weaker relationships with school conditions than any of the other sources of leadership measured.

These results do not suggest a simple, linear, 'more is better', relationship between total leadership and school effects. Beyond some, as yet unclear, optimal level of total leadership, perhaps more leadership actually detracts from clarity of purpose, sense of mission, sufficient certainty about what needs to be done to allow for productive collective action in the school, and the like. Because robust, quantitative evidence about the effects on schools of leadership from sources other than teachers and principals is almost non-existent, we believe these results call for considerable caution on the part of those who argue that everyone should become a leader. However attractively egalitarian and democratic that may seem, perhaps schools benefit most from the leadership of a small number of easily identified sources.

Conclusion

Our study examined the effects, on student engagement with school, of principal and teacher leadership, as well as the total amounts of leadership offered by others. We assumed that, whatever the effects of leadership on students, these effects are more likely to work through their influence on such characteristics of the school as its culture and structure, for example, rather than directly. Also, we assumed that contributions of families' educational cultures would need to be accounted for if we were to detect the unique contributions of leadership to student engagement.

Results of our analysis of this evidence suggest that the leadership of principals has a modest but significant effect on student engagement, an effect no greater and probably no less than the leadership of teachers. The effects of both principal and teacher leadership appear to influence approximately the same features of the school. And it appears that there is no advantage in encouraging widely distributed forms of leadership (total leadership) at least with respect to student engagement. Results of the study support the distribution of a larger proportion of current leadership development resources to the development of teacher leadership.

Appendix: tables

Table 4.1 Teacher ratings of school and classroom conditions and transformational leadership, as well as student ratings of family culture and engagement (N=110 Schools)

	Mean	SD	Scale reliability (Cronbach's Alpha)
Teacher ratings of school conditions:			
School Conditions (Aggregate)	3.82[1]	0.31	0.87
Culture	4.03	0.31	0.89
Information collection and decision making	4.04	0.33	0.88
Mission and goals	3.88	0.49	0.95
Planning	3.61	0.40	0.92
Structure and organization	3.58	0.40	0.87
Teacher ratings of classroom conditions:			
Classroom conditions (aggregate)	3.97	0.22	0.78
Policy and procedures	3.77	0.25	0.79
Instructional strategies	4.17	0.22	0.88
Teacher ratings of leadership:			
Principal	3.40[2]	0.47	n/a
Teacher	3.10[2]	0.35	0.76
Total Leadership	13.57[3]	2.28	0.53
Student ratings of family educational culture:			
Family Educational Culture	4.02	0.33	0.79
Student ratings of engagement with school:			
Participation	3.49	0.26	0.81
Identification	3.94	0.27	0.93

Notes: [1]Rating scale: 1=Disagree strongly; 5=Agree strongly.
[2]Rating scale: 1=Minimal to 4=Very strong influence.
[3]Total leadership is the sum of influences from all seven sources, with 1 as the minimum and 28 as the maximum.

Table 4.2 Factor pattern matrix resulting from analysis of teacher ratings of conditions within their schools (N=110 Schools)

	Factors	
	1 School conditions	*2* Classroom conditions
1. School culture	0.78	
2. Information collection and decision making	0.63	
3. School mission	0.79	
4. Planning	0.84	
5. Structure and organization	0.84	
6. Policy and procedures		0.80
7. Instructional strategies		0.92
Eigenvalue	3.75	1.25
Percent of explained variance	53.6	17.9

Note: Principal components extraction with varimax rotation was used to analyse the seven school conditions to estimate the number of factors measured by the specific conditions. The school conditions loaded on two factors; one factor included most items concerned with school-wide conditions, and the second factor included most items concerning classroom practices, as well as policies about such practices.

Table 4.3 Effects of principal and teacher leadership influence on school and classroom
conditons (N=110 Schools)

Dependent variables	Principal influence		Teacher influence	
	Adj R2	F ratio	Adj R2	F ratio
School conditions:				
School conditions mean	0.36	61.18***	0.34	56.33***
Planning	0.32	51.96***	0.39	72.13***
Mission	0.26	39.71***	0.18	25.49***
Culture	0.26	38.74***	0.15	20.24***
Structure and organization	0.18	24.88***	0.29	45.24***
Information collection	0.15	19.37***	0.12	15.37***
Classroom conditions:				
Classroom conditions mean	0.05	6.87**	0.07	9.21**
Instruction	0.01	2.06	0.02	3.55
Policy and procedures	0.09	10.44**	0.09	12.40***

*** $p<0.001$; ** $p<0.01$.

Note: Each row in the table summarises two separate regression analyses run to determine
how much of the variation in the school or classroom variable was explained by
principal leadership and how much was explained by teacher leadership. Degrees of
freedom for F equations were (1,108).

Table 4.4 Effects of Different Forms of Leadership on Student Engagement with School

	Total effects on	
	Participation	Identification
Principal leadership	0.04	0.08
Teacher leadership	0.10	−0.04
Total leadership	−0.07	−0.02
School conditions	0.09	0.26*
Classroom conditions	0.03	0.08
Family educational culture	0.84*	0.76*

Note: *Significant effect. The effects of the non-leadership variables varied slightly (<0.10)
depending upon the form of leadership used in the analysis.

References

Banner, D.K. and Gagné, T.E. (1995) *Designing Effective Organizations: Traditional
and Transformational Views*, Thousand Oaks, CA: Sage Publications.

Barnard, C.I. (1968) *Functions of the Executive*, Cambridge, MA: Harvard University Press.

Bascia, N. (1997) 'Invisible leadership: teachers' union activity in schools', *The
Alberta Journal of Educational Research* 33(2/3): 69–85.

Bloom, B.S. (1984) 'The search for methods of group instruction as effective as
one-to-one tutoring', *Educational Leadership, May*, 4–17.

Bosker, R.J., Kremers, E.J. and Lugthart, E. (1990) 'School and instruction effects
on mathematics achievement', *School Effectiveness and School Improvement* 1(4):
233–48.

Bridge, R., Judd, C. and Moock, P. (1979) *The Determinants of Educational outcomes*, Cambridge, MA: Ballinger.

Bryman, A. (1996) 'Leadership in organizations', in S. Clegg, C. Hard and W.R. Nord (eds), *Handbook of Organization Studies*, Thousand Oaks, CA: Sage Publications, pp. 276–92.

Coleman, J.S. *et al.* (1966) *Equality of educational opportunity*, Washington, DC: US Government Printing Office.

Conley, D.T. (1993) *Roadmap to Restructuring: Policies, Practices, and the Emerging Visions of Schooling*, Oregon: ERIC Clearinghouse on Educational Management.

Creemers, B.P.M. (1994) *The Effective Classroom*, London: Cassell.

Creemers, B.P.M. and Reezigt, G.J. (1996) 'School level conditions affecting the effectiveness of instruction', *School Effectiveness and School Improvement* 7(3): 197–228.

Daft, R.L. (1988) *Organization Theory and Design* (third edition), St Paul, MN: West Publishing Company.

Duke, D., Showers, B. and Imber, M. (1980). 'Teachers and shared decision making: the costs and benefits of involvement', *Educational Administration Quarterly* 16: 93–106.

Dukelow, G.A. (1993). 'A statistical analysis of educational variables that influence high school students' grades and participation', University of Victoria, unpublished Masters thesis.

Finn, J.D. (1989) 'Withdrawing from school', *Review of Educational Research* 59(2): 117–43.

Finn, J.D. and Cox, D. (1992) 'Participation and withdrawal among fourth-grade pupils', *American Educational Research Journal* 29(1): 141–62.

Firestone, W.A. (1996) 'Leadership: roles or functions?' in K. Leithwood *et al.* (eds), *International Handbook of Educational Leadership and Administration*, The Netherlands: Kluwer Academic Publishers, pp. 395–418.

Foster, W. (1989) 'Toward a critical practice of leadership', in J. Smyth (ed.), *Critical Perspectives on Educational Leadership*, London: Falmer Press, pp. 39–62.

Fullan, M. (1993) *Change Forces*, Toronto: Falmer.

Fullan, M. and Hargreaves, A. (1991) *What's Worth Fighting For? Working Together For Your School*, Toronto: Ontario Public School Teachers Federation.

Galbraith, J.R. (1977) *Organization Design*, Reading, MA: Addison-Wesley.

Hallinger, P., Bickman, L. and Davis, K. (in press) 'School context, principal leadership and student achievement', *Elementary School Journal*.

Hallinger, P. and Heck, R.H. (1996a) 'Reassessing the principal's role in school effectiveness: a review of empirical research, 1980–1995', *Educational Administration Quarterly* 32(1): 5–44.

—— (1996b) 'The principal's role in school effectiveness: an assessment of methodological progress, 1980–1995', in K. Leithwood *et al.* (eds), *International Handbook of Educational Leadership and Administration*, The Netherlands: Kluwer Academic Publishers, pp. 723–83.

Hannay, L.M. and Denby, M. (1994). "Secondary school change: the role of department heads', paper presented at the annual meeting of the American Educational Research Association, New Orleans, April.

Hannay, L.M. and Ross, J. (1997) 'Initiating secondary school reform: the dynamic relationship between restructuring, reculturing, and retiming', *Educational Administration Quarterly* 33(supplement): 576–603.

Hargreaves, D. and Hopkins, D. (1991) *The Empowered School*, London: Cassell.

Hart, A.W. (1995) 'Reconceiving school leadership: emergent views', *The Elementary School Journal* 96(1): 9–28.

Heller, M.F. and Firestone, W.A. (1995) 'Who's in charge here? Sources of leadership for change in eight schools'. *The Elementary School Journal* 96(1): 65–86.

Hosking, D. and Morley, I.E. (1988) 'The skills of leadership', in J.G. Hunt, B.R. Baliga, H.P. Dachler and C.A. Schriesheim (eds), *Emerging Leadership Vistas*, Lexington, MA: Lexington Books, pp. 80–106.

Howell, J. (1997) 'Substitutes for leadership: their meaning and measurement – a historical assessment', *The Leadership Quarterly* 8(2): 113–16.

Hudson, J. (1997) 'Ethical leadership: the soul of policy making', *Journal of School Leadership* 7(5): 506–20.

Jermier, J.M. and Kerr, S. (1997) 'Substitutes for leadership: the meaning and measurement – contextual recollections and current observations', *The Leadership Quarterly* 8(2): 95–101.

Kerr, S. (1978) 'Substitutes for leadership: some implications for organizational design', *Organization and Administrative Sciences* 8: 135–46.

Kerr, S. and Jermier, J. (1978) 'Substitutes for leadership: their meaning and measurement', *Organizational Behavior and Human Performance* 22: 375–403.

Leithwood, K. and Aitken, R. (1995) *Making Schools Smarter: A System for Monitoring School and District Progress*, Thousand Oaks, CA: Corwin Press.

Leithwood, K. and Duke, D. (in press) 'A century's quest to understand school leadership', in J. Murphy and K. Louis (eds), *Handbook of Research on Educational Administration*, Washington, DC: American Educational Research Association.

Leithwood, K. and Jantzi, D. (1998) 'Distributed leadership and student engagement in school', paper presented at the annual meeting of the American Educational Research Association, San Diego, April.

Leithwood, K. and Menzies, T. (1998) 'Forms and effects of school-based management: a review', *Educational Policy* 12(3).

Lieberman, A., Saxl, E.R. and Miles, M.B. (1988) 'Teacher leadership: ideology and practice', in A. Lieberman (ed.), *Building a Professional Culture in Schools*, New York: Basic Books, pp. 148–66.

Little, J.W. (1995) 'Contested ground: the basis of teacher leadership in two restructuring high schools', *The Elementary School Journal* 96(1): 47–63.

Lloyd, D. (1978) 'Prediction of school failure from third-grade data', *Educational and Psychological Measurements* 38: 1193–200.

Malen, B., Ogawa, R.T. and Krantz, J. (1990) 'What do we know about school-based management? A case study of the literature – a call for research', in W.H. Clune and J.F. Witte (eds), *Choice and Control in American Education, 2: The Practice of Choice, Decentralization, and School Restructuring*, New York: Falmer, pp. 289–342.

Meindl, J.R. (1995) 'The romance of leadership as a follower-centric theory: a social constructionist approach', *Leadership Quarterly* 6(3): 329–41.

Mortimore, P. (1993) 'School effectiveness and the management of effective learning and teaching', *School Effectiveness and School Improvement* 4(4): 290–310.

Murphy, J. and Beck, L.G. (1995) *School-Based Management as School Reform*, Thousand Oaks, CA: Sage Publications.

Ogawa, R. and Hart, A. (1985) 'The effects of principals on the instructional performance of schools', *Journal of Educational Administration* 23(1): 59–72.

Ogawa, R.T. and Bossert, S.T. (1995) 'Leadership as an organizational quality', *Educational Administration Quarterly* 31(2): 224–43.

Oxley, D. (1997) 'Theory and practice of school communities', *Educational Administration Quarterly* 33(supplement): 624–43.

Pitner, N.J. (1986) 'Substitutes for principal leader behavior: an exploratory study', *Educational Administration Quarterly* 22(2): 23–42.

Pounder, D.G., Ogawa, R.T. and Adams, E.A. (1995) 'Leadership as an organization-wide phenomena: its impact on school performance', *Educational Administration Quarterly* 31(4): 564–88.

Reavis, C. and Griffith, H. (1993) *Restructuring Schools: Theory and Practice*, Lancaster, PA: Technomic Publishing Co.

Reynolds, D., Sammons, P., Stoll, L., Barber, M. and Hillman, J. (1996) 'School effectiveness and school improvement in the United Kingdom', *School Effectiveness and School Improvement* 7(2): 133–58.

Rumberger, R.W. (1983) 'Dropping out of high school: the influence of race, sex, and family background', *American Educational Research Journal* 20: 199–220.

—— (1987) 'High school dropouts: a review of issues and evidence', *Review of Educational Research* 57(2): 101–21.

Scheerens, J. (1997) 'Conceptual models and theory-embedded principles on effective schooling', *School Effectiveness and School Improvement* 8(3): 269–310.

Scott-Jones, P. (1984) 'Family influences on cognitive development and school achievement', in E. Gordon (ed.), *Review of Research in Education, III*, Washington, DC: American Educational Research Association.

Stringfield, S.C. and Slavin, R.E. (1992) 'A hierarchical longitudinal model for elementary school effects', in B.P.M. Creemers and G.J. Reezigt (eds), *Evaluation of Effectiveness*, ICO – Publication 2.

Taylor, D.L. and Bogotch, I.E. (1994) 'School level effects of teachers' participation in decision making', *Educational Evaluation and Policy Analysis* 16(3): 302–19.

Walberg, H.J. (1984) 'Improving the productivity of America's schools', *Educational Leadership* 41(8): 19–27.

Wasley, P.A. (1991) *Teachers as Leaders: The Rhetoric of Reform and the Realities of Practice*, New York: Teachers College Press.

Whitaker, T. (1995) 'Informal teacher leadership: the key to successful change in the middle school', *NASSP Bulletin, January*, pp. 76–81.

5 Leadership in the creation of world-class schools

Brian J. Caldwell

A world-class school meets the high expectations that are set for all of its students, as determined by the community of the school and, more broadly, for all schools in a system, state or nation. It enables its students to engage successfully, in a global and lifelong network of learning opportunities in a knowledge society (based on Caldwell and Spinks 1998). According to Michael Barber, Head of the Standards and Effectiveness Unit, Department for Education and Employment in the UK, in the twenty-first century, world-class standards will demand that everyone is highly literate, highly numerate, well-informed, capable of learning constantly, and confident and able to play their part as a citizen of a democratic society. This implies a curriculum that provides a firm grounding for everyone in literacy and numeracy but also goes far beyond this. A world-class education service provides all pupils, whatever their backgrounds, with the opportunity to become highly expert in one or more fields, highly creative and innovative, and capable of leadership (based on Barber 1998).

Many nations have embarked on reform programs in an effort to create systems of world-class schools along these lines. Central concerns are the extent to which this effort has met with success and what more must be done, given that expectations are high and there is every sign of further dramatic change in the nature of schooling. The purpose of this chapter is to illuminate these issues, paying particular attention to the role of leaders at the school level.

The starting point is an examination of evidence that recent reforms have had an impact on outcomes for students, with particular attention being given to the findings of research on large-scale reform in Australia. This evidence suggests that a new and richer role for the teacher as a professional is emerging, one which will flourish as the school is further transformed with the impact of information and communications technology. Strategies for action at the school level are organised according to two sets of ten 'strategic intentions' around which a professional development or training programme can be organised or a long-term strategy can be devised, as a school seeks to become world class. Leaders have an important role to play, and the concept of 'strategic conversation' is invoked to suggest how the process can be energised.

School reform is seen as proceeding on three tracks: Track 1 involves the building of systems of self-managing or locally managed schools; Track 2 calls for an unrelenting focus on learning outcomes; Track 3 entails the creation of schools for the knowledge society, underpinned by advances in information and communications technology. These are not stages or sequences; there are developments on each track everywhere, with schools and systems at different points in respect to how far down each track they have travelled.

Impact of structural reform on learning outcomes

After a decade of structural reform on Track 1 ('building systems of self-managing schools'), it is fair to ask about the extent to which there has been an impact on outcomes for students, and how such reform can make a contribution to further reform on Track 2 ('unrelenting focus on learning outcomes').

It is sobering to note the consistent finding in research over many years that there appear to be few if any direct links between local management or school-based management or self-management, on the one hand, and learning outcomes, on the other (Malen, Ogawa and Kranz 1990; Summers and Johnson 1996; Whitty, Power and Halpin 1998). Some observers have noted that such gains are unlikely to be achieved in the absence of purposeful links between capacities associated with school reform and what occurs in the classroom, in learning and teaching and the support of learning and teaching (see Bullock and Thomas 1997; Cheng 1996; Cheung 1996; Hanushek 1996, 1997; Leithwood and Menzies 1998; Levacic 1995; OECD 1994; Smith, Scoll and Link 1996). Bullock and Thomas go to the heart of the issue:

> If learning is at the heart of education, it must be central to our . . . discussion of decentralisation. It means asking whether, in their variety of guises, the changes characterised by decentralisation have washed over and around children in classrooms, leaving their day-to-day experiences largely untouched. In asking this question, we must begin by recognising that structural changes in governance, management and finance may leave largely untouched the daily interaction of pupils and teachers.
>
> (Bullock and Thomas 1997: 219)

Evidence of how 'purposeful links' have been made are now emerging, especially in Chicago (Bryk 1998) and in Victoria (Cooperative Research Project 1998; Wee 1999).

Mapping the links

Particular attention is given at this point to the processes and outcomes of the most recent wave of reform in the State of Victoria, Australia which has occurred since early 1993 under the rubric of Schools of the Future. Almost 90 per cent of the state's budget for public education has been decentralised to schools for local decision-making within a curriculum and standards framework in eight key learning areas. Schools have a capacity to select their own staff, who remain employed by the central authority, with provision for annual and triennial report to the local community and the state Department of Education on a range of indicators.

Findings are drawn from several research projects. The primary source is the Cooperative Research Project, a joint endeavour of the Department of Education, the Victorian Association of State Secondary Principals, the Victorian Primary Principals Association, and the University of Melbourne. The Cooperative Research Project began in mid-1993 and concluded in mid-1998, completing on schedule a planned five-year longitudinal study of the processes and outcomes of Schools of the Future. Seven state-wide surveys of representative samples of principals were conducted and these covered virtually every aspect of the reform, including its impact on learning outcomes for students.

More recent work is under the umbrella of an international collaborative project which pools research from Australia (University of Melbourne), Britain (Open University) and the United States (University of Wisconsin at Madison). There are two purposes of this larger effort, which is supported by a large grant from the Australian Research Council: first, the development of models that transcend national boundaries for matching resource allocation to special educational need; and, second, investigation of the impact of school-based decisions about resource allocation on learning outcomes for students.

The potential for linkage is present in the Victorian reform because of its comprehensive and coherent nature, with the shift in authority, responsibility and accountability for key functions shifting from the centre to the school, all occurring within a curriculum and standards framework in eight key learning areas, and realignment of important personnel functions. Principals provided ratings on the extent of realisation of expected benefits or extent of achievement of certain outcomes.

Successive surveys in the Cooperative Research Project have consistently shown that principals believe there has been moderate to high level of realisation of the expected benefit in respect to improved learning outcomes for students. In the most recent survey, 84 per cent gave a rating of 3 or more on the 5–point scale (1 is 'low' and 5 is 'high').

This finding is noteworthy but it does not illuminate the extent to which the capacities fostered by the reform have a direct impact on learning outcomes for students. Structural equation modelling was employed in the analysis of findings in each of the last three surveys, using LISREL 8 (Jöreskog and Sörbom 1993). This approach allows the analysis of ordinal-scale variables such as those utilised in this research. The model reported here derives from the most recent survey (Cooperative Research Project 1998).

The first step was to create clusters of related items and to treat these as constructs. These seven constructs were created from a total of forty-five items in the survey instrument, with their titles shown in italic in the text that follows. Figure 5.1 contains the explanatory regression model that shows the interdependent effects among variables (in this instance, latent variables that represent the constructs) on the variable *Curriculum and Learning Benefits*. Standardised path coefficients are shown, representing the direct effects (all paths are statistically significant beyond the $p < 0.05$ level by univariate two-tailed test). The fit between the data and model is very good indeed, with an Adjusted Goodness of Fit Index of 0.969 indicating that almost all (96.9 per cent) of the variances and co-variances in the data are accounted for by the model.

The path coefficients may be interpreted in this manner. The direct effect of *Personnel and Professional Benefits* on *Curriculum and Learning Benefits* is indicated by a path coefficient of 0.299. This indicates that an increase in the measure of *Personnel and Professional Benefits* of 1 standard deviation, as reflected in ratings of principals, produces an increase in the measure of *Curriculum and Learning Benefits* of 0.299 of a standard deviation.

The model shows that three variables have a direct effect on *Curriculum and Learning Benefits* (which includes improved learning outcomes for students), namely, *Personnel and Professional Benefits* (which reflects ratings for realisation of the expected benefits of better personnel management, enhanced professional development, shared decision-making, improved staff performance, more effective organisation following restructure, increased staff satisfaction and an enhanced capacity to attract staff*); Curriculum Improvement due to CSF* (which reflects ratings for improvement of capacity for planning the curriculum, establishing levels and standards for students, moving to a curriculum based on learning outcomes and meeting the needs of students); and *Confidence in Attainment of SOF Objectives*.

Noteworthy are the pathways of indirect effects, illustrated for *Planning and Resource Allocation Benefits*, which is mediated in respect to its effect on *Curriculum and Learning Benefits* through *Personnel and Professional Benefits* and *Confidence in Attainment of SOF Objectives*. Expressed another way, realising the expected benefits of better resource management, clearer sense of direction, increased accountability and responsibility, greater financial and administrative flexibility, and improved long-term planning, will have no direct effect on *Curriculum and Learning Benefits* but will have an indirect effect to the extent they impact on *Personnel and Professional Benefits* which in turn have a direct effect on *Curriculum and Learning Benefits*.

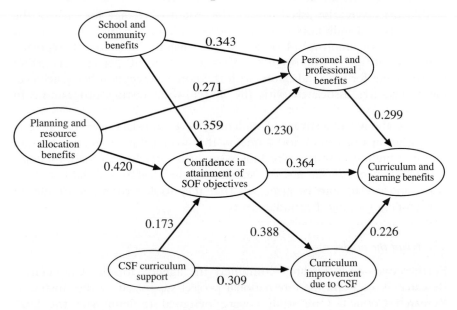

Figure 5.1 Explanatory regression model showing interdependent effects among
factors influencing perceived *Curriculum and Learning Benefits*
(Cooperative Research Project 1998)

Also noteworthy are the constructs that have direct effects on *Confidence
in Attainment of SOF Objectives*. High ratings of confidence were associated
with high ratings for the achievement of *Planning and Resource Allocation
Benefits, School and Community Benefits* and *CSF Curriculum Support*. The
likely explanation is that unless principals experience benefits in these last
three domains, they are unlikely to have confidence in the reform.
Modelling of this kind has been done for findings in each of the last three
surveys and there is now stability in the model, with only small variations in
the directions of effects and the size of path coefficients.

Indicators of improvement in learning outcomes

Principals were asked to indicate the basis for their rating of the extent to
which the expected benefit of improved student learning had been realised.
They were asked to rate the importance of certain achievement measures and
indicators of attendance, time allocations in curriculum, participation rates,
exit/destination data, parent opinion, staff opinion and level of professional
development (a total of twenty-three indicators was provided). Most principals
indicated moderate to high importance for these indicators in arriving at their
ratings, with the most notable exception being the low level of importance
attached to the system-wide testing programme in primary schools.

Principals were also asked to rate the extent of change for each of the aforementioned indicators, with a 5–point scale of 'decline' (1 or 2), 'no change' (3) or 'improve' (4 or 5). A large majority of principals reported either no change or improvement, with more than 50 per cent reporting improvement for most indicators, with the notable exception being achievement measures associated with the system-wide testing programme in primary.

In the absence of a stream of student achievement data over several years among groups of comparable students that would put the matter beyond doubt, a high level of trustworthiness ought be attached to these findings, given consistency in ratings, the stability of the model over the last three years, and declarations by principals that they took account of a range of indicators in forming their judgements.

Verifying the model

Further case study research combined the agenda for the Cooperative Research Project and the international project supported by the Australian Research Council. Case studies were designed to illuminate the links illustrated in the model in Figure 5.1 under conditions where principals report improved learning outcomes. Are the linkages evident in the model confirmed in deep on-site investigations in particular schools where improvement is claimed?

The starting point in the research design for several projects to date was a set of schools where principals made a claim of improved learning outcomes. The first task was to test the validity of these claims, drawing on evidence in the particular schools selected for study. The second task was to seek explanations for how such improvement occurred and then to match it against the linkages or pathways that are shown in the model in Figure 5.1. A third task was to highlight, in particular, the role of the principal and other leaders in achieving these linkages.

The first such study by Julie Wee (1999) was conducted in late 1997 when the pool of indicators was well developed and a substantial body of evidence was available to test claims of improved learning outcomes. A feature of her study was the relentless probing for evidence and an extended pursuit of explanations to account for improvement where this was found.

The research was carried out in four primary schools in the Western Metropolitan Region in Melbourne. Eight primary schools had expressed a willingness to participate in a case study following the survey of principals in 1996 and were invited to name up to three areas of the curriculum where improvement in student learning had occurred and where they believed evidence was available to substantiate their claim.

Findings reveal that schools can cite evidence that their efforts have led to improved outcomes for students. They draw on many sources of data in recognising improved student learning in their schools. This illustrates the capacity being developed in the system to gather information about the performance of schools. It was noted above in connection with the findings of the most recent survey of principals in the Cooperative Research Project that most respondents had been able to draw on up to twenty-three indicators in making their judgement of the extent to which there had been improvement in learning outcomes for students.

Maps of direct and indirect links were prepared by Wee for each school using the rigorous approach to data collection, data display and data reduction for qualitative research proposed by Miles and Huberman (1994). These maps are consistent with the explanatory model in Figure 5.1. A new link was identified, being the impact of monitoring, including assessment and reporting, which was not contained in the explanatory model. Developing a capacity at the school level for gathering and utilising a wide range of techniques for monitoring student progress has impacted directly on improvement in student learning and on the way staff have implemented the curriculum and standards framework. Taken together, this mapping of links between self-management and learning is consistent with the outstanding conceptual work of Cheng (1996) that provided a framework for several related research projects (for example, Cheung 1996).

Strategic intentions

What implications can be drawn from these and related findings for leaders who are determined to ensure that structural reform is linked to learning in schools that aspire to be world class? The formation of strategic intent is one of several elements in a comprehensive approach to the management of strategy.

Max Boisot is Professor of Strategic Management at ESADE in Barcelona and Senior Associate at the Judge Institute of Management Studies at the University of Cambridge. He provided a helpful classification of management responses in the exercise of strategic leadership (Boisot 1995). As illustrated in Figure 5.2, there are four, namely, emergent strategy, strategic planning, intrapreneurship and strategic intent. Which are possible and appropriate depends on the level of turbulence in an organisation's environment ('turbulence') and the capacity of the organisation to extract and process useful information from that environment ('understanding'). If used appropriately, these provide a repertoire of responses for strategic management in the learning organisation (see Davies and Ellison 1999 for other ways to utilise the Boisot model).

Using this model we can deduce the following:

- When turbulence and understanding are low, an *emergent strategy* is all that may be possible and hence appropriate, being an 'incremental adjustment to environmental states that cannot be discerned or anticipated through a prior analysis of data' (Boisot 1995: 34, based on Mintzberg). These are not the conditions that face schools at this time.

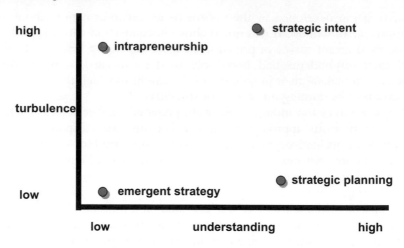

Figure 5.2 A model for strategic management (after Boisot, 1995).

- When turbulence is low and understanding is high, *strategic planning* is possible and appropriate, being the setting of medium- to long-term plans on the basis of an environmental scan. These were the conditions that faced schools until about the mid-1990s but they are fast receding. ('The thinking that underpins strategic planning is a legacy of more stable times when the environment was changing sufficiently slowly for an effective corporate response to emerge from methodical organisational routines' (Boisot 1995: 33).)
- When turbulence is high and understanding is low, '*intrapreneurship*' may be appropriate (a similar concept to 'entrepreneurship' except that it is carried out within the organisation). Intrapreneurship is an approach to management that encourages individual initiative when it is not possible to formulate a coherent and integrated organisational response. Some efforts may pay off and be incorporated later in an organisation-wide strategy. For schools, intrapreneurship may be appropriate, for example, for some developments in information technology.
- When turbulence is high and understanding is high, *strategic intent* is the desirable response, adapted from Boisot as follows

  Strategic intent describes a process of coping with turbulence through a direct, intuitive understanding of what is occurring in order to guide the work of a school. A turbulent environment cannot be tamed by rational analysis alone so that conventional strategic planning is deemed to be of little use. Yet it does not follow that a school's response must be left to a random distribution of lone individuals acting opportunistically and often in isolation as in a regime of intrapreneurship. Strategic intent relies on an intuitively formed pattern or *gestalt* – some would call it a vision – to give it unity and coherence (Boisot 1995: 36).

In the opinion of Boisot (1995: 41) strategic intent is 'the distinguishing mark of the learning organisation and, by implication, an essential component of its strategic repertoire'. This should be the case for schools, faced with a level of turbulence that is unprecedented. Leaders and managers ought to strive for a level of understanding of their environment, and develop a capacity for acquiring and processing information that will ensure a timely and effective response in any circumstance.

Strategic intentions for linking self-management to learning outcomes

Ten strategic intentions are offered as a guide to schools that seek to link structural reform, in this instance, the increased authority, responsibility and accountability that comes with self-management, to learning outcomes for students. For each, the name of a particular school can be inserted at the appropriate place in each statement. A professional development programme or an agenda for action over several months can be based around one or more of these.

These strategic intentions reflect the outcome of a form of 'backward mapping', starting from the primary purpose of schooling – learning – and then drawing on research findings to develop an agenda (see Dimmock 1995 for illustrations of the concept of 'backward mapping').

1 The primary purpose of self-management is to make a contribution to learning, so schools that aspire to success in this domain will make an unrelenting effort to utilise all of the capacities that accrue with self-management to achieve that end.
2 There will be clear, explicit and planned links, either direct or indirect, between each of the capacities that come with self-management and activities in the school that relate to learning and teaching and the support of learning and teaching.
3 There is a strong association between the mix and capacities of staff and success in addressing needs and priorities in learning, so schools will develop a capacity to optimally select staff, taking account of these needs and priorities.
4 There is a strong association between the knowledge and skills of staff and learning outcomes for students, so schools will employ their capacity for self-management to design, select, implement or utilise professional development programmes to help ensure these outcomes.
5 A feature of staff selection and professional development will be the building of high performing teams whose work is needs-based and data-driven, underpinned by a culture that values quality, effectiveness, equity and efficiency.

6 There is a strong association between social capital and learning outcomes, so schools will utilise their capacities for self-management to build an alliance of community interests to support a commitment to high achievement for all students.

7 Self-managing schools will not be distracted by claims and counter-claims for competition and the impact of market forces, but will none-theless market their programmes with integrity, building the strongest possible links between needs and aspirations of the community, programme design, programme implementation and programme out-comes.

8 Schools will have a capacity for 'backward mapping' in the design and implementation of programmes for learning, starting from goals, objec-tives, needs and desired outcomes, and working backwards to determine courses of action that will achieve success, utilising where possible and appropriate the capacities that accrue with self-management.

9 Incentive, recognition and reward schemes will be designed that make explicit the links between effort and outcomes in the take-up of capacities for self-management and improvement in learning outcomes, ack-nowledging that as much if not more attention must be given to intrinsic as to extrinsic incentives and rewards.

10 A key task for principals and other school leaders is to help make effective the links between capacities for self-management and learning outcomes, and to ensure that support is available when these links break down or prove ineffective.

New professionalism

What are the important dimensions of professional practice that emerge from the research and from accounts of success, especially in areas such as early literacy, where 'success for all' is now feasible?

Teachers acquire new knowledge and skill in a learning area for which they were already qualified to teach. They are skilful in using an array of diagnostic and assessment instruments to identify precisely what entry levels and needs exist among their students, and these are different in each classroom. Every child is treated as an individual, in reality as well as in rhetoric. Teachers have a capacity to work in a team and devote much time out of class to preparation and in briefing and de-briefing meetings, to assess the effectiveness of approaches and to plan new ones. Cross-cultural communication and the effective involvement of parents as partners in the enterprise are also required. Also evident is a commitment to the vision, appreciating that existing approaches were not good enough, though good enough to get by in the past.

These are the hallmarks of the new professional in teaching. None of these capacities call for abandonment of the traditional tenets of profession-alism. They are reinforced, extended and enriched. The effective professional in the past will likely be well-suited to the new circumstance, albeit with an updating of knowledge and skill. But there should be no doubting that there is a more sophisticated body of knowledge and skill than in the past, and a new and very demanding set of expectations to live up to.

One contrast with past practices in the profession is in order, as is a comparison with professional practice in other fields. In respect to the former, it is clear that the isolation of the past has gone. This is not a teacher working alone, who is expected or expects to teach her or his class behind closed doors. This is a professional who is at ease working in a team and at ease in sharing complex sets of data about student entry points, progress and outcomes. This calls for a willingness to share and also a willingness to be vulnerable.

The comparisons with other professions, particular the caring professions, are immediately apparent. One expects doctors, general practitioners and specialists, to make use of an increasingly sophisticated battery of tests and select a treatment. There is distress at the prospect that doctors might not keep up to date with the latest developments in their fields, through their private reading and successful participation at regularly organised programmes of professional development, that are provided as a matter of course by their professional associations. At a place where there is a concentration of doctors, such as a clinic or a hospital, there is an expectation of regular conferences where there is a sharing of information about what does or does not work. We expect full accountability. This comparison with the health care field is not new. David Hargreaves has employed it to good effect (Hargreaves 1994, 1997). It is not an entirely appropriate comparison, for education involves concern about students who are learning, whereas, in medicine, doctors deal with patients who have an ailment. It is, however, entirely appropriate to show that the new professionalism for teachers can be as fully professional as for doctors, whose status in this regard is held in society to be unquestionable.

1   There will be planned and purposeful efforts to reach higher levels of professionalism in data-driven, outcomes-oriented, team-based approaches to raising levels of achievement for all students.

2   Substantial blocks of time will be scheduled for teams of teachers and other professionals to reflect on data, devise and adapt approaches to learning and teaching, and set standards and targets that are relevant to their students.

3   Teachers and other professionals will read widely and continuously in local, national and international literature in their fields, consistent with expectations and norms for medical practitioners.

4   Teachers and other professionals will become skilful in the use of a range of information and communications technology, employing it to support learning and teaching, and to gain access to current information that will inform their professional practice.

5   Schools will join networks of schools and other providers of professional services in the public and private sectors to ensure that the needs of all students will be diagnosed and met, especially among the disabled and disadvantaged, employing the techniques of case management to ensure success for every individual in need.

6   Professionals will work within curriculum and standards frameworks, as well as other protocols and standards of professional practice, with the same level of commitment and rigour as expected in medicine.

7   Schools will advocate, support and participate in programmes of unions and professional associations that are consistent with the new professionalism in education.

8   Working within frameworks established for the profession, incentives, recognition and reward schemes will be developed at the school level that are consistent with the strategic needs of the workplace, with components that are skill-based and contain provision for collective rewards, gainsharing and team-based performance awards where these are possible and appropriate.

9   Staff will seek recognition of their work that meets or exceeds standards of professional practice, and will support and participate in the programmes of professional bodies established for this purpose.

10   Schools will work with universities and other providers in a range of programmes in teaching, research and development that support and reflect the new professionalism in education.

Creating schools for the knowledge society in reform on Track 3

The third track for change in school education cannot be described in detail but may be presented as a vision, illustrated in a *gestalt* in Figure 5.3: a perceived organised whole that is more than the sum of its parts.

It is schooling for the knowledge society, because those who manage information to solve problems, provide service or create new products form the largest group in the workforce, displacing industrial workers, who formed the largest group following the industrial revolution and who, in turn, displaced agricultural and domestic workers who dominated in pre-industrial times.

Strategic intentions for the transformation of learning (G1–G3 in Figure 5.3)

1   Approaches to learning and teaching will change to accommodate the reality that every student in every setting will have a laptop or hand-held computer, making the new learning technologies as much a part of the learning scene as books have been since the advent of systems of public education.

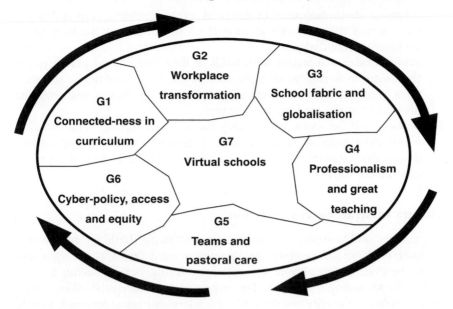

Figure 5.3 A vision for schooling in the knowledge society illustrated in a *gestalt*.

2 Subject boundaries will be broken and learning will be integrated across the curriculum as the new learning technologies become universal, challenging rigidity in curriculum and standards frameworks, without removing the need for testing in discrete areas as well as in learning that spans the whole.
3 Schools will critically examine their approaches to the teaching of literacy and numeracy to ensure that the new learning technologies are incorporated, and every effort will be made to resource the latter without sacrificing targets for success in the basics for every student.
4 Rigidity in roles, relationships and approaches to school and classroom organisation will be broken down, with multiple but rewarding roles for teachers and other professionals, more flexibility in the use of time, and abandonment of narrow specifications of class size that are rendered meaningless in the new workplace arrangements.
5 School buildings designed for the industrial age will be re-designed to suit the needs of the knowledge society.
6 Staff in self-managing schools will have critical roles to play in school design, sharing needs, aspirations and visions with architects who are tuned to the requirements of schooling for the knowledge society.
7 Information technology will pervade school design for the knowledge society.
8 Schools that serve the middle years in the Grade 5 to Grade 8 range, or thereabouts, will require major changes in school design, reflecting what

is known about the causes of flattened levels of achievement and motivation across the years of transition from the traditional primary to the
traditional secondary.

9 School design will feature high levels of flexibility and adaptability, with
   the former referring to multiple uses of the same facilities in the short
   term, and the latter to a capacity for major re-design with minimal
   disruption in the medium to long term.

10 Schools will be adept at analysing the relationship between function,
    form and culture in school design, helping to bring to realisation a
    design that contributes to making schools exciting and uplifting places
    of work for staff and students.

The art of strategic conversation

The generic skill in strategic management is strategic thinking, described by
Mintzberg (1995) in refreshingly straightforward terms as seeing ahead,
seeing behind, seeing above, seeing below, seeing beside, seeing beyond,
and above all, seeing it through. This suggests that strategic thinking should
be a continuous activity on the part of leaders and managers and, for this
reason, it should be given expression. The concept of 'strategic conversation' is central, as illustrated in Figure 5.4.

Larry Hirschhorn is wary of formalising planning processes, at least in the
early stages: 'High-stakes strategic issues stimulate executives to use more
formal planning methods. These methods, in turn, create more superficial
and less meaningful decisions' (Hirschhorn 1997: 123). The alternative is
strategic conversation:

> In this context, I believe that executives must learn to have what I call
> 'strategic conversations' with one another and with their subordinates.
> Such conversations, while supported by data and by rigorous think-
> ing . . . should be as freewheeling as possible. (Hirschhorn 1997:
> 123–4)

Kees van der Heijden (1996) suggests that scenario formulation is an
important tool in strategic management, and that strategic planning can
inform a strategic conversation, with the aim of the latter being to create a
shared view about the direction of the organisation:

> If action is based on planning on the basis of a mental model, then
> institutional action must be based on a shared mental model. Only
> through a process of conversation can elements of observation and
> thought be structured and embedded in the accepted and shared organ-
> isational theories-in-use. Similarly new perceptions of opportunities and
> threats based on the reflection on experiences obtained in the environ-
> ment can only become institutional property through conversation. An

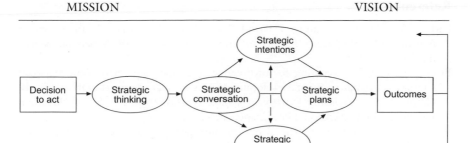

Figure 5.4 Strategic conversation at the heart of strategic management.

> effective strategic conversation must incorporate a wide range of initially
> unstructured thoughts and views, and out of this create shared inter-
> pretations of the world in which the majority of individual insights can
> find a logical place.
>
> (van der Heijden 1996: 41–2)

For a school wishing to thrive in a climate of continuing change, it needs first a decision to act. It needs a capacity for strategic thinking that should be widely dispersed and utilised in a range of structures and processes in which various strategic conversations are conducted. An outcome of strategic conversation may be the selection of an appropriate response. The environ-ment may be stable enough, and information of action may be understandable enough, for strategic plans to be formulated immediately. On the other hand, the level of turbulence may be so high that the school ought to form clear strategic intentions and proceed on that basis or, alternatively, some intra-preneurial effort might be encouraged (described as 'strategic creativity' in Figure 5.4). As suggested in the figure, there can be some interaction among the elements. Action will follow and outcomes will be secured, yielding data that can inform further strategic conversations in the future. Figure 5.4 also illustrates how these events should be framed by the mission and vision of the school, with a cultural foundation in the values and philosophy of the school.

Leaders in schools that seek to become world class may start the journey through strategic conversation with their colleagues. The aim is to reach a shared understanding as far as vision and strategies for realisation are con-cerned. There will, of course, be countless conversations for a host of strategies, each of which might be energised by strategic intentions of the kind illustrated in this chapter. The reader can bring these intentions to life by inserting the name of a school in each statement, around which a professional development or training programme can be organised or more detailed plans prepared as the school embarks on its journey to achieve world-class status.

References

Barber, M. (1998) 'Creating a World Class Education Service', Incorporated Association of Registered Teacher of Victoria (IARTV), IARTV Seminar Series, no. 71, February.

Boisot, M. (1995) 'Preparing for turbulence: the changing relationship between strategy and management development in the learning organisation', in B. Garratt (ed.) *Developing Strategic Thought: Rediscovering the Art of Direction-Giving*, London: McGraw-Hill, Chapter 3.

Bryk, A. S. (1998) 'Chicago school reform: linkages between local control, educational supports and student achievement', presentations with colleagues in the Consortium on Chicago School Research in a Symposium at the Annual Meeting of the American Educational Research Association, San Diego, April.

Bullock, A. and Thomas, H. (1997) *Schools at the Centre: A Study of Decentralisation*, London: Routledge.

Caldwell, B. J. and Spinks, J. M. (1998) *Beyond the Self-managing School*, London: Falmer Press.

Cheng, Y. C. (1996) *School Effectiveness and School-Based Management: A Mechanism for Development*, London: Falmer Press.

Cheung, W. M. (1996) 'A study of multi-level self management in school', unpublished thesis for the degree of Doctor of Philosophy, Chinese University of Hong Kong.

Cooperative Research Project (1998) *Assessing the Outcomes,* report of the Cooperative Research Project on 'Leading Victoria's Schools of the Future', Department of Education, Victorian Association of State Secondary Principals, Victorian Primary Principals Association, The University of Melbourne (Fay Thomas, Chair) [available from Department of Education].

Davies, B. and Ellison, L. (1999) *Strategic Direction and Development of the School*, London: Routledge.

Dimmock, C. (1995) 'School leadership: Securing quality teaching and learning' in C. W. Evers and J. D. Chapman (eds) *Educational Administration: An Australian Perspective*, St Leonards, NSW: Allen and Unwin, Chapter 16.

Garratt, B. (ed.) (1995) *Developing Strategic Thought: Rediscovering the Art of Direction-Giving*, London: McGraw-Hill.

Hanushek, E. A. (1996) 'Outcomes, costs, and incentives in schools' in E. A. Hanushek and D. W. Jorgenson (eds) *Improving America's Schools: The Role of Incentives*, Washington, DC: National Academy Press, Chapter 3, pp. 29–52.

—— (1997) 'Assessing the effects of school resources on student performance: an update', *Educational Evaluation and Policy Analysis* 19(2): 141–64.

Hargreaves, D. (1994) *The Mosaic of Learning: Schools and Teachers for the New Century*, London: Demos.

—— (1997) 'A road to the learning society', *School Leadership and Management*, 17(4): 9–21.

Hirschhorn, L. (1997) *Re-Working Authority: Leading and Authority in the Post-Modern Organisation*, Cambridge, MA: MIT Press.

Jöreskog, K. G. and Sörbom, D. (1993) *LISREL 8: User's Reference Guide*, Chicago: Scientific Software, Inc.

Leithwood, K. and Menzies, T. (1998) 'A review of research concerning the implementation of site-based management', *School Effectiveness and School Improvement* 9(3): 233–85.

Levacic, R. (1995) *Local Management of Schools: Analysis and Practice*, Buckingham: Open University Press.

Malen, B., Ogawa, R. T. and Kranz, J. (1990) 'What do we know about site-based management: a case study of the literature – a call for research' in W. Clune and J. Witte (eds) *Choice and Control in American Education Volume 2: The Practice of Choice, Decentralisation and School Restructuring*, London: Falmer Press, pp. 289–342.

Miles, M. B. and Huberman, A. M. (1994) *Qualitative Data Analysis: An Expanded Sourcebook*, second edition, Thousand Oaks: Sage Publications.

Mintzberg, H. (1995) 'Strategic thinking as "seeing",' in B. Garratt (ed.) *Developing Strategic Thought: Rediscovering the Art of Direction-Giving*, London, McGraw-Hill, Chapter 5.

OECD, Directorate of Education, Employment, Labor and Social Affairs, Education Committee (1994) *Effectiveness of Schooling and of Educational Resource Management: Synthesis of Country Studies*, Points 22 and 23, Paris: OECD.

Smith, M.S., Scoll, B.W. and Link, J. (1996) 'Research-based school reform: the Clinton Administration's agenda' in E. A. Hanushek and D. W. Jorgenson (eds) *Improving America's Schools: The Role of Incentives*, Washington, DC: National Academy Press, Chapter 2, pp. 9–27.

Summers, A. A. and Johnson, A. W. (1996) 'The effects of school-based management plans' in E. A. Hanushek and D. W. Jorgenson (eds) *Improving America's Schools: The Role of Incentives*, Washington, DC: National Academy Press, Chapter 5, pp. 75–96.

Van der Heijden, K. (1997) *Scenarios: The Art of Strategic Conversation*, New York: John Wiley & Sons.

Wee, J. (1999) 'Improved student learning and leadership in self-managed schools', unpublished thesis for the degree of Doctor of Education, University of Melbourne.

Whitty, G., Power, S. and Halpin, D. (1998) *Devolution and Choice in Education: The School, the State and the Market*, Buckingham: Open University Press.

6 Global and national perspectives on leadership

Lejf Moos

There are many internal contradictions embedded in the strategies for managing the public sectors – especially public education – in Western European countries such as England and Denmark. These contradictions arise from the dissociation between traditional, national cultures (as expressed in the expectations of key stakeholders such as teachers, parents and students) and the governmental strategies for changing or 'improving' public sector organisations. The contradictions are best captured in the streams in the applied research literature that are identified with 'New Public Management' and the concept of 'the learning organisation', and are derived from research and experiences in all kinds of private and public organisations. These applied research streams are not attentive to national or local cultures, but reflect a pattern of globalisation of management and policy theory and practice.

In the first part of this chapter I will elaborate the nature of globalisation, the dismantling of the welfare state and emergence of the New Public Management. I will then present some of the contradictions between the New Public Management and the knowledge and experiences of learning organisations. Finally, I will outline differences in national culture and differences and similarities in the expectations of effective school leadership as expressed by students, teachers, parents and heads themselves in our study: 'Effective School Leadership in a Time of Change'.[1]

Globalisation and the New Public Management

The word 'globalisation' is often used as a shorthand explanation for the rapid rate of change in our education systems and other areas of the public sector over recent years.[2] The transformations, in what we used to call the welfare state, are often presented as a consequence of an external phenomenon over which nation-states have little or no control. From my perspective, 'globalisation' is not just an economic phenomenon, but signifies a set of cultural and social changes that alter our perceptions of the everyday world – as least as we experienced it when we were growing up. These changes include:

- the ease with which ideas, finance, manpower and goods can be moved around the world, which makes the concept of the 'global village' a reality and forms the conditions in which governments have to act;
- the increasing prominence of transnational companies: the 40,000 companies that play off one state against the other in a search for profit (Martin and Schumann 1997);[3]
- the increasing influence of international organisations such as the OECD and the European Parliament;
- the erosion of the autonomy of national governments through transnational trade agreements;
- the changing pattern of world employment consequent on both the emergence of the major trading zones and the development of technology.

For many Europeans, these trends have struck at the heart of certainties which characterised the early life-experiences of the current middle-aged generation. The notion of a job for life, for example, at least for white middle-class men, has given way to 'the portfolio career', which appears to many, as a one-way ticket to job insecurity and attendant anxieties about how to pay the next set of bills. The relations between sexes and between generations are changing fundamentally. Some of the changes have been made possible through revolutions in communications and technology. Accessibility to electronic information, at least for those who can afford it, has promoted the flow of both information and knowledge that is both anti-educational and educative, and anti-social as well as beneficial to society (MacBeath, Moos and Riley 1996). It offers new opportunities for criminal activity on a transnational basis (from the multi-million dollar electronic movement of money, to street level drug exchange or sex trafficking in women and children) whilst also allowing students in Denmark to correspond on a daily basis with school children in the US to explore weather patterns, or to conduct experiments.

As the world is characterised by increasing interpenetration and the crystallisation of transnational markets and structures, states themselves act increasingly as market players, shaping their policies to promote, control, and maximise returns from economic forces in an international setting (Cerny 1990: 230). This provides a convenient pragmatic explanation for the negative effects of new policies which are nipping hardest at the heels of the most vulnerable members of our societies. The poverty gap widens, an increasing number of mentally ill people are turned over to 'community care' (which may consist of a cardboard box on the street), and the children most in need of resources are channelled into the schools that have the fewest supports to provide them; at the same time, more policy-makers proclaim their helplessness in addressing these issues.

In contrast, our project, 'Effective School Leadership in a Time of Change', found evidence which challenged the concept of the wholly deterministic power of the global market. We found that countries were adopting differing responses to the demands that education systems become more accountable, more responsive, more efficient and more effective. We concluded there are choices to be made in how these demands are met and one of our central messages was the need to understand what has occurred in England in the name of global competition. In what follows I will rely primarily on a comparison between England and Denmark.[4]

In the UK and in Denmark, the preoccupation with increasing the competitiveness of the nations in the global economy is very pervasive. The UK government's pages on the Internet include, for example, a clear statement about the importance of competitiveness:

> Competitiveness is important because if a nation is uncompetitive, its living standards deteriorate and it has difficulty in maintaining high standards of education, health, infrastructure and in preserving its quality of life.
>
> (Competitiveness Division 1996, no page number)

And in Denmark:

> Education is a decisive precondition for the competitiveness of economic life. The Danish Education, therefore, must be part of the world elite.
>
> (Ole Vig Jensen, Former Secretary of Education, National Competence Development 1997)

On the one hand, statements like these signal that the education sector is supposed to meet the challenges of meaning and function in contemporary society. Northern European countries have traditionally regarded education as part of the socialisation of children, enabling them to become citizens that are aware of and conditioned to live in the actual culture and the actual society. The word education has different meanings in different languages. For example, the German expression: 'bildung' or the Dutch word 'ontwikkeling' may also be translated as 'development'. In Danish, the expression 'dannelse' means both education and development, like the German 'bildung'. In this sense education is regarded as part of the formation of national culture.

In contrast, current educational policy discussions focus on schooling as a competitive national instrument for training manpower for the production and service sectors. With this shift comes a tendency to focus on the best students, the elite, and to forget about the average students and those with special learning needs. In other words, current trends suggest the potential for developing new 'class societies' within countries that have worked for a half century to minimise class differences. When students are seen as workers rather than citizens, some will be well off and others will be left to the margins. However, the precise contribution of schooling to economic well-being is controversial, and the belief that national prosperity depends on high levels of knowledge and skill is clearly a political rather than an empirical presumption. This conviction underpins the preoccupation with a particular account of school effectiveness and defines the priorities of schooling (Mahony and Hextall 1997a). At the same time, if one driving force in policy reform has been the need for increased 'effectiveness' in global competition, another has involved the pressure to cut taxes (or, at least, corporate taxes), which has lead to reductions in public expenditure and calls for efficiency in the public sector.

Among the international policy agencies, a clear message to the European countries – first sounded by the OECD to its members – was to decentralise finances and administration of all public sectors, permitting decisions about what and whom to cut out of the system to be less visible. The new New Public Management (NPM) has now been introduced in most OECD countries (Shand 1996) and some analysts claim to have witnessed a universal shift in the philosophy and delivery of welfare (Osborne and Gaebler 1992), although not everyone would agree. There is increasing evidence to suggest, however, that different countries and sectors have introduced NPM in different ways according to their diverse historical and cultural traditions. England has witnessed the introduction of management, reporting and accounting approaches in the public sector along the lines of 'best commercial practice', and the negative impact of the establishment of quasi-markets, including the introduction of competition, in every area of the public sector has been documented in what is now an enormous literature. Denmark is at an earlier stage in the introduction of NPM, as I shall discuss later in this chapter. The argument being put forward is that even if we accept that NPM is the new paradigm for reinvented government, the details of what it means and how it is implemented are problematic. I now turn to the main principles of NPM.

An early version of NPM operating in England has been identified by Hood (1991) as being based on seven principles or doctrines. These are:

- Hands-on professional management ('active, visible, discretionary control of organisations from named persons at the top');
- Explicit standards and measures of performance (clear definition of goals, targets or indicators of success preferably in quantitative form);
- Greater emphasis on output controls (with resource allocation and rewards linked to measured performance and a stress on results rather than procedures);
- Break up of large organisations into smaller units operating on decentralised budgets;
- Introduction of competition (often involving contracts and public tendering procedures);
- Stress on commercial styles of management, replacing the former goal of a 'public service ethic';
- Stress on doing more for less (ibid., pp. 4–5).

Hood's description carries a familiar ring to those working in the English context over the past decade but it is less recognisable to those in the Danish system. In the educational sector, England has witnessed the devolution of financial management, alongside greater centralised control of the curriculum and a weakening of Local Education Authorities. In contrast, in Denmark the devolution of financial management of schools in 1991 was carried through by giving the powers to the Local Authorities (the communes) and letting them, if they wished, devolve further to each individual school. Local Authorities are currently choosing to devolve powers to the schools.

In both countries, centralised knowledge objectives and performance objectives have been introduced. However, in Denmark the tendency towards greater centralised control of the curriculum and a national programme of evaluation is not nearly as strong as it has been (and continues to be) in the UK. In England, the introduction of competitive quasi-markets through published 'league tables' of exam performance and inspection reports have combined to exert pressure on schools to achieve good examination results so that parents will exercise 'choice' in their favour. In Denmark, although the rhetoric of economic competitiveness is occasionally in evidence, examination results are not published and there is no inspection system. The policy instruments to 'involve the customer' are also different: in England, parents have been empowered by their inclusion in governing bodies with statutory responsibilities for the effective running of the school, whereas in Denmark parents have been given more power on the school board which has a purely advisory role.

Recent policy analysis points to an emerging professional/managerial split in the social welfare sectors – a growing divide between the orientations of those who see themselves as occupying client-related professional positions and those who administer the sector as a whole. As a corollary, power and influence in these areas is also viewed as shifting towards managerial 'leaders' and away from professional control (Taylor-Gooby and Lawson 1993). In some public service areas managers have increasingly been recruited from careers outside the social welfare system altogether. In addition, 'professional supervisory positions' have been redefined as 'managerial' with attendant retraining and job-respecification. Writing specifically about the redesignation of the headteacher's role in the context of the increasing impact of managerialism in education Fergusson (1994) says:

> In essence, the headteacher is ceasing to be a senior peer embedded within a professional group who has taken on additional responsibilities including a significant administrative function, and is becoming a distinctive and key actor in an essentially managerialist system, in which the pursuit of objectives and methods which are increasingly centrally determined is the responsibility of managers who must account for their achievement and ensure the compliance of teaching staff.
>
> (ibid. p.94)

In virtually all sectors operational decentralisation has been accompanied by the development of new accountability and performance management systems. Such systems – like the OFSTED: Office of Standards in Education – seem designed to both monitor and shape organisational behaviour and encompass a range of 'top down' techniques including performance review, staff appraisal systems, performance-related pay, quality audits, customer feedback mechanisms, and comparative tables of performance (Hoggett 1996: 20). These transformations have not been universally welcomed. As the public sector in England has been progressively remodelled and evaluated on the basis of 'delivery of products' in cost effective ways, commercial style contracts have replaced traditional forms of political accountability (Mahony and Hextall 1997b). 'Consumer democracy' has, in the eyes of some, led to an increasing deficit in democratic participation that involves debate and discussion (Weir and Hall 1994). As we shall see, this becomes important in considering what the role of the headteacher or school principal should be.

New contradictions and organisational learning

In many versions of NPM, states have decentralised financial and administrative responsibilities to municipalities or institutions whilst at the same time trying to hold on to the management of the content of schooling and the details of teaching. The powerful concept of the Learning Organisation (LO) has been introduced in many public sectors, as a companion of NPM. Senge (1990) has described the Learning Organisation in the following terms:

- *Systems Thinking* – 'Each has an influence on the rest, an influence that is usually hidden from view. You can only understand the system of a rainstorm [or of an organisation, my note] by contemplating the whole, not any individual part of the pattern' (p. 7).
- *Personal Mastery* – 'is the discipline of continually clarifying and deepening our personal vision, of focusing our energies, of developing patience, and of seeing reality objectively' (p. 7).
- *Mental Models* – 'are deeply ingrained assumptions, generalisations, or even pictures or images that influence how we understand the world and how we take action' (p. 9).
- *Building Shared Vision* – 'Where there is a genuine vision (as opposed to the all-too-familiar 'vision statement'), people excel and learn, not because they are told to, but because they want to. But many leaders have personal visions that never get translated into shared visions that galvanize an organization' (p. 9).
- *Team Learning* – 'We know that teams can learn; . . . The discipline of team learning starts with 'dialogue', the capacity of members of a team to suspend assumptions and enter into genuine 'thinking together' (p. 9).

Behind the concept of the Learning Organisation lies the notion or the theory of *Human Resource Management* (Keldorf 1997 pp.161–95). Analysis of the needs of production, service enterprises and public institutions tells us that employees should be innovative, creative, aware of quality and open to consumers and able to develop both professional and personal competencies in order that 'It shall be fun to be used fully' (Keldorf 1997: 169–98). But, the enthusiasm for Learning Organisations reveals the internal contradictions of the NPM. On the one hand, strong, hands-on leadership, vision from the top, performance-related wages, stress on output and explicit standards and measures of performance are advocated. All of these features seem to leave little room for professional discretion and for symmetrical dialogue and the collaboration of teachers and school principals. And yet, productivity through the development of personal and professional competencies on the 'ground floor' are also advocated. These contradictions are manifested in a number of ways:

Explicit standards and measures of performance   As part of the move towards the three virtuous 'Es' of economy, efficiency and effectiveness, teaching in England is being radically transformed. The government, through its agency The Teacher Training Agency (which is responsible only for England), is in the process of developing a whole raft of changes which centrally define both what it means to teach and the structure of the teaching profession. The formulation of national standards and national professional qualifications for newly qualified teachers, expert teachers, subject leaders and school leaders is central to these changes.

Strategic direction and development of the headteachers   Of particular interest to me is the way in which the role of the headteacher is conceived within a particular and (I would argue), narrow definition of the effective school (TTA 1997). This approach defines clear, but limited responsibilities. The first relate to 'management'. Headteachers will be expected to:

> T1. Build an ethos and provide educational vision and direction supported by parents and the local community . . .
> T2. Create and implement a strategic plan which identifies appropriate priorities and targets . . . increasing teacher effectiveness and school improvement . . . which relates to overall financial planning.
> T3. Ensure that there is commitment to the aims . . .
> T4. Ensure that the management, finance, organisation and administration of the school supports its vision . . .
> T5. Monitor, evaluate and review the effects of policies, priorities and targets . . . and take the necessary action for improvement.

The role of headteachers in developing the learning climate and outcomes of the school is also specified, but these responsibilities are also clearly focused on management and accountability:

T6. Create and maintain an environment conducive to effective learning, good teaching, good behaviour and discipline.

T7. Establish a clear school code where cultural, social and religious differences are respected . . .

T8. Monitor and evaluate the quality of teaching and the quality and standards of all pupils' learning and achievements . . .

T9. Ensure policies and practices take account of recent research and inspection evidence.

T10. Monitor, evaluate and review the curriculum and its associated assessment in order to identify areas for improvement.

This account of headship is a somewhat hierarchical, 'hands-on' management model which places other participants in the school community in a largely responsive relationship to the head's vision. As Angus (1994) argues:

> Other organisational participants, such as teachers, parents and students, . . . are generally viewed as essentially passive recipients of the leader's vision. . . . on the basis of this account of leadership, the main skill required of most participants is for them merely to adopt the leader's vision and slot into the leader's definition of school culture. . . . The elitist implication of this view is that leaders are more visionary and trustworthy than anyone else.
>
> (ibid. p. 86)

We know from our experience of working with headteachers in the project and from the growing literature on the subject that there are alternative models of leadership (Fullan and Hargreaves 1992; Murphy and Louis 1994). In the Danish context, where policy is less centrally driven, the Folkeskole (common school for all students until age 16) is not the embodiment of the headteacher's beliefs or values. The vision or mission of the school is not disseminated from the top downwards. Instead, a discussion of goals and values takes place and it is a shared dialogue between teachers and administrators – an approach enshrined in legislation:

> It is the duty of the school leader to stimulate the development of the shared values and pedagogical attitudes of the school and to further the subject matter and pedagogical co-operation of teachers. e.g. in encouraging to team building.
>
> (The Act on the Folkeskole, remarks to § 45)

The expectation in England appears to be that the head should bring her/his vision into the school, whereas in Denmark, the head is expected to initiate the dialogue with the teachers in order to build a shared vision together with them.

Some differences in tradition and culture

The particular forms which the NPM takes can be influenced by a country's culture and traditions. In the UK, there is a traditional class culture represented in hierarchical school structures. For example, it would not uncommon be in larger schools to find between seven and eight levels of status and hierarchy: head, deputy heads, assistant heads, senior teachers, heads of department, deputy heads of department, teachers with specialised assignments, and those without.

In Denmark, on the other hand, there is a long tradition of very flat structures consisting of head, deputy and teachers.

The cultural expectations regarding leadership behaviour are also different. In the UK, decision-making tends to be the head's prerogative, whilst in Denmark there is a tradition of full participation of teachers in democratic decision-making (the teachers council used to be powerful in most aspects of school life). In the Danish context , the headteacher's freedom to manage would have to take account of the values of the society as expressed in the structure of schools.

In the UK, the older tradition of school and teacher autonomy over content (at least in primary schools – secondary school content has traditionally been influenced by the A- and O-level examination system) has given way to control by central government of the curriculum. In Denmark, traditionally strong beliefs in teacher autonomy have largely been maintained with broad descriptions of the aims and objectives of school and no inspection. In the Danish context, the 'politics' of curriculum, and explicit standards and measures of performance, are mitigated by the social value accorded to stakeholder involvement in developing social policies and practices.

In the UK, formal cooperation between schools and parents has tended to be a matter for the school, with the head issuing invitations for parent involvement. In Denmark, the relationship has been organised at a classroom level with the class teacher initiating contact. (To date, the introduction of the NPM in Denmark has not affected this basic practice, although it will be interesting to monitor whether efforts to shift control to named persons at the top of the organisation removes this activity from class teachers.) The two countries place different emphasis on the relationship between parents and school in the education of children. In the UK this is expressed in the following terms:

> It shall be the duty of the parents of every child of compulsory school age to cause him to receive full-time education suitable to his age, ability and aptitude, either by regular attendance at school or otherwise.
>
> (Education Act (England and Wales) section 76, 1988)

In contrast, Denmark's statutes emphasise the mutual responsibility of schools and parents:

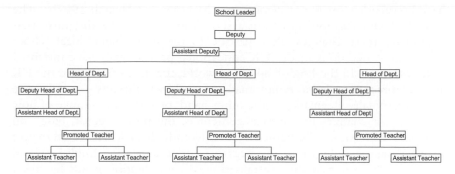

Figure 6.1 Typical school structure in England.

Figure 6.2 Typical school structure in Denmark.

> The Folkeskole shall – in co-operation with parents – further the pupils'
> acquisition of knowledge, skills, working methods and ways of expressing
> themselves and thus contribute to the all-round personal development of
> the individual pupil.
>
> (Folkeskole Act of 1993, article 1.1)

Since co-operation with parents is an aspect of legal code, there are inherent
limitations on the control of schooling by higher authorities.

The differences in tradition and culture appear to have affected the
application of the NPM within the two contexts. Less centralisation fits
within the Danish tradition of participatory democracy, while the English
political system relies far more heavily on representative democratic institutions and a very hierarchical bureaucracy. One implication of this is that it is
not possible to transport the top-down leadership model emerging in the
English context to Denmark. As we shall see in the next section, differences
in tradition and culture also appear to make a difference in how parents and
teachers conceptualise good leadership.

Education for democracy

There is growing evidence that the market-driven policies of the UK have
produced greater degrees of inequity for school students (Young and Budge
1997), and also that the dynamics of educational policy-making processes

have become less open and democratic (Mahony and Hextall 1997b). The 'threat of globalisation' has been a significant part of the discourse that legitimates these changes. Perhaps due to the more hierarchical school organisation traditions in the UK educational professionals have mounted little resistance. In the English-speaking world, the developments in the UK are sometimes regarded as symptomatic of world-wide trends – or at least as a cautionary tale. Denmark, on the other hand, provides an example of how demands for changes in the management of the public sector, based on economic context, can be framed very differently. It provides an alternative to what many would see as the negative consequence for English school leaders of the way that the centralisation/decentralisation nexus has been resolved.

In their 1994 report *Quality in Education*, the OECD stressed the importance of an appropriate balance between 'state controlled, profession controlled and consumerist accountability . . . Otherwise there is a danger that the power is kept where it is, while the blame is being decentralised' (OECD 1994: 12). This caution points to the potential vacuum which may occur if the school's crucial role in educating future citizens in their rights to participate in an inclusive model of political decision-making is abrogated. It also demonstrates the way the excessive application of the New Public Management model may ignore the responsibility of schools 'to develop their students' capacity for democratic deliberation, critical judgement and rational understanding', with the attendant danger that 'future generations of democratic citizens will disappear' (Carr and Hartnett 1996: 195–6).

By contrast, article 3 of the Folkeskole Act (1993) states:

> The school shall prepare the students for participation, sharing of respons-ibilities, rights and duties in a society with freedom and democracy. The education in the school as well as the daily life of the school therefore must build on intellectual liberty, equality and democracy.

The Act reflects the wide acceptance of the need for student participation in decisions about their education, and the correlative obligation of teachers and heads, to provide democratic role models for them. Collaboration is needed between students and teachers and between teachers and heads, and in a speech in August 1997, the former Minister for Education, Ole Vig Jensen, was very direct in rejecting a model of education based on the economic rationalism arguments that are popular in the UK:

> A democratic challenge to education is the way to go if we want to develop our democracy. If an education must prepare for democracy it must be democratically organised. Our educational system shall not be a product of a global educational race without thinking of the goals and ideals we want in Denmark. We don't postulate a connection between democracy and education. We insist on it.

(Vig Jensen 1997: 2)

In the context of the Danish response to current transformations, it is likely that school leaders and their supervisors will become concerned with teaching and learning, not through the kinds of monitoring practices introduced in the UK, but through working with teacher teams in planning, teaching and evaluating their classroom practice. The responsibility of 'the leader' is to assist teachers in becoming 'more professional' through critical reflection on classroom practice and ethics. The other role for the head will be to provide organisational leadership, concerned with the whole school's development towards a learning organisation. In this 'leaders' will be responsible for initiating and maintaining dialogue with staff, students, the school board, parents and the community about values and goals (visions) and for working through the inevitable conflicts which arise over different interpretations of these.

Leadership theories and leadership traditions

An international perspective on leadership theories has been offered by Ken Leithwood who has been influential in arguing that there is a need to move from the concept of 'transactional leadership' to 'transformational leadership': The former 'is based on an exchange of services (from teachers, for example) for various kinds of rewards (salary, recognition, and intrinsic rewards) that the leader controls, at least in part' (Leithwood 1992: 9). Leithwood argues that 'transformational leadership' is needed to develop the school into a learning organisation with shared, defensible values and goals, with good communication and problem-solving routines. In the learning organisation, the school leader supports teachers in achieving goals and in developing their personal/professional capacities. The differences between the two types of leadership are often described as involving single loop and double loop learning – or first- and second-order learning.

While Leithwood's arguments are reasonable in the context of the hierarchical organisation of schools in the UK (and, presumably, Canada), in Denmark their applicability is less obvious since heads have never had a role in teachers' classroom practice: the notion of school heads as 'instructional leaders' is foreign. Teachers have always been considered 'professional' and autonomous both in their choice of teaching methods, and in their selection of the content of the curriculum (provided they adhered to broad national and local guidelines). Berg (1995) suggests that in the current context, a deal has been struck whereby in return for increased administrative and financial power, heads will continue to have no role in teachers' decisions about curriculum content and methods of teaching. The Danish school leader is thus not in a position to move from an established 'transactional leadership' role to a 'transformational leadership' role, or from first-order to second-order learning because the first order – authoritative leadership by designated individual – that is assumed in the English-speaking countries has never existed.

This suggests that there are limitations on the transportability of leadership theories across national traditions and cultures which follow from the way in which the role of the head is conceptualised within different political presumptions, as well as the purposes of education and the nature of the 'ideal' society. Such diversities in tradition and culture account for differences in how managerialism and models of leadership in education have been interpreted within the two contexts being discussed in this chapter. A less centralised, tightly framed, regulatory framework seems to fit within the Danish tradition of decentralised participatory democracy which, throughout the Effective Leadership project, was explicitly mentioned by Danish heads as something to be valued and retained. As we shall see this is reiterated locally.

Stakeholder views about leadership

Parents, teachers and students

One element of the 'Effective School Leadership in a Time of Change' (Moos, Mahony and Reeves 1998: 60) project involved asking the sample of teachers, students and their parents referred to earlier, what counts as a good headteacher. We asked a variety of different open and closed questions through questionnaires (which enabled us to check for internal validity) and we conducted card-sort exercises with two groups of about six from each category in order to provoke discussion and to follow up any issues emerging from the questionnaire. Taking all the data from the questionnaire responses together with all the responses from the card-sort activity and the notes taken of the discussion, certain trends emerged very clearly and these are summarised below.

One of the tasks put to parents and teachers was to tick the definition of leadership closest to their own view in the column marked 'Best' (and the definition furthest from their own view in the column headed 'Worst').

The results of the parents' and teachers' responses are given in Table 6.1 and provide a clear overview of differences in expectations. Danish parents want a leader who looks ahead and the English parents want a head that has a clear view. In both countries, parents dislike leaders who let teachers get on with their job and who protects them from outside pressures. Danish teachers agree with Danish parents in preferring a leader that looks ahead and prepares his/her staff. Danish teachers dislike a pragmatic school leader, whilst English teachers are less concerned about this.

Parents' and governors' views

The responses of parents and governors were virtually identical, so for the purposes of this analysis, I shall include governors (the 'school board' in Denmark) in the data on parents. English parents consistently identified

Table 6.1 Definitions of leadership

	Leadership Definition	Parents %				Teachers %			
		Danish		English		Danish		English	
		Best	Worst	Best	Worst	Best	Worst	Best	Worst
Personal Vision	A headteacher should have a clear view of what makes for a good school and be able to inspire people to make it happen	**23**	8	**38**	1	12	24	**29**	24
Role model	A good headteacher leads by example. S/he should work in the classroom alongside the teachers and encourage them to take responsibility for improving things	6	16	4	12	**26**	6	**26**	6
Teachers	Good school leaders let teachers get on with the job and protect them from too many outside pressures	5	**53**	0	**46**	12	10	6	17
Look ahead	A good headteacher should know what's going on and be able to look ahead and make sure staff are ready for what's coming so that they are able to deal with change confidently and in a planned way	**48**	3	25	3	**47**	2	15	10
Pragmatic	Good leaders know how to use the system to get the best for their own school. They know how to negotiate and when to compromise.	6	9	3	9	0	**50**	7	**29**
No answer		13	10	30	29	4	8	15	15

qualities of 'good communication skills', 'assertive or strong leadership', 'effective management skills', 'accessibility and approachability', 'the maintenance of discipline' and 'understanding of and empathy with pupils, parents and staff'. According to English parents, the good head 'encourages and motivates people', acts with 'consistency and fairness', has the 'ability to compromise' and is 'flexible, dedicated and committed'. Danish parents thought that the good head is someone who has a 'good overview', is 'co-operative', 'inspiring', 'visionary' and is 'a good and well qualified '. S/he has 'effective management skills, 'encourages and motivates people', 'understands and empathises with pupils, parents and staff and 'delegates effectively'.

In some respects there does not appear to be a great deal of difference between English and Danish parents. One might conclude that the earlier introduction of site-based management in the UK does not seem to have affected parents' expectations of the good head, despite the feeling of heads themselves that this restructuring has altered the balance of their duties. However, 'effective management skills' have very different meanings in the two countries. For the English parents, effective management is strongly associated with 'assertive or strong leadership' – an expression which Danish parents simply do not use. There was also a clear difference in the domain in which these skills were assumed to be exercised. In England the good head came across as a more public figure who was expected to take an active and direct role in interactions with parents and the direction of young people. Running through the responses from Danish parents was the belief that good heads were 'co-operative' and 'collaborative'. Such language did not figure at all in the responses from English parents.

In both countries there was surprisingly little support for statements such as 'promoting the image of the school', even in England where a school's survival in the competitive market might depend on it. Neither group wanted an entrepreneurial or business-orientated head. While the survey of Danish parents indicated a preference for school leaders who would help prepare staff for change, neither their comments nor those of English parents placed much emphasis on leaders as a source of productive change. Being innovative and keeping up with new developments was only mentioned by a handful of respondents, which suggests that this discourse is limited to the profession itself.

In the area of interpersonal skills there were several categories consistently identified by parents. In England the essential quality was that of being a good communicator. Over and over again, responses mentioned the importance of the head being able to listen to others and to operate with consistency and fairness – all notable for their absence from the national 'standards'. Sometimes being a good communicator and being able to listen to others was amplified in the discussions to include the way in which heads are often seen as the final arbiters and adjudicators between different stakeholders, with each group wanting their particular needs to be understood, represented and responded to.

Accessibility and approachability were also rated very highly by English parents but were not mentioned by the Danes (as noted above, the relationship between parent and school is organised at a class level with the class teacher initiating contact). Danish parents did not emphasise direct 'hands-on' monitoring and control of teachers (thus reflecting the tradition of professional autonomy). On the other hand, the importance of being a 'good and well-qualified teacher' indicated that Danish parents see the main role of the school leader as being about promoting dialogue about good professional practice, rather than ensuring staff compliance – for that would not be 'the Danish way'. Discipline, regarded as important by English parents, was not mentioned by the Danes. Cultural difference could explain this. Perhaps the UK places much more emphasis on 'masculine' values of discipline and correction while Denmark favours the more 'feminine' values of permissiveness and compromise.

Teachers' views

Interview data from teachers in both countries again revealed some interesting similarities and differences. English teachers identified the good head as having 'communication skills', being able to 'motivate and inspire staff and pupils', as well as possessing a 'clear direction or vision' and being 'accessible and approachable'. The good head was skilful in finance and administration (here reference was frequently made to the impact on staff jobs when heads did not manage the budget well). S/he demonstrates 'empathy and caring', 'strong and assertive leadership' and 'consistency and fairness'. S/he is also someone who 'commands respect' and 'maintains discipline'. In Denmark, teachers identified 'vision', an ability to 'preserve the overview', to 'inspire others', to 'listen' and to be 'loyal to staff and pupils'. The good head is 'able to delegate', is 'visible to pupils and staff','humane', 'engaged' and has 'pedagogical insight'.

Both English and Danish teachers mentioned 'vision' but the meaning attached to the word was different. The English teachers were more inclined to use the term to indicate the head's ability to point out a clear direction (part of the role as defined in England). For the Danish teachers, 'vision' meant that the headteacher should maintain a dialogue with the staff and other involved groups about the direction in which the school should progress, again in line with the importance the Danes attach to their traditions of participatory democracy. In the card-sort activity, issues of social justice emerged as being particularly important for English teachers and as something which they took for granted as integral to the definition of a good leader. In Denmark, where educational opportunities and facilities are more equalised through the tradition of the Folkskole (common school), social justice may not be viewed as something to be sorted out in the school setting.

The fact that the Danes did not explicitly mention good communication skills seemed to be because leadership operates within flatter structures. In the UK, where much more power and responsibility for direction or vision is invested in the head, teachers felt that they could only follow the head's lead, if it had been communicated successfully in the first place.

Overall, looking at the views of parents and teachers in both countries, a much greater emphasis on the need for 'strong leadership' or 'assertive leadership' emerged from the English data. Whereas in Denmark, the good school leader was conceptualised as being co-operative and able to 'preserve a good overview' (rather than creating or building it, which would be the way of expressing it in the English national standards).

Younger children (ages 5–11)

From a simplified questionnaire (which included the opportunity to draw) and focus group discussions it became apparent that many of the younger children found difficulty in distinguishing between what a headteacher (presumably theirs) actually is or does, and what a good headteacher is like. Nevertheless, embedded in the data were real glimpses of headship from the child's point of view.

In Denmark, the head 'pays attention to unhappy kids', and 'makes an aerial ropeway'. In England s/he 'talks about the good news', 'cheers you up' and 'protects education'. For English children, the head (or good head) 'tells children off if they're naughty', s/he is a 'good organiser' and 'helps teachers and children'. S/he 'buys things for the school', 'sorts out arguments and problems', is 'friendly to parents', 'teaches classes', 'praises children' and 'makes sure children are safe'. For Danish children, the head was (or ought to be) 'kind' and 'sympathetic'. The phrase 'tell children off if they're naughty' did recur, as did its opposite 'doesn't tell you off', but 'telling off', in general did not feature so prominently as in the English responses. S/he 'keeps school orderly' (including keeping it clean), 'solves problems', 'arranges good outings', is 'happy', and generally 'good to kids'.

The differences in the extent to which children saw the role of the headteacher as 'telling off' appear to reflect the distinguishing features of school staffing and structure. In England, it is not uncommon for the class teacher, as a last resort, to send children who misbehave to the school leader for adjudication. In Denmark, responsibility is allocated to the class teacher who often follows the class for several years (up to nine years) and is the main link with parents. Thus, discussions of disciplinary action beyond the usual daily routines is more likely to involve parents than formal school leaders.[5]

Older students

Beneath some superficial differences in expression, there was a large measure of agreement between the older students from both countries. The data was laden with statements such as 'listens', 'talks with pupils', ' is kind to pupils', 'takes care of pupils', 'understands pupils', 'establishes good relationships', is 'accessible' and 'approachable'. If, as was suggested during the discussions, these are taken as falling under a broader category of 'establishing positive relationships', then the data is overwhelming. Along with a concern that heads should be just in their dealings with pupils, 'positive relationships' is the most important criterion of what makes for a good headteacher.

There were, however, some differences in responses which paralleled those of younger children. In responding to a question which asked them to rank a list of statements, the English students rated 'makes sure there is good behaviour in the school' as very important, whereas it appeared way down the list for the Danes: good behaviour was a matter for the class teacher. Similarly, the word 'strict' peppered the English data but did not figure at all for the Danes in any of the data sets. Older students from both countries expressed the need for a good head to be involved in the school and to visit classes. Danish students seemed not to share the concern expressed by their heads, that visiting classes might well be construed as 'spying on colleagues'. On the contrary, a significant number of Danish students, believe that a good head ensures that 'teachers are teaching well'.

Unlike teachers, English students did not mention the financial management of schools in their depiction of a good head. For them, the emphasis was almost entirely on the quality of relationships s/he ought to establish and what personal qualities a good head would have. S/he should be 'human (not like a robot)' and 'friendly', and be able to 'support pupil/teacher relationships'. Danish students also thought these were important but did include being 'financially knowledgeable'. For the Danes 'lively', 'resolute', 'devoted to work', 'creative' and 'not old-fashioned' all commanded a fair measure of support.

New school and leadership structures

I have argued so far that the culture and traditions of a country influence the forms taken both by the NPM and preferred models of leadership. UK schools are hierarchical and contain many differentiated roles (at least in larger secondary schools). By contrast, in Denmark, the tradition of flatter structures and the influence of Teachers' Councils have resulted in high levels of trust for teachers' professionalism. However, in both countries there are changes occurring. In Denmark the 'flatarchy' is gradually being transformed in many schools (including the schools in our project), in part because of the difficulties in 'leading' a staff of 30 – 60 teachers and other members, but also due to the wish to abolish the 'silent contract' between teachers and leaders not to get in each other's way (Berg 1995). This contract is a hindrance to the development and learning of the school. In England, on the other hand, the new policies relating to teacher professionalisation have yet to be fully realised, and their impact on the highly differentiated role structure of schools is as yet unknown.

In some Danish schools an attempt has been made to introduce a kind of middle manager (e.g. heads of department, where a department usually would consist of one-third of the teachers of the school). There has been two different models for middle-leaders: one model is that of functional leader in charge of some administrative matters, including finances, special needs education and so on. This kind of middle leader is accepted by the teachers. The other model is the pedagogical middle leader in charge of the pedagogical dialogue and leadership of part of the school. In a small research and and development project (Moos 1997), I found strong evidence, that the teachers would – unwillingly – accept the school leader as the pedagogical leader, but they would certainly not accept the middle leader in that role. The teachers strongly opposed and obstructed the attempt.

Rather than this kind of middle leader, and what is seen as the 'UK-hierarchy', Danish heads, parents and teachers seem to favour a project-group structure. That is a starburst organisation that stems from the tradition of a strong and leading class teacher because it seems to be consistent with the collaborative, democratic traditions and culture. The Danish Education Act of 1993 supports this trend: there are requirements for teachers to work in teams, at times in cross-curricular ways and to teach and assess through project work. This kind of team is often responsible for planning, carrying through and evaluating the teaching and everyday life of one or more groups of students. The class teacher is very often the co-ordinator or leader of the team (Moos and Thomassen 1997). Reliance on a team leader structure does not excuse the school leader from his/her responsibilities for the quality, the effectiveness and development of teaching, but it makes it possible to fulfil this task through the teams. In interviews or dialogues with the team s/he can monitor the progress of the teachers and s/he can support the team learning and the learning of the individual teacher (Harrit and Moos 1997).

Concluding reflections

In both England, Scotland and Denmark we saw new contradictions and dilemmas for school leaders. Different variations of New Public Management demanded strong, hands-on managers who were prepared and able to manage through low-trust arrangements, such as strong hierarchy, monitoring, control, national standards and output control. At the same time, the transformation of schools into learning organisations is dependent on school leaders creating shared visions, shared values and mental models for the development of the school and assisting the teachers to become members of teams that would be learning through continuous dialogue. School leaders are also expected to become increasingly sensitive to 'the customer' and to comply with the expectations of children, parents, school boards and teachers – even if they are contradictory.

The largest contradiction, however, is not in the local stakeholder groups.

Most of the expectations expressed by stakeholders – and equally the demands for transforming schools into learning organisations or learning communities – assume trust and dialogue based on human values of civility, respect, fairness and love of children. In contrast, the New Public Management models are driven by financial values and depend on low-trust, external regulation and command. The leadership challenge facing school heads today may be to collaborate with the local community in sheltering the school – and its attendant developmental functions – from the worst effects of the New Public Management.

Notes

1 'Effective School Leadership in a Time of Change'. Members of the Research Team were: Chresten Kruchov, Lejf Moos and Johnny Thomassen from Danmarks Laerhojskole, Copenhagen (The Royal Danish School of Educational Studies); Kathryn Riley and Pat Mahony from the Roehampton Institute London, England; John MacBeath, Joan Forrest, and Jenny Reeves from QIE, University of Strathclyde, Scotland.
2 Parts of this paper come from Pat Mahony and Lejf Moos: 'Central and local expectations of school leadership in England and Denmark' (paper for the 'Leadership in a Time of Change' conference in Lancashire. January 1998).
3 However, the very terms multinational and international would suggests an inter-relationship with the national rather than some uncontrollable juggernaut propelled along by its own momentum.
4 Our data suggests that Scotland is currently in between these two but (as one might expect), travelling down the road forged by the government that is shared by England and Scotland.
5 An alternative explanation which cannot be explored here lies in broader cultural differences in the expectations of children and child-development.

References

Angus, L. (1994) 'Sociological analysis and education management: the social context of the self-managing school', *British Journal of Sociology of Education*, 15(1): 79–91.

Berg, G.(1995) *Skolkultur – nyckeln till skolans utveckling*, Gothia: Göteborg.

Carr, W. and Hartnett, A. (1996) *Education and the Struggle for Democracy*, Buckingham: Open University Press.

Cerny. P. (1990) *The Changing Architecture of Politics: Structure, Agency and the Future of the State*, London: Sage

Christensen, A. (ed.) (1997) *Den lærende organisations begreber og praksis*, Ålborg.

Danish Ministry of Education (1993) *Act on the Folkeskole*, Copenhagen: Minstry of Education.

English Ministry of Education (1988) *Education Act (England and Wales)*, London: HMSO.

Fergusson, R. (1994) 'Managerialism in education', in J. Clarke, A. Cochrane and E. MacLaughlin (eds) *Managing Social Policy*, London: Sage.

Fullan, M. and Hargreaves , A. (1992) *What's Worth Fighting For in School Leadership*, New York: Teachers College Press.

Harrit, O. and Moos, L. (1997): *Skoleledelse – kvalitetsudvikling og evaluering*, Copenhagen: Royal Danish School of Educational Studies (RDSES).

Hextall, I. and Mahony, P. (1998) ' Effective teachers for effective schools', in R. Slee, S. Tomlinson and G. Weiner (eds) *Effective for Whom?*, London: Falmer.

Hogget, P. (1996) 'New modes of control in the public service', *Public Administration* 74, Spring, pp. 9–32.

Hood, C. (1991) 'A public management for all seasons, *Public Administration*, 69, Spring pp. 3–19.

Keldorf, S. (1997) 'Voksen og følsom [Adult and Sensitive]', in Christensen, A. (ed.) *Den Lurende Organisations Begreber og Praksis*, Aalborg: Aalborg University.

Leithwood, K. (1992) 'The move towards transformational leadership', *Educational Leadership* 49(5): 8–12.

MacBeath, J., Moos, L. and Riley, K.A. (1996) 'Leadership in a changing world', in K.A.Leithwood, K.Chapman, C. Corson, P. Hallinger and A. Hart (eds) *International Handbook for Educational Leadership and Administration*, The Netherlands: Kluwer Academic Publishers, pp. 223–250.

Mahony, P. and Hextall, I. (1997a) *The Policy Context and Impact of the TTA: A Summary*, London: The Roehampton Institute London.

Mahony. P. and Hextall, I. (1997b) 'Problems of accountability in reinverted government: a case study of teacher training agency', *Journal of Education Policy*, 12(4): 267–78

Martin, Hans-Peter, and Schumann, Harald (1997) *The Trap of Globalisation*, Copenhagen: Borgen.

Moos, Lejf (1997) *Hillerød skolelederudvikling*, Copenhagen: CLUE, RDSES.

Moos, L. and Thomassen, J. (1997): *Der er dømt skoleudvikling*, Copenhagen: RDSES.

Moos, L., Mahony, P. and Reeves, J. (1998) 'What teachers, parents, governors and pupils want from their heads', in J. MacBeath (ed.) *Effective School Leadership – Responding to Change*, London: Sage/Chapman Publishing, pp. 60–79.

OECD (1994) *Quality in Education,* Paris: Organisation for Economic Co-operation and Development.

Murphy, J. and Louis, K.S. (eds) (1994*) Reshaping the Principalship: Insights from Transformational Schools,* London: Corwin.

Osborne, A. and Graebler, T. (1992) *Reinventing Government: How the Entrepreneurial Spirit is Transforming the Public Sector*, Reading MA: Addison Wesley.

Senge, P. M. (1990) *The Fifth Discipline,* London: Century Business.

Shand D. (1996) 'The New Public Management: an international perspective', paper presented to Public Service Management 2000 Conference, University of Glamorgan.

Taylor-Gooby, P. and Lawson, R. (eds) (1993) *Markets and Managers: New Issues in the Delivery of Welfare,* Buckingham: Open University Press.

TTA (1996) *Corporate Plan,* London: Teacher Training Agency.

—— (1997) *National Standards for Headteachers*, London: Teacher Training Agency.

Weir, S. and Hall, W. (1994) *EGO TRIP: Extra-governmental Organisations in the United Kingdom and their accountability,* London: Charter 88 Trust.

Vig Jensen, O. (1997) 'Demokrati og uddannelse', in *Uddannelse* 30(6): September.

Young, S. and Budge, D. (1997) 'Two nations under Tories', *Times Educational Supplement*, no. 4217, April 5.

Part 2

The capacity of local systems to respond to educational reform and change and rethink their local leadership role

7 Caught between local education authorities

Making a difference through their leadership?

Kathryn A. Riley, Jim Docking and David Rowles

Introduction

Intermediary authorities are the grey areas of local governance: the tier between schools and national or state governments which is wheeled into the spotlight at the moments of crisis that feature periodically on our education landscapes (Riley 1998). By and large, however, the public in general, and the media in particular, have been far more interested in what governments have to say about education and in what schools are actually doing than in the effectiveness and leadership of intermediary authorities. Until recently, school leadership has become the more pressing policy issue: an integral component of the drive for more effective schools, raised achievement and greater public accountability (Riley and McBeath 1998).

Intermediary authorities come in various shapes and sizes. Local education authorities (LEAs), the English version of the middle tier in the vertical partnership between government and schools, can be responsible for as few as ten, or as many as 800 schools. Their responsibilities, funding and accountability arrangements differ widely. European municipalities and authorities tend to be part of an elected local government, whose diverse responsibilities can include housing, refuse collection, street lighting and economic regeneration, as well as education and social services. The North American model – the school district – is more likely to be a free standing, single-issue organisation.

Whether they are local education authorities, school districts or municipalities, intermediary authorities share the same intractable problem: how to counteract assertions that they are failing to do their job, and provide evidence that they are. If all is going well in any school system, central government will take the credit for having set the agenda, and schools for having raised pupil achievement. Much of the work of intermediary authorities is hidden from public view. Parents only tend to have direct experience of them at transition points in the education life of their child (starting school, or moving to a senior or high school), or at crisis points (lack of funding or facilities for a child with special educational needs).

Over recent years, however, the situation has begun to change. 'Failing' authorities have hit the headlines, and those which aspire to be successful have endeavoured to find ways of conveying their goals and activities to their local communities. Many school boards in the US now publicise how they use their local tax dollars. Municipalities in Europe try and engage local residents in debates with about their goals, and many LEAs have developed consultative mechanisms with parents, particularly those who have children with special educational needs. Nevertheless, there is still considerable confusion about the roles and responsibilities of intermediary authorities, and the ways in which their effectiveness can be judged.

In this chapter we examine the nature of the leadership role of intermediary authorities and assess their effectiveness from the perspective of those who are closest to them: users and providers of local services. To do this, we draw on findings from an extensive research study on local education authorities, *The Changing Role and Effectiveness of LEAs*, as well as research evidence from elsewhere (particularly from North America) to answer the following questions: Can LEAs make a difference, and if so, how? What are the characteristics of effective intermediary authorities, and what are the ways in which they contribute to the local leadership climate?

Local education authorities in the spotlight

Questions about the effectiveness of intermediary authorities come to the fore when things go wrong: a massive overspend, a school in crisis, an intractable dispute with teacher unions. Each country has its own 'cause celebre'. One of the most notorious examples in the UK was William Tyndale Junior School which made national press headlines over many months in the 1970s. It was depicted as the 'School of Shame', created by a headteacher 'who thought writing was obsolete' and teachers who had become left-wing ideologues and 'classroom despots' (Riley 1998: 21–22).

The Public Inquiry set up to resolve matters laid the blame on the teachers, the school managers (the governors of the school) and the local education authority – the Inner London Education Authority, the ILEA.[1] The teachers were blamed for their intransigence and their failure 'to strike the right balance between direction by teachers, and freedom of choice by the child'. The school managers were blamed because they had acted irresponsibly, and the ILEA because it had failed to act strategically and had been too bureaucratic and unwilling to intervene in the school when things went wrong (ibid., p.46). The Tyndale 'affair' created shock waves which reached the ears of the prime minister of the day, Jim Callaghan, influencing his thinking about education.

Tyndale also contributed to the growing scepticism in the UK about LEAs, re-enforcing the view of the Thatcher administrations of the 1980s and early 1990s, that local education authorities were responsible for many of the supposed education evils of the day. Over a period of years, LEAs were shunted into the wings, no longer star players as they had been for many decades but forced to audition for the 'bit' parts – which some did with more success then others. Through the introduction of a national curriculum, national tests and inspection, national government assumed increasing control of key aspects of education and devolved many respons-ibilities previously carried out by LEAs to schools and colleges. As their roles, resources and prestige diminished, pundits of the day assumed that LEAs would wither on the vine.[2] But LEAs survived – although only just.

The election of a Labour government in 1997 generated fresh specul-ation about the future of LEAs, and the prognosis for their future remains uncertain. Under the Labour government, LEAs have been brought back centre stage and given a defined role in helping the government achieve its targets for improvement. They are expected to deliver higher performance and greater value for money and are part of the new Labour agenda for education: key elements in the drive for standards. However, the govern-ment also perceives LEAs as a potential problem area that needs to be tightly regulated. LEAs are now required to produce Education Develop-ment Plans, detailing a planned programme of activity in support of school improvement, and indicating 'robust mechanisms for self-evaluation' (DfEE 1997). They will have to satisfy the stringent requirements of external scrutiny, since like schools, they have now become subject to national inspection (Ofsted 1997).

The Labour government's approach has been to issue LEAs with a challenge – to engage actively with improving school performance, or risk being sidelined by other local approaches in education, such as education action zones (Riley *et al.* 1998; Riley and Watling, forthcoming). LEAs are far from being monopoly suppliers and education management companies are on the horizon. In January 1999, the government advertised for private sector and other organisations willing to take over the running of 'failing' LEAs.

LEAs also have a number of other challenges to contend with. As well as seeking to raise standards in schools, the government also intends to tackle social disadvantage through a range of developments. As a consequence, LEAs are being pulled in two directions: towards a sharper focus on school improvement and towards a broader set of policy challenges about tackling social exclusion, regenerating communities, improving community safety and supporting life-long learning (Riley and Skelcher 1998). Whether they are able to achieve those twin goals remains to be seen.

Attempts to redefine the role of LEAs and improve their effectiveness also have to be seen in the context of ongoing scepticism from the media about their capabilities. A 1998 article in *The Economist* began with the following headline, 'Councils of despair. Does the Government want to get local councils out of the education business?' The article went on to suggest that the government was in two minds about LEAs (*Economist* 1998). Their local leadership role in education is hotly contested by leading figures in education, most notably by the Chief Inspector of Schools, Chris Woodhead who argues that the role of LEAs should be limited to providing support to those 2–3 per cent of schools that have 'failed' their inspection by the Office for Standards in Inspection (Ofsted), and to the further 10 per cent which have been judged to have 'serious weaknesses' (Woodhead 1998; Hackett 1997). Support for LEAs from government ministers is equivocal, and to some extent LEAs are on probation, needing to demonstrate that they can win 'the trust and respect of schools' and champion 'the value of education in its community for adults, as well as children' (White Paper 1997: 69).

The study

We began the first stage of the study, 'The Changing Role and Effectiveness of LEAs' in late 1995. The context for our work was one in which the 'opting out' provision had existed for several years, and yet the vast majority of schools still remained within the local education authority.[3] Typically, this fact had been described in negative terms – the schools had not chosen to opt out. However, if one looked at this as a positive decision, i.e. 'the schools had *opted for* LEA *membership*', then a number of questions emerged which provided a starting point for our research. We wanted to look at what benefits accrued to those schools that had retained LEA 'membership', what type of schools (primary, secondary, special) had benefited most, and whether such perceptions varied amongst personnel (heads, teachers, governors)? We also wanted to try and establish the characteristics of an effective LEA.

Our study has focused primarily on the relationship between LEAs and schools but has also looked at other aspects of the LEA's role and we have tried to capture the essential features of each participating authority. What, according to local politicians and officials, were they trying to achieve and what, according to the users of their services, did they achieve? How have they fared in comparison with each other and what can we learn from our study about the effectiveness of the LEA and its leadership role? We wanted to see whether we could construct a template of how leadership is expressed and exercised. We also wanted to consider the extent to which such a template was unique to the UK context, or had elements that were relevant to school districts, or municipalities in other countries.

To date, twenty-three LEAs from different parts of England have been involved in the study, and here we report on aspects of our findings from eighteen of them. The LEAs involved vary in size, location and ethnic composition. Some cover vast rural areas and small town communities, others suburban areas, others still cover diverse inner-city communities. One common factor has been that they have chosen to 'opt' into our study in order to get an external perspective on their own performance ,and to learn from the experience of others.

Some comparative findings

We derived our data from surveys and interviews. For all surveys, we circulated a questionnaire to Education Department staff, members of the Education Committee, headteachers, teachers and governors to ascertain their views about the authority's overall performance, management practices, styles of working, the effectiveness of services and service priorities.[4] The total number of respondents in the eighteen authorities was 6,085, representing an average response rate of 35 per cent. In over half the authorities, we have also conducted two sets of interviews: one with individual head-teachers, senior officers and local politicians; the other with groups who represented the authority's 'clients' (typically headteachers, school governors and teacher association representatives) but also other members of the LEA's workforce, such as frontline staff.[5]

First of all, we should make clear that perceptions of the effectiveness of education authorities, as for any institution, are not easy to compare. People's expectations of performance vary according to what seems realistically achievable given the contextual features of the locality. What a community in one authority counts as 'effective performance' may, therefore, be different from what a community in another authority deems appropriate, since the circumstances and challenges there are not the same.

That said, our findings have revealed marked differences between authorities in respondents' evaluations of overall performance (which had been assessed on a scale from 'poor' to 'excellent'), and these differences are highly significant in statistical terms. The combined ratings for 'competent' and 'excellent' ranged from just 19 per cent in one authority to 87 per cent in another, with ratings of 'excellent' alone varying from zero to 19 per cent (Figure 7.1). These overall ratings reflect similar differences in judgements concerning the effectiveness of most individual services – particularly advisory support for curriculum development, assessment of special educational needs (SEN), and SEN support for teachers.

The service most widely regarded as of high quality was training and support for school governors. With some exceptions, seven other services were generally perceived to be very effective: managing school admission processes; support for education in the early years; teachers' professional development opportunities; the educational welfare service; personnel advice; dealing with parents' complaints; and monitoring standards of pupil achievement. In contrast, provision for excluded pupils and the maintenance of school buildings were usually seen as ineffective, though one authority attracted clearly positive evaluations of the former service and four authorities attracted respectable ratings for the latter.

The marked differences in judgements about the *effectiveness* of individual services stood in contrast to the narrow range of evaluations concerning their *importance*. In every authority, a clear and usually large majority of respondents agreed or strongly agreed that each of the services

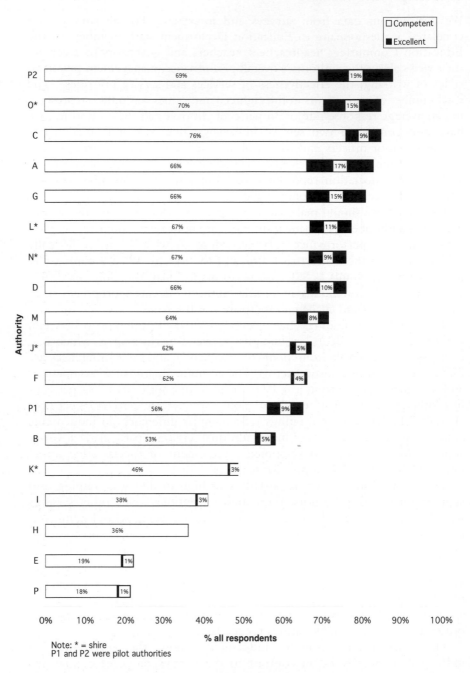

Figure 7.1 Evaluations of overall current performance.

currently provided should continue to be so (though schools – especially secondary – sometimes also wanted more delegated funds to 'buy back' certain services from the authority or to look elsewhere). However, when comparisons were based only on ratings of *strong* agreement, marked differences in the level of priorities became evident. Services judged to be especially important included, not surprisingly, assessment of special educational needs, support for teachers of children with special needs, and nursery provision – but not early admission to reception classes.

We also asked respondents to say how far they agreed/disagreed with twenty-two statements (some positively and some negatively worded) about aspects of the authority's performance. From those statements, we constructed three effectiveness scales to evaluate the extent to which a LEA was considered to be:

- efficiently managed
- responsive to needs
- improvement orientated (i.e. focused on improving school performance)

Here, too, responses varied remarkably between authorities, which fell into three bands ranging from unsatisfactory to clearly satisfactory (Figure 7.2). In general, LEAs that performed well on one of the three aspects of performance did so on the others, and vice-versa. Differences were also marked for most of the individual items. An example is shown in Figure 7.3, which indicates the extent to which respondents agreed or strongly agreed that the LEA had clear plans for the future. In one authority (M), as many as four in five returned positive responses and in another five authorities (A down to P1) more than three in five did so; yet in three authorities (P, E and H) the proportion responding positively was only about two in five.

When we asked respondents to indicate how they expected their authority to perform in the future, most (65 per cent to 95 per cent) said that they thought performance would improve at least 'a bit' (Figure 7.4 – the pilot authorities were not given this question). However, expectations that performance was set to become '*much*' better varied more between authorities, with as few as 7 per cent expressing confidence in one LEA (D), to as many as 60 per cent doing so in another (M). The relationship between ratings for overall current performance and future expectations was not straightforward. Respondents in some but not all authorities that returned low ratings for current performance showed considerable optimism about the future (often when there had been a change in leadership or new structures had only recently been put in place), but two authorities occupied the high ground on both measures.

Differences in evaluations arose not only between authorities but also among different respondent groups within each authority. On the whole, staff of the Education Department and councillors on the Education Committee were the most positive and teachers the least, with headteachers

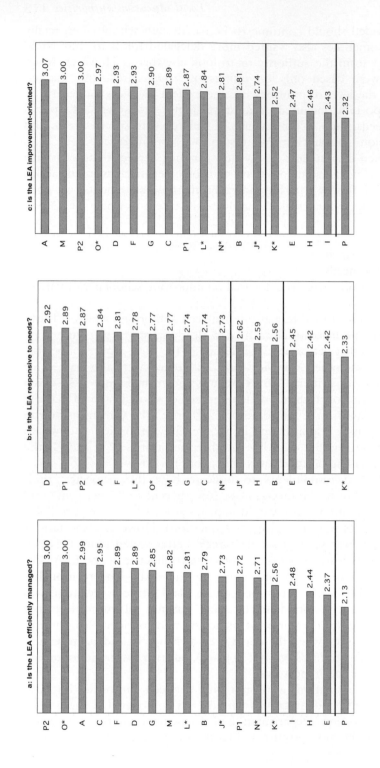

a: Is the LEA efficiently managed?

P2	3.00
O*	3.00
A	2.99
C	2.95
F	2.89
D	2.89
G	2.85
M	2.82
L*	2.81
B	2.79
J*	2.73
P1	2.72
N*	2.71
K*	2.56
I	2.48
H	2.44
E	2.37
P	2.13

b: Is the LEA responsive to needs?

D	2.92
P1	2.89
P2	2.87
A	2.84
F	2.81
L*	2.78
O*	2.77
M	2.77
G	2.74
C	2.74
N*	2.73
J*	2.62
H	2.59
B	2.56
E	2.45
P	2.42
I	2.42
K*	2.33

c: Is the LEA improvement-oriented?

A	3.07
M	3.00
P2	3.00
O*	2.97
D	2.93
F	2.93
G	2.90
C	2.89
P1	2.87
L*	2.84
N*	2.81
B	2.81
J*	2.74
K*	2.52
E	2.47
H	2.46
I	2.43
P	2.32

Notes: * = shire

Ratings are based on a scale from 1 (strongly disagree) to 4 (strongly agree)

1) *Differences between authorities.* For all three measures, the range of mean ratings was considerable, and differences between authorities were highly significant in statistical terms. The bold horizontal lines separate authorities whose mean ratings differ significantly from the others. 2) *Differences within authorities.* For efficient management and improvement-orientation (Figures 7.2a and 7.2c), LEA respondents typically returned more positive ratings than schools and governors, and differences reached significance in most cases. For responsiveness to needs (Figure 7.2b), differences between respondent groups were narrower and significant in only a few authorities.

Figure 7.2 Aspects of performance: mean ratings.

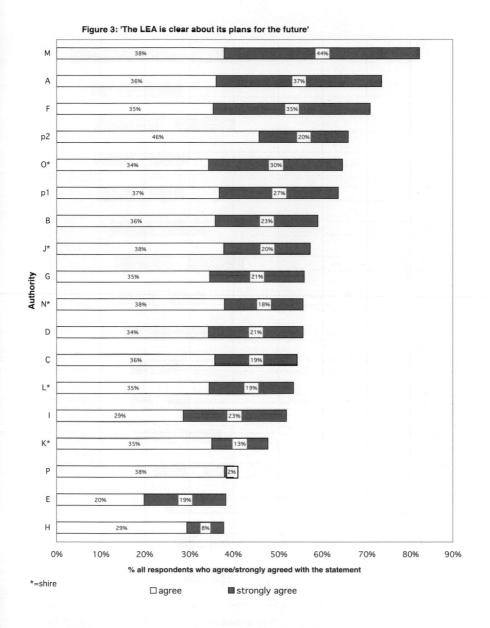

Figure 3: 'The LEA is clear about its plans for the future'

*=shire

□ agree   ■ strongly agree

Figure 7.3 'The LEA is clear about its plans for the future'.

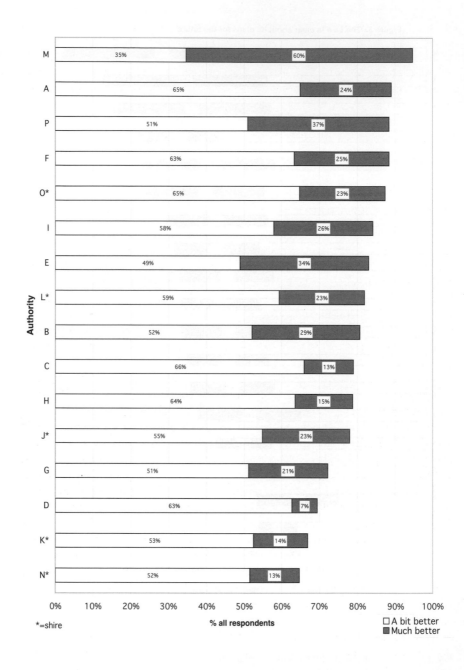

Figure 7.4 Expectations of future overall performance.

and governors coming in between (perhaps because they were more closely involved with the authority). For many services, primary schools were also frequently more positive than secondary schools. We also found some evidence to suggest that whilst school staff overall clearly valued local curriculum initiatives and other examples of practical classroom support, not least for children with special needs, many teachers – although not head-teachers – were relatively less enthusiastic about the role of local authorities in monitoring standards and providing statistical information about perfor-mance. On the whole, school staff valued in-service courses for teachers and support for curriculum development and school improvement (Riley, Docking and Rowles, 1998).

What makes a good LEA?

Evidence from the ratings

What is it that leads an education community to be satisfied with its authority? This is not an easy question to answer, not least because some of our data (as in most educational research) has yielded some paradoxical findings. For instance, in one authority the ratings for overall performance were fairly low compared with those of other authorities, yet the ratings for most individual services were perfectly respectable. In another LEA, respondents expressed high confidence that the authority's performance would improve while only a minority agreed that it had clear plans for the future.

None the less, we have tried to test three hypotheses to explain vari-ations in the ratings for overall current performance (Figure 7.5). Our first hypothesis was that LEAs with high levels of social disadvantage would be more likely to have below-average ratings for overall performance, and vice-versa. The argument was that 'being an effective LEA' is especially difficult in those localities where schools need so much support. Using eligibility for free school meals at age 10 as a rough indication of social hardship, we did find a fair relationship between this factor and judgements of overall current performance. The three 'best performing' authorities (P2, C and O) had the fewest number of children eligible for free meals (8 per cent to 10 per cent), while the three 'weakest performing' authorities ((E, H and P) were among those with the highest rates (33 per cent–40 per cent). Yet the association was far from perfect. For example, one authority (M) had quite high ratings for overall current performance (more than 7 in 10 thought it to be competent or excellent) but also one of the largest proportions of pupils eligible for free meals (34 per cent). Also, authorities that were 'statistical neighbours' (e.g. M and P), according to Ofsted's measures of the social characteristics of an area, could have markedly different ratings. In short, it looks as though LEAs can make a difference.

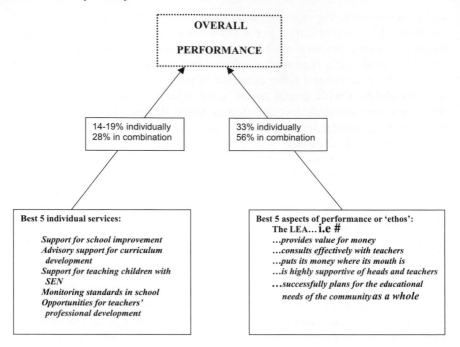

Figure 7.5 Variance of current overall performance predicted by (a) ratings for individual services and (b) general aspects of performance.

We then put forward two hypotheses to explain judgements of overall current performance in terms of respondents' evaluations for more particular aspects of the authorities' work. One hypothesis was related to perceptions of the effectiveness of specific services: the assumption being that a LEA was as effective as the quality of its core services for schools, such as support for curriculum development or special needs. The other hypothesis was that evaluations of overall performance would be associated with perceptions of an authority's general policies and practices, that is the extent to which it was seen to be efficiently managed, focused on improvement and responsive to needs (according to ratings on the three scales described in the previous section). The argument here was that an authority would be judged to be generally 'doing a good job' if people responded favourably to factors that characterised its general 'ethos' – its reputation for efficiency, its relationships with schools, its leadership qualities, and so on.

What emerged from our analysis (using multiple regression techniques) was that a *combination* of factors was more important in predicting evaluations of overall performance than any single factor. Among the specific services, the five most strongly associated with overall performance in almost all authorities were those that were particularly concerned with improving standards – support for school improvement, curriculum development, and teaching children with special educational needs, along with monitoring standards in schools and providing opportunities for teachers' professional development. Individually, across all authorities these predicted only 14–19 per cent of the variance in overall performance ratings, but in combination they predicted more than a quarter (Figure 7.5).

Similarly, the more general aspects of performance – those concerned with an authority's efficiency, responsiveness to needs and orientation towards improvement (which themselves were quite strongly inter-correlated) – were more powerful predictors of overall performance when taken in combination. Of the individual statements that made up the scales to measure these qualities, the five that emerged as most important were that *the LEA gives value for money, consults effectively with teachers, 'puts its money where its mouth is', is highly supportive of heads and teachers, and plans successfully for the educational needs of the community as a whole*. Individually, these predicted on average about a third of the variance in overall performance, but in combination they predicted well over half (56 per cent).

The evidence suggested that overall performance was more strongly related to these more ambivalent measures of performance than to specific services. The value of these five general factors in predicting overall performance was only slightly increased (to 59%) when ratings for the five individual services listed above were added to the equation. It seemed as if the 'ethos' of an authority carried rather more weight with respondents than the quality of its specific services.

The LEA and educational leadership: what appears to make a difference?

The next stage in our analysis was to try and explore some of the *how* questions: *How do LEAs create a positive ethos? How do they show that they value education?* and to then use this information to examine the *what* questions: *In what ways does leadership style appear to make a difference? What does educational leadership mean in practice in a LEA?*

Drawing on our interview data, as well as the analysis from questionnaires, we have constructed a template that attempts to capture some of the features of successful educational leadership on the part of the LEA. This template is illustrated in Table 7.1. The evidence from our study is that by its focus, style and activities, LEAs can and do make a difference. These differences are expressed in:

- The values which an LEA articulates
- How it defines its strategic direction;
- The climate that it creates
- How it exercises its leadership role
- How it operates on a day to day basis; and
- How it focuses on its activities

Table 7.1 The LEA and educational leadership: what makes a difference?

Core elements	What this means in practice	How this filters to the school level	Points of tension
Values expressed	• Education as a public service and a basic entitlement • Schools as part of a local education community	Affirmation of sense of community: *Belief in a coherent whole: the strong supporting the weak*	Providing support to schools *vs* acting as advocate of children and parents
Strategic direction	• Clarity of purpose • Context specific: local interpretation of need, as well as pursuit of national goals • Dependent on interaction between the professional and political	Schools understand both local and national agendas Even controversial policies are respected, if they're decisive and have been reached after extensive consultation	Assessment of local need and priorities *vs* legislative boundaries and financial constraints set by central govt
Climate	• Rising aspirations and expectations • Momentum, enthusiasm, commitment, trust	Climate promotes professional debate and exchange of good practice	Competing expectations within the local sytem
How the leadership role is exercised	• Clear, well-defined and enabling leadership but no exercised aspirations of the heroic • Partnership and consultation: relationships matter	Schools feel valued: *The director holds schools so tightly in her regard that they are never forgotten*	New initiatives e.g. Education Action Zones may fragment connections in a locality
Mode of operation	• Challenge and support • Intervention if a school is in trouble • Services are efficiently managed and well-targeted	Schools and governors feel well supported Schools receive high-quality services provided by dedicated professionals	Autonomy of schools *vs* responsibilities of LEA
Focus of activities	• Improvement orientated • 'Fresh start' where needed	Teachers have access to school-improvement initiatives, advisory services and challenging training and development opportunities	School standards agenda *vs* broader social inclusion agenda

Values and vision are key, and the authorities that were highly rated expressed common core values about the nature of education as a public service and about the concept of education entitlement. These LEAs did not see themselves merely as agencies of central government – the means through which government policies could be transmitted to schools – but as organisations which re-interpreted those policies within the context of local aspirations. Values and vision were embedded in the strategic direction and the strong value statements that underpinned the local partnership, and they were reflected in the connections between education and other local authority services, such as social services. The UK's national public audit office (The Audit Commission) found a similar set of dynamics:

> Effective local authorities view their education services not as discrete entities but as services that are intimately connected with other parts of the authority, working together to implement an agenda that is deter-mined as much by elected members and local stakeholders, as by the requirements of central government.
>
> (Audit Commission 1998: 10)

In one LEA in our study, for example, the local vision was based on a recog-nition of the importance of education for human growth and fulfilment, as well as for economic well-being. Interviewees shared the view that some groups within the local community were disenfranchised by their lack of education opportunities – groups such as young people without the skills and confidence to move forward, as well as women who had left work for family commitments and returned to low paid, unskilled jobs. The LEA became the vehicle through which the boundaries of local expectations could be made clear – no more 'failing' schools, higher aspirations for young people and opportunities to return to 'learning'.

The strength of those LEAs identified in our study as being the most effective sprang from a well-defined educational partnership with schools and a clear political-professional partnership between officers and local politicians. The partnership philosophy underpinned all the activities and was reflected in the aspirations of the local education community. As one headteacher put it:

> What is referred to as the education partnership is coming to mean a belief in a coherent whole, the strong supporting the weak and the need to work towards a common vision jointly. It also means a belief very firmly in a public education service, rather than market forces.

The partnership in this authority was tangible and a top priority for both officers and councillors, whilst headteachers saw it as one of the greatest assets of their LEA 'membership'. It was based on a relationship of mutuality, and sustained by good communications with staff and trade unions (through bulletins and a system of regular meetings), with schools and governors (through a range of forums, formal and informal meetings and newsletters), and for all concerned by events such as an annual conference which involved representatives from all parts of the the local education community.

The professional–political interface was critical, and local politicians played a key role in setting the local agenda and contributing to the educational leadership of the authority. The professional/political inter-action appeared to contribute to the effectiveness of the LEA by helping create a healthy challenge, and a clear and localised focus. One councillor described the symbiotic nature of the political/professional partnership in the following terms:

> The department is responsible for delivering the political will, but the political will is informed by a two-way process between members and officers and informed by the professional expertise of senior officers.

The impact of local politicians is highly significant. In a number of the LEAs that were rated as being poor by schools and governors, the local politicians had been unclear about their priorities, and working relationships between politicians and officers were often unproductive. At their most extreme, councillors saw themselves as embattled, with schools and head-teachers as problems that needed to be sorted out, and education adminis-trators as officers who needed to be controlled. How far this was down to the politicians, or to the officers, or indeed to schools themselves is often difficult to disentangle.

The directors of those LEAs which were highly rated aspired to be educ-ation leaders, and in the views of other interviewees succeeded in achieving this goal. They were respected as professionals who had clear views about what could be achieved and how, and they demonstrated a determination to influence the educational discourse. The leadership style was typically open and responsive with a strong sense of purpose that made an impact on the organisation as a whole. For example, one director (from authority 'P2' which was one of the highest rated LEAs) was described by a local head-teacher as, ' having a very particular style . . . she treats everybody's remarks as important,' and by another as 'holding schools so tightly in her regard that they are never forgotten'. Another director of a large LEA (Authority 'L') was seen by a head as having made an impact on the organisation through raising the aspirations of his staff:

> What we clearly have at the moment is somebody who has vision and is a leader, somebody who is taking us in a new direction. What is very interesting to me is that a number of people who perhaps are coming to the end of their careers certainly suddenly feel invigorated, and that is remarkable.

Where appropriate, the director had to signal to the organisation that changes were on the way. One explained it this way:

> When I first started, the department was in culture shock. No one worked together. There was no unifying theme, so I had to do the development plan. The initial ideas came from me but we consulted extensively for about a year and the plan is now very widely owned.

Context, as well as the attributes and experiences that the leading figures brought to it influenced effective leadership of LEAs.

During the course of interviews, we also asked directors of education about their preferred leadership style, and we asked other interviewees to give their perceptions of the leadership of the organisation. We found little evidence of 'heroic' leadership, and much evidence of shared leadership. Below are examples from the directors of two highly rated authorities:

> I see my job, I suppose, in Drucker's terms as enabling others to succeed. . . . I'm not looking for people to be subservient, I am looking for people to take a lead in their own context and to feel that they have a vibrant role to play, so that they can take initiative. I suppose the modern jargon is 'empowering'.

> In the end what you have to do is give everyone the capacity to take on their areas of responsibility, have an expectation that everyone can do that.... I would characterise the leadership of the organisation (and that's not just me) in terms of educational leadership. . . . It's about using but not controlling the education debate . . . creating a climate of thinking and challenge about education.

In both instances, local politicians, headteachers, governors and officers shared the same perceptions.

Leadership is also about substance. Those LEAs which were highly rated excelled in their administrative practices and had efficient monitoring and evaluation schemes for schools. They had also adopted a 'working with you' approach (which provided schools with clear data and analysis of performance and support for tackling such issues as pupil behaviour, or attendance), and they had expertise in key areas (such as curriculum, personnel and finance). The nature of the partnership with schools was based on mutuality and was expressed through a climate of professional challenge and enquiry.

Our findings suggest that through their leadership LEAs can have a significant impact on the local climate, shaping expectations and aspirations. When LEAs are focused on improvement and maximise their educational leadership potential through the local partnership, schools reap the benefits.

Effective training and development opportunities and well-focused advisory services can serve to generate the climate of professional challenge and debate in which schools thrive. Good morale in schools is critical to improvement and, from the evidence of our study, effective educational leadership by the LEA can contribute to raised teacher morale and a climate in which schools move forward together. Such a climate is characterised by school improvement projects which stimulate professional debate and contribute to the development planning processes in schools, equipping them to evaluate their own progress. Governors receive supportive inform- ation, such as briefing papers. Headteachers receive professional advice and support which includes interpretation of changing national expectations and information about curriculum innovation or developments in pedagogy. All of this practical support is linked to a clear vision of education in the locality, and sustained by a clear model of educational leadership.

Managing change at a local system level is about managing boundaries, as well as responding to competing demands. It is about managing the political/professional interface in the locality and at national level. Roles and relationships have to be redefined with schools, trade unions, local agencies (including local businesses and training agencies) and national government agencies (responsible for curriculum, inspection, testing, etc). The change process itself is likely to be stuttering and drawn out, requiring the identific- ation of existing constraints and obstacles, as well the capacity to design new strategies and embed these within the LEA itself and within the locality.

Not surprisingly, we detected a number of points of tension for LEAs in all aspects of their activities that contribute to the complexities of managing the change process (Table 7.1). These tensions exist at both the local and national level. LEAs find themselves caught between the expectations of schools and the pressures of national government. Schools quite rightly expect LEAs to be supportive of their endeavours, but the LEA must also be the advocate of parents and pupils; and in extreme situations, such as the exclusion of a pupil from a school, this may bring them into conflict with the school. LEAs must also be prepared to make decisions for the benefit of a whole community (which may go against the aspirations of individual schools) and to intervene in a school if performance is slipping, whilst at the same time encouraging school self-development.

Intermediary authorities: the wider picture

How do the findings from our study compare with the research evidence from elsewhere? How effective have LEAs – or their school district counter- parts – been? Researchers looking at American urban schools have con- cluded that the politics of control at school district level have consumed the energy of many American school leaders, distracting them from their principal task of developing a professional community (Louis and Kruse 1995). In a similar vein, Canadian researchers have concluded that school leaders tended to see the policies and procedures of the local district as hurdles to be overcome rather than as supportive agencies (Leithwood, Begley and Cousins 1994).

However, researchers from both North America and the UK have also found evidence to suggest that, through targeted resources and support which enables teachers and headteachers to concentrate on specific areas of student learning, LEAs and school districts can make a significant contribution to school improvement (ibid; Coleman and LaRocque 1990; Riley and Rowles 1997a and b). International evidence from an OECD study supports this analysis. The OECD study of eleven countries found many positive elements in the school/local authority relationship, and concluded that schools which exhibited unusually high levels of teacher quality shared a number of characteristics. These included 'a symbiotic relationship' between the school, its district authority and community that involved pressure and support at all levels within the context of shared educational values (OECD 1994). The research evidence to date, therefore, is mixed: school districts or LEAs can be a hindrance, but they can also be a help.[6]

In looking at the comparative research findings, we were also interested to discover how other researchers and analysts had described the characteristics of effective intermediary authorities. On the basis of analysis of a number of LEAs, the Audit Commission (1998) has highlighted the features that, in its view, effective LEAs appear to have in common. These appear to coalesce around three areas:

- Strategy: the ability to assess the needs of the locality, aided by a clear understanding of boundaries, resources and national expectations.
- Processes: the ability to gather, distribute, utilise and disseminate information, and to co-ordinate activities, not only across the education department but also across other local authority departments and with other agencies.
- Culture: features of trust and partnership that characterise the relationship between schools and the LEA, and the nature of the leadership.

The Audit Commission's analysis has a strong resonance with our own findings.

We were also particularly struck by the similarities between the findings from our study and those from a US study of Texan school districts (Asera, Johnson and Ragland 1999). The Texan researchers began their investigation by identifying school districts in which at least one-third of the pupils from 'high-poverty' schools were achieving particularly high ratings in the State's assessment tests. They were keen to examine what it was that happened at the levels of the superintendent, school board and central office to support high levels of academic achievement in those schools and came to three broad conclusions. Firstly, that the districts had created a 'sense of urgency' and 'efficacy' about academic achievement. Second, that they had created an environment in which improving academic performance became the primary focus of schools in their locality. And third, that the district leaders recognised that having challenging goals was not sufficient if schools did not know how to improve instruction.

Concluding thoughts

We conclude this chapter with a number of broad observations. The first is that whilst the jury is still out on LEAs, the evidence from our study, at least, is that they can make a significant contribution to their local education community. Whether in the future they can all deliver in comparable ways remains to be seen.

The second is about what it is LEAs do that appears to make a difference. What seems to matter is the relentless drive on issues of teaching and learning that was reflected in the strong focus on the five service areas identified earlier, which are all linked to school improvement. The third observation is about how LEAs go about achieving their objectives. *How* they do it seems increasingly to be as important as *what* they do. The 'how' is about providing a climate of challenge and support for schools, linking resources to agreed objectives, focusing on teaching and learning, and planning successfully for the needs of the community as a whole. The 'how' is about the ethos: the expectations and aspirations and the ways in which things are done to bind an education community together: the absence of which can fragment a community.

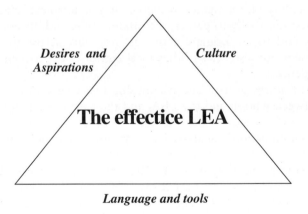

Desires, dreams and aspirations for the local community; a climate of continuous improvement and an urgency for change; the language of education and the tools for improvement.

Figure 7.6 Elements characterising effective interrmediary authorities.

Our final observation is about replicability. Leadership in education, whether at a school or school district level, is bounded in history, culture and context. We are hesitant about proposing a universal model against which the effectiveness of all intermediary authorities can be measured. Nevertheless, we would invite others to test out the validity of the model presented in this chapter in other cultures and contexts. Having said that, on the limited comparative evidence that we have, there may be three inter-connected elements that can be seen as characterising effective intermediary authorities and contributing to the local leadership of education (Figure 7.6):

Notes

1 The Public Inquiry led by Robin Auld, now Lord Chief Justice Auld, took evidence over a period of 62 days and 9 evenings from 107 witnesses who were represented by 11 barristers, as well as considering a further 600 pieces of written evidence before reaching a conclusion (Riley 1998).

2 Senior Conservative politicians, such as Kenneth Clarke and Michael Heseltine, argued for the demise of LEAs – a view shared by others. In June 1991, the *Independent* newspaper published a 'Schools' Charter' which included the following proposal, 'We recommend the eventual abolition of local education authorities – not because they are solely to blame for the performance crisis but because their role is withering away and the ground must be cleared'. (quoted in Riley 1998: 3).

3 The 'opt out' provision allowed schools to vote (through a parental ballot) to become independent of the local education authority and to be nationally funded as a grant-maintained school. Under the 1997 Labour government, this provision has been rescinded.

4 The project has been conducted in three overlapping phases, the first two of which have now been completed. In *phase I*, pilot work in two London borough enabled us to refine our questionnaire (distributed to 2,210 respondents), test the internal consistency of the performance scales, and make changes to the interview schedule. In *phase II*, the revised questionnaire was circulated to 4,173 respondents in a further nine London boroughs. (For a detailed analysis of the findings from phase II, see Riley, Docking and Rowles 1999.) *Phase III* has involved six shire authorities, one metropolitan authority and one newly created unitary authority. These latter surveys are more intensive than in Phase II, and include extensive interviewing. The questionnaire has been further adapted in the light of Phase II experience, with the items varying somewhat from one authority to another to accommodate the particular services offered, though a core has been retained for comparative purposes.

5 During these group interviews, we have used a card-sort ranking exercise based on twenty statements about the LEA which had been drawn from previous interview data.

6 A UK Rowntree Foundation project concluded that the quality of relationships and services had become key factors in the way that schools appraised their LEA (Radnor, Ball and Vincent 1997).

References

Asera, R., Johnson, Jr., J.F. and Ragland, M. (1999) 'Successful Texas school Districts', paper to the International Congress for School Effectiveness and Improvement (ICSEI), January, San Antonio, Texas.

Audit Commission (1998) *Changing Partners*, London: Audit Commission.

Coleman, P. and LaRoque, L. (1990) *Struggling to be Good Enough: Administrative Practices and School District Ethos*, London: Falmer Press.

DfEE (1997) *Framework for the Organisation of Schools: Technical Consultation Paper*, Department for Education and Employment, London: HMSO.

Economist (1998) 'Councils of despair', 24 Jan., pp. 27–8.

Hackett, G. (1997) 'Chief inspector seeks to limit role of councils in improving schools', *Times Educational Supplement*, (14th November) p. 5.

Independent (1991) 'A charter for schools', 5 July.

Leithwood, K. A., Begley, P. T. and Cousins, J.B. (1994) *Developing Expert Leadership for Future Schools*, London: Falmer Press.

Louis, K. S., Kruse, S.D. and Associates (1995) *Professionalism and Community*, California: Corwin Press.

OECD (1994) *Quality in Teaching*, Paris: Organisation for Economic Cooperation and Development.

Ofsted (1997) *Framework for the Inspection of Local Education Authorities*, London: Office for Standards and Inspection in Education.

Radnor, H.A., Ball, S.J. and Vincent, C. (1997) 'Whither democratic accountability in education? An investigation into headteachers' perspectives on accountability in the 1990s with reference to their relationships with their LEAs and governors', *Research Papers Education* 12(2): 205–22.

Riley, K.A. (1998) *Whose School is it Anyway?*, London: Falmer Press.

Riley, K.A. and MacBeath, J. (1998) 'Effective leaders and effective schools', in J. MacBeath (ed.) *Effective School Leadership: Responding to Change*, London: Paul Chapman, pp. 140–52.

Riley, K.A., Docking, J. and Rowles, D. (1998) 'LEAS on probation – will they make the grade?', *Education Review*, Summer, 12(1): 30–4.

—— (1999) Can Local Education Authorities make a difference? The perceptions of users and providers', *Educational Management and Administration* 27 (1) 29–44.

Riley, K.A. and Rowles, D. (1997a) *From Intensive Care to Recovery: Schools Requiring Special Measures*, London: London Borough of Haringey.

—— (1997b) 'Inspection and school improvement in England and Wales: national contexts and local realities', in T. Townsend (ed.) *Restructuring, Quality and Effectiveness: Problems and Possibilities for Tomorrow's Schools*, London: Routledge, pp. 81–99.

Riley, K. A. and Skelcher, C. (1998) *Local Education Authorities: A Schools' Service, or a Local Authority Service?* London: Local Government Management Board.

Riley, K.A., Watling, R., Rowles, D. and Hopkins, D. (1998) 'Some lessons learned: the first wave of Education Action Zone applications', London: The Education Network.

Riley, K. A. and Watling, R. (forthcoming) 'Education Action Zones: an initiative in the making', *Public Money and Management*.

The White Paper (1997) *Excellence in Schools*, London, HMSO.

Woodhead, C. (1998) 'Yin versus Yang', *Guardian Education*, 3 March, pp. 2–3.

8 Local leadership
Policy implementation, local education authorities and schools

John Fitz, William A. Firestone and Janet Fairman

Introduction

Recent writing in educational policy and administration has emphasised the extent to which education systems are composed of loosely coupled domains (eg Fuhrman *et al*. 1988: Spillane 1998). In this scenario, each domain has its own structure, rules, focus and capacity for policy determination and decision-making. The relative insulation of one domain from another, it is argued, accounts for some of the difficulties of embedding policy intentions formulated at the macro level, in practices at the micro-level.

This chapter builds on these insights in a consideration of educational leadership in two ways. First, we draw on the perspective broadly known as 'new institutionalism' to argue that leadership has to be considered in relationship to the institutions which regulate the boundaries of authority of agencies and actors, the scope and direction their decision-making and their capacity to govern (Steinmo *et al*. 1993; John 1998; Rhodes 1997). Second, we draw on an empirical study of policy implementation conducted in the USA and England and Wales (for brevity sometimes referred to as E-W), which focused on local responses to centrally generated assessment policies. In this connection, we survey the different meanings attached to notions of 'the centre' and 'the local', following through the implications for the translation of policy intentions into pedagogic and assessment practice.[1]

Our thesis is that education systems evoke varieties of educational leadership, and varieties of educational leaders, regulated and positioned by the institutional arrangements that constitute the various domains or arenas, of which systems are composed. These are fundamental units of analysis, we argue, when policies are tracked from their formulation at the centre to their impact on the ground. The model proposed here has two features. We suggest that centrally generated policies not only have substantive components, they also distribute power and control across local agencies and actors and thus determine whom is responsible to whom, and who is accountable for what. Second, the model proposed here also embraces the view that local agencies and actors are key participants in the detailed interpretation, and translation, of policy into practice.

This chapter is organised into the following sections. The first considers the theoretical underpinnings of the conception of leadership we have sketched above. The second section reviews our research on local responses to central testing programmes. The third section compares and contrasts the composition and occupants of various domains of policy-making in relation to assessment in the US and UK. The fourth section focuses on the local interpretations of policy and explores the relationship between local educational authorities and schools in the US and Britain. The last section reviews the varieties of leadership and the interconnections between them in our comparative study.

Institutions, the policy process and educational leadership

We begin with brief consideration of institutions. From the perspective of 'new institutionalism', institutions 'matter' and they do so for two reasons. First, institutions matter insofar as their regulations, rules and procedures structure politics and policy-making in very powerful ways, by determining who can participate, who is privileged and who is not. They provide, amongst other things, a particular bias towards certain values and voices. Second, the configuration of institutions, their character and the relationship between them, differentiates between one polity and another. We only have to consider the two liberal democracies which feature in this study to appreciate the significance that institutions have in shaping two very different systems, evidenced in the governance, organisation and provision of education in the USA and the UK. For example, a written constitution in the US sustains the delicate balance between state power and individual freedom, federal government authority and states' rights, and maintains a division between state and church. It constrains what federal governments can do in the field of education and it also prevents tax dollars being spent in religiously affiliated schools. In the UK, where parliamentary sovereignty is paramount, as successive administrations have demonstrated, that there are few defences against a determined national government that seeks to diminish the power, control and accountability of local democratic institutions. A notable recent example here is the changing importance of local education authorities (LEAs). The consequences for educational policy of these contrasting institutional ensembles are evident in this paper.

For the purpose of this chapter, the policy process is conceptualised as a series of levels, hierarchically related. Each level is theorised as an ensemble of structured positions, occupied by institutions and agents, related in a struggle to become the authoritative shapers or interpreters of policy texts. Following Bernstein (1996), conceptually, occupants in each successive level are engaged in the interpretation and recontextualisation of the policy text made available and legitimate by the occupants of the preceding level.

In this chapter we employ the 'institutions' and 'levels' framework to examine the local implementation and impact of centrally generated assessment policies. Our analysis has identified three levels where policy as successively interpreted recontextualised and refocused. The first, the *central level*, denotes the institutional ensemble where policy is formulated, promulgated as legislation or as administrative action. What constitutes the centre, however, is one important difference between the UK and the US. In the latter case, schooling is primarily the responsibility of the states, whilst in the UK, central government has assumed the lead role in curriculum and assessment policy, via the creation of a National Curriculum and an associated testing programme since 1988. The *local level* denotes local education authorities – in the US, the school district or its nominative equivalent – and in the UK, its counterpart, the local education authority (LEA). The *schools' level* is self-explanatory, and signifies the institutional sites where policies are further interpreted, adjusted and realised as curriculum and pedagogical and assessment practices, in policy texts, organisational principles and interactions between teaching staff and students. 'Leadership' in this model is differentially distributed across the three levels.

Methods of enquiry

Firestone and his colleagues undertook the first phase of the research reported here in two American states, Maine and Maryland, selected because state testing programmes were linked, differentially, to the application of formal policy instruments designed to monitor and, in one state, Maryland, to take over schools (Firestone, Mayrowetz, and Fairman 1997). Thus, they varied in the 'stakes' that were likely to be attached to levels of student attainment. In each state, interviews were undertaken with state officials, district level administrators, school principals and maths teachers responsible for teaching maths to 8th grade students. The researchers further investigated the impact of testing on instructional practices via the observation of maths lessons in the sample schools. The study focused on ten schools and featured interviews with twenty-four heads of English, social studies and maths departments, and subsequent interviews with, and observations of, twenty-five maths teachers across the two states.

The second phase of the fieldwork was undertaken in four *secondary* schools, two in Cardiff and two in Bristol in the period May–June 1997. The selection of secondary schools was designed to addressed an imbalance in the British research base on assessment, where hitherto, research had been conducted mainly in primary schools with 6–10-year-olds (e.g. Gipps *et al.* 1995; Pollard *et al.* 1994).

To match Firestone's sample schools in the Maine–Maryland study, the UK schools chosen were *middle* and *low* ranking in terms of levels of student attainment, as ranked by published GCSE scores – one in each category – in Cardiff and Bristol. GCSE scores, coincidentally, are also a good indication of the social composition of schools in Britain. Unlike the American study, however, we did not collect data at the equivalent of the school district (local education authorities) for these are less central in relation to the funding and governance of schools than are their US counterparts. This was subsequently emphasised in our interviews with school administrators.

School-based research focused on Key Stage 3 assessments taken by all 14-year-olds in public schools. Again, this matched the sample age range in the American study. Interviews were conducted with headteachers, curriculum directors/deputy heads and the heads of the maths departments at each of the four schools. Interview schedules employed in the American study were revised and provided the basis for interviews with the above respondents. Our purpose here was to elicit perspectives on the national policy framework from key actors who had both the responsibility for, and capacity to shape, the schools' responses to policy assessment imperatives.

Classroom-based research included two interviews with four maths teachers in each of the focus schools and two observations of maths classes taught by the sample teachers. This research was intended to explore teacher interpretation of school policies and national assessment programmes, gather data on teaching experience, subject knowledge, teachers beliefs and classroom practices and pedagogic processes. Again, interviews and observations were based on schedules employed in the American study and modified, where appropriate.

Assessment in context: defining the centre

United Kingdom

Included in the interlocking policy initiatives which formed the 1988 Education Reform Act, was an ambitious programme to test all children in maintained schools at ages 7, 11, 14 and 16. The tests were set alongside a National Curriculum (NC) composed of ten subjects and a number of cross-curricular themes. For the first time, then, central government created the mechanisms through which it could determine the sequence, pace and content of the school curriculum. It wrested control of the curriculum and assessment from local education authorities and schools. Paradoxically, alongside the central determination of the curriculum, the 1988 Act also devolved considerable financial and managerial independence to schools, which, in turn, were to compete in a per capita funded regime of school choice. This has been examined elsewhere and will not be discussed here (Ball 1990: Maclure 1988, 1998; Chitty 1989).

The distinctive features of the 1988 system of assessment programme were its scale, that it was government controlled, its overt regulative purpose in seeking to ensure that schools followed the NC, and the 'stakes' attached to it. Publication of test attainments was justified as providing information to parents on which they could base their choice of schools. In the competitive admissions' market created by the 1988 Act, test results became critical for schools seeking institutional survival. While educationalists were prepared for, and gave a cautious welcome to, a National Curriculum (indeed, some had advocated it), the reception of national testing was more hostile.

Another distinctive feature of the post-1988 period was the creation of succession of agencies appointed by ministers. These were intended to take forward, with maximum efficiency, the government's educational initiatives legislated in the 1988 Act. For example, in order to take its curriculum and testing ambitions forward, central government created new agencies, the National Curriculum Council (NCC) and Schools Examination and Accreditation Council (SEAC) and the Task Group on Assessment and Testing (TGAT). These were merged in 1994 to form the Qualifications and Curriculum Authority. The creation of these agencies moved curriculum and assessment leadership away from LEAs and teachers and firmly located it at the centre. In addition, education policy was also put under scrutiny by a range of new right and 'cultural restorationist' 'think tanks', allied to the Conservative government. The politics of policy-making became a rich confection of political and bureaucratic interests and values (Ball 1990; Maw 1993; Taylor 1995).

It was the Task Group on Assessment and Testing (TGAT), chaired by Paul Black, which was asked it to bring forward proposals for a national testing programme for the four stages of assessment identified in the legislation. It reported in 1988 (Black 1994). TGAT's proposals included a combination of externally generated standard assessment tasks (SATs) and teacher assessment (TA). It proposed a form of testing that was intended to be formative and summative, within a programme that aimed to match the relative progress of students across age-related stages. It employed criterion referencing and also drew on state-of-the-art research. TGAT's proposals were attractive to the educational professionals but were also sufficiently rigorous to calm the standards-obsessed voices of the new right. Classes and schools could be compared, in a system which proposed external SATs as a measure to moderate teacher judgements on students' learning, on the basis of a range of assessments they had devised and on attainments they had recorded.

The radical proposals in the TGAT report encountered trouble on three fronts: the political, the ideological and the operational (see Black 1994; Daugherty 1995). There was a 'drift', in Black's terms, from TGAT's classroom-centred programme of assessment, organically linked to the teaching taking place within the classroom, to the 'examination' model which we observed in our KS3 maths assessment research in 1997 (Fitz, Fairman and Davies 1998) cannot be discussed in detail here. The drift proceeded via the over-elaboration of the testing programme by SEAC, and a Secretary of

State sympathetic to voices which called for the return of time-limited, uncomplicated test and transparent tests scores. In 1992/93, there followed a sustained action by teachers (supported by their governing bodies and many parents) against the load placed on class time by testing arrangements. The outcome was a review of the National Curriculum and its associated tests (Dearing 1993) and the subsequent demise of a Secretary of State. At the time we undertook our research, the KS3 assessment of maths gave prominence to externally set and marked, time-limited SATs. Teacher assessment continued and was the basis of judgements about student attainment in AT1 (using and applying maths) – the investigative element in the assessment. National testing at KS1–3 is now the responsibility of the QCA.

TGAT exemplifies the route subsequently adopted by central government in its determination to control the scope, pace and direction of curriculum and assessment reform. In the period 1992–4, the creation of other meso-level, ministerially appointed, and upwardly accountable institutions, extended central government controls over other areas of the system. Most prominent was the new system of inspection in which all school were subject to a full inspection, on a regular (4 years in England, 5 years in Wales) cycle. Other agencies established with influence over the operation of schools were the Teacher Training Agency and the Funding Agency for Schools. In combination with new powers granted to Education Secretaries to intervene in schools, these meso-level institutions were the means through which the centre asserted its pedagogic authority over teachers and schools, and diminished the powers of LEAs (Fitz, Halpin and Power 1997).

United States

The governance of education in the US is very different. Under its federal structure, control over education is located at the level of the states. Federal governments have power to influence the scope and direction of education via a system of grants, but does not have at its disposal the kinds of policy levers that successive British governments have been able to assemble and employ.

That being the case, there has been, nevertheless, a family resemblance in the school reforms in both countries (Boyd 1995) and policy-makers have sought to learn the 'lessons' from developments taking place on either side of the Atlantic (Boyd 1996; Stearns 1996; Firestone 1997). Attention has been focused, for example, on the contribution self-managing schools, parental choice programmes and competition between schools might make, to the shared goal of levering up standards. And although there is no exact equivalent to the National Curriculum in the US, the 1994 '*Goals 2000: Educate America Act*' can be interpreted as an expression of the concern of federal governments to influence curriculum and assessment policy (Jennings 1998). The proposals included financial support for states and school districts willing to adopt a defined standards and curriculum framework, a rigorous testing programme, the creation of opportunities to learn (Boyd, 1995) and the devolution of financial and managerial responsibilities to schools. Subsequent changes in the political composition of the House of Representatives and the return of a large Republican majority made it unlikely that the 'Goals 2000' would progress much further. Even its limited ambitions were interpreted on the right, and in the Representatives, as a threat to local democracy and for the more extreme opponents, also a threat to the family (Jennings 1998). The episode emphasizes how constrained federal governments are in seeking to lead nationally effective policies in education and training, in comparison with their British counterparts,

In the US, though, there is considerable latitude for sub-government and private agencies, with federal encouragement, to create and promote curriculum and assessment policies and 'standards' and argue for their adoption on a national basis. Some examples include the National Council on Education Standards and Testing, the National Science Foundation, and the one most relevant to our study, the National Council of Teachers of Mathematics (NCTM). It was the NCTM which published influential proposals on content, pedagogy and age-related targets for schools maths (NCTM 1989). The NCTM proposals were widely credited with exerting influence on state standards reforms, such as those published in Maryland in 1990 and the 'Learning Results' standards published in Maine in 1997. In the US, then, there has been a considerable role for subject associations, testing agencies and educational foundations – the professional educational community – to drive forward curriculum and testing programmes. This is in stark contrast to Britain, where in the past, similar organisations have been seen as barriers to, rather than partners in, the drive to raise standards.

By no means a national curriculum, the NCTM proposals, nevertheless, provided a template of good practice that was influential, both at state and school district levels. In Maine and Maryland, for example, the NCTM 1989 document suggested the maths topics which ought to be covered and identified skills which should be acquired by the 8th grade. In the context of our American study, the document influenced the construction of the state-wide assessments in our focus states.

Of these states, Maryland corresponds more closely to the aspirations set out in 'Goals 2000'. It has proactively promoted two state tests (MSPAP and the Functional Test), has set high school graduation targets for schools and has a well-defined curriculum framework. The state also requires schools to establish School Improvement Teams (SITs) which are responsible for the creation and reporting of an annual school development plan, linked to school strategies to improve their MSPAP scores. Maryland has consolidated into twenty-four districts, which meet the Maryland State Education Department (MSED) on a regular basis. The MSDE also facilitates state-wide co-ordinating meetings between district superintendents, testing officers and subject specialists. While these meetings alerted districts about state expectations and policy trends, our research also suggests the direction of influence ran primarily from the state to local level.

Moreover, the state has one policy lever that assures a considerable degree of alignment between its curriculum and assessment policy and local level practices. 'Reconstitution' is the policy instrument that enables state intervention in schools where performance indicators demonstrate under-achievement against state-determined targets. MSPAP scores have been employed as a principle, but not the only indicator of relative school performance. Over fifty schools have been subject to 'reconstitution'; the great majority of which have been in Baltimore. Although school districts can undertake to apply special measures to schools in order to lever up standards, the institutional arrangements in Maryland suggest that the centre has the capacity to regulate directly what schools do.

Maine offers an interesting contrast. Compared with Maryland, it is an example of a strongly de-centralised system. Local governance of schools is distributed amongst 188 local authorities (school districts, towns, super-visory unions and school administrative districts – SADs). The small and declining, State Education Department has limited capacity either to devise policy or oversee its implementation. Thus, although it has a state-testing programme (The Maine Education Assessment – MEA) which commenced in 1984–5, the Department's assessment unit has recently been reduced from five staff to one. The autonomy of school districts and the indepen-dence from state regulation enjoyed by its schools, aligns Maine with the model of educational governance promoted by the Republican critics of the 'Goals 2000' programme (Boyd 1995). Nevertheless, district-level institu-tions had a mediating and directive role in relation to schools in their respective administrative areas. How these mediations shaped the state-testing programme in Maine and Maryland is something we shall return to later. Their counterparts in the England–Wales study, the local education authorities (LEAs), post-1988, had their powers to determine and support curriculum and assessment policies greatly constrained. But how are LEAs situated as local leaders?

Local education authorities and policy

The 1944 Education Act created a clear framework for Local Education Authorities (LEAs) in the UK. They were primarily responsible for the provision of school places for all children of compulsory school age and formerly held budgets for schools and were the direct employers of heads, teachers and support staff. Historically, they also provided curriculum support and monitored school performance. Under the Local Management of Schools arrangements in the 1988 Act (which transferred 90 per cent of local school budgets to schools – 95 per cent in Wales) and via policy initiatives that increased parental choice, the planning and provision of education moved away from LEAs to schools. Moreover, for nearly a decade after the 1988 Education Reform Act, LEAs had no secure role in curriculum and assessment matters in relation to their schools and were bypassed in central discussions on curriculum and testing issues. In addition, central government indicated that schools were primarily accountable to the centre and to parents. The resources at the disposal of LEAs for curriculum leadership and innovation also varied one from the other. From the perspective of schools in our study, they were relatively small, and in practice, operated primarily through in-service days for schools. We should add, however, that under the Labour government, LEAs have recently been given a more strategic role in the drive to raise standards (DfEE 1997, 1999) which we will discuss in more detail later.

The relationship in the UK between the centre and schools is very direct. Accountability for performance lies with schools, and the power to intervene in schools which fail to provide education of a satisfactory standard, resides with central government, where the Secretary of State, who on the advice of the schools' inspectorate (Ofsted), may effectively take over schools. As if further to endorse the subordinate status of LEAs, like schools, they are now subject to inspections judgements made about their efficiency and effectiveness.

Our interviews with headteachers in England and Wales shed considerable light on how they viewed the relative importance of central and local authority influence in curriculum and assessment matters. The data also highlighted how little say in curriculum matters LEAs in our study had. One head noted that although LEAs are accorded a statutory role in curriculum matters,

> In practice, [they have] very little. They have certain statutory obligations, especially special education needs. The rest of the curriculum is the National Curriculum. You follow that? . . . LEAs try to provide support for the curriculum through specific projects and advisory teachers, but they face a challenge.

From the schools' perspective, the responsibility to interpret and respond to National Curriculum and assessment frameworks rests primarily with them. Seen in this light, the relationship between national policy and schools was direct *and regulative* in curriculum and assessment matters, and the relationship between LEAs and schools was *advisory and developmental,*

There is some contrast to this situation in our American study. In Maine, school districts and schools respond in relatively muted ways, to the state-testing programme in the absence of central administrative censure. This, and also the absence of direct market implications for schools, meant that state testing was not a priority for school districts or schools. In Maryland, where 'reconstitution' has serious implications for the local control of schools, school superintendents and district-level administrators have a considerable stake in testing outcomes at the school level. They are able to exert downward pressure on schools in ways school districts in Maine and LEAs in the UK were not.

Arising from state testing, there were also informal, but nevertheless pervasive, and important implications for many of the school district interviewees in Maryland, and also in Maine. Interviewees expressed the view that poor performance by schools in their districts shed them in a poor light. Whilst sensitive to the possibility of negative comparison, the interviews with administrators and principals evinced almost no concrete evidence of a direct connection between negative comparisons and serious consequences for the careers of public officials, or for the market reputation of schools.

That being said, the American study found Maryland schools involved in significantly more practices related to state-testing programmes than was the case in Maine. Moreover, district-level administrators exerted downward pressure on schools to take account of state tests in their curriculum. This process involved one-to-one meetings between school district officers and principals, where the latter were asked to account for low test scores. Maryland school districts also pressured schools to attend to state-testing goals through the leadership efforts of the superintendent, and through professional development activities, organised for teachers and by district subject supervisors. Pressure was also exerted via the operation of site-based School Improvement Teams (SITs) who were required by the state to draft formal plans for improving student skills that were particularly weak. The SIT report back to the district office, and a copy is forwarded to the state department of education. Although SITs could ostensibly initiate curriculum reform at the school level, by encouraging teachers to recommend specific changes, in practice, they operated more as an arm of the state or district administration to ensure compliance with state assessment policy.

For example, in the rural, poor district of Frontier, the superintendent had been hired from a higher income state with a history of strong central control over educational policy. Although he did not wholly agree with the shift away from basic skills toward more critical thinking skills emphasized by the state performance assessment (MSPAP), he nonetheless made improvement of test scores one of his main priorities. He stated: 'Frontier was behind the times. Some teachers thought the MSPAP would go away with the new Governor in January, 1995 but it didn't.' The superintendent instituted a monthly writing assessment for all grades, which teachers administered in various subjects, to prepare students to handle the open-response format on the new assessment. His counterpart in Chesapeake district regarded the improvement of test scores as a legal mandate, whether or not he considered the testing programme as useful or not. He said his local board of education set goals for him that were based on the MSPAP and local priorities, and that 'assessment is driving what we are doing'.

School principals in Frontier felt pressured by the superintendent to show improvement in test scores, as a component of their job evaluation process.

While the superintendent said: '[The media] don't make a big deal out of [test scores]. The pressure comes from me'. A school principal concurred: 'I have to be honest with you, the man's my boss. He wants us to advance and we're trying to do that and, yes, there's some pressure.'

In contrast to the Maryland districts, Maine superintendents did not place high priority on improvement of test scores or alignment of curriculum with state learning goals. Replacement of ageing school buildings, local school budgets, and parents' demand for traditional curricula occupied the attention of district administrators. Moreover, interviews with Maine administrators consistently revealed a stronger attitude of independence vis-à-vis state authority over local curricular decisions.

In one school district, Farm Town, the newly hired superintendent was regarded by teachers as having the potential for leading improvement in curriculum, but was too busy with budgetary and administrative matters to be involved in curriculum. The assistant superintendent, ostensibly the curriculum co-ordinator, worked mostly to obtain funding to replace two pre-Civil War middle school buildings. Teachers did comment on the superintendent's support of their professional development efforts, which was signalled by a substantial increase in district spending to send teachers to outside conferences or bring in speakers requested by teachers. In River City, another school district, district administrators had backed away from introducing the middle school philosophy in one school, when parents' opposed new instructional approaches.

In summary, then, how school districts in Maine and Maryland chose to interpret and respond to state-testing programmes was an important variable in explaining the degree to which schools aligned their practices with state-testing regimes (Firestone *et al.* 1997). In our England–Wales study we argue that LEAs had few powers to mediate the alignment between centrally driven testing policy and school-based pedagogic and assessment practice. The constitutional framework in the US continued to preserve a place for local democracies such as school districts, and states proceeded with relative caution in directing their activities and in interfering with the relationship between districts and schools. The LEA situation was much more fragile at the time we conducted our research; an outcome of legislation designed to curtail their direct influence over schools. The comparative findings also reveal the power of the threat of school take-overs as a policy lever. Where this exists local policies and practices were closely aligned with centrally determined programmes. That in turn diminished the capacity of district-level officials to devise local and community oriented strategies for teaching and learning. In our next section we extend our comparative analysis to schools.

Schools and responses to assessment frameworks

We noted earlier that schools in England and Wales were located within two kinds of external policy frameworks, each of which exerted pressure on their operations. The first was administrative pressure, which required them to conform to curriculum and assessment policies and to perform well against a number of centrally determined performance indicators. The second was the pressure exerted by local educational markets, within which schools are required to develop strategies for institutional survival (see Woods *et al.* 1998). This has had an impact on how schools are managed and led (see also Levacic 1995; Whitty, Power and Halpin 1998; Fitz *et al.* 1997).

Our evidence suggests that it was headteachers and their senior management teams (SMTs) that organised and took responsibility for creating an institution judged to be financially sound, administratively efficient, and effective, and also for sustaining their market share of students. Within the school, it was subject heads who had assumed considerable responsibility for the detailed interpretation and implementation of national policies on curriculum and assessment (see also Turner 1996; Brown and Rutherford 1998).

In the England–Wales study, for example, we asked the headteachers what were the biggest challenges they faced. One of our headteachers reported what this meant for him:

> The two big issues for this school are academic achievement and student behaviour . . .buildings and resources are also an issue. The big two are achievement and behaviour. Those two are clearly linked.

He went on to note that his student population was:

> Mixed, regarding social class, mainly white, 10% ethnic background. In terms of ability, reasonably mixed but we do not have our fair share of more able children when compared with the national norms. [We believe] the professional classes prefer to send their children to the private sector or out of Bristol to the leafy suburbs [away from] the terrible influence of estate children. We have busloads of children going to South Gloucestershire. . . . People perceive their children getting better exam results there.

In the market, then, schools need to recruit to their standard number, or physical capacity, to survive as institutions, but in order to secure their market position they also perceive the need to recruit academically high attaining students. In consequence, national assessment scores, employed as performance indicators by parents or by central state agencies, have high stakes attached to them.

A Cardiff head explained a similar point of tension:

> The big problem has been intake, the quality of intake. Our ability profile is slipping to the left quite rapidly. There is a constant drift up from

schools like us to the better schools because of parental perception. That's the way this government at the moment has given us the hurdles to jump. The way they published our achievement is totally scientific but statistically inaccurate. Schools are compared, even though the intakes are totally different. They compare year-on-year but the intake is different year-on-year.

The challenges presented by choice and competition policies and recruitment is further emphasised by another Bristol headteacher:

The big problem for Bristol is the large number of children going outside the city because of parental choice. In this locality, many parents do not make a positive choice, they send their children to the nearest school, ourselves. A quarter send their children to other comprehensive(s) [schools] nearby. Sometimes, they go outside the city. Many parents want their children to go off the estate and away from the influence of the key individuals amongst their peer group.

Our fourth school in Cardiff was, by contrast, a 'winner' in the competitive market but for demographic reasons, and not because it had recruited a disproportionate number of high achievers. Its location, next to a rapidly growing peri-urban development, which did not as yet have its own secondary school, caused this school to be over-subscribed.

Schools' responses to assessment policy relate directly to their location in an educational market, within which test scores feature as a mark of quality. Headteachers are required to engage in 'educational' leadership *and* to maximise the survival chances of the school in an arena of 'manufactured uncertainty'. Against this background, it is not surprising that some aspects of the schools' operations were devolved within schools, notably responsibility for curriculum and assessment. Certainly, all the subject heads in our study acknowledged their lead role in the area of curriculum and assessment matters and we asked heads of maths departments who was responsible for teaching and learning activities in their schools. A typical response was as follows:

Ultimately, me. I took over the department in September. I haven't changed the curriculum from last year, though hopefully I have improved it slightly. Ceri is doing a lot of work at KS3. I check the syllabus coverage there to cover the National Curriculum. I pass around schemes of work to the rest of the staff for comments. I take these into account.

How the teaching and learning processes relate to a whole school response to the challenges posed by national testing is somewhat complex because this involved resource and student grouping issues which are negotiated between the head, the senior management team and the subject departments. A vignette of how one Cardiff school managed these tensions best illustrates this.

'Ty Glas' is a middle range school, where GCSE (age 16+ tests) scores broadly match the national average. Whole school policies arrange the nine forms of entry into mixed ability groups in the Year 7. In Years 8 and 9, the student population is divided into two blocks, and subjects are also block timetabled in such a way that all subject teachers teach together. This also enables subject departments to determine student grouping policy. In this school, the mathematics' department allocated students to groups or 'sets' based on ability in Years 8 and 9. Many other subjects did not. It is also the school policy to have the more able children in larger classes, sometimes nearly double the size of classes with the least able students.

Ability grouping is a matter for each department. The development of the schemes of work designed to cover National Curriculum requirements, and detailed assessment arrangements, are also their responsibility. In this school, and in others in our study, a half-hour unseen test is given at the end of each unit of work. This is aggregated, along with the profile of work related to what is known as AT1 – Using and Applying Maths, independent investigations conducted by students – to form the Teacher Assessment element of KS3 assessment.

KS3 also had an impact via the 'tiering' of papers, regarded by all our respondents as a nuisance. In this maths department, the top two sets are not entered for the top tier paper. Failure in this paper has punitive consequences for the students and indirectly for the school. Four or five students, carefully selected, may, from time to time, be permitted to sit the paper in order to achieve the highest grade, level eight. Again these decisions are made primarily at departmental level. At Ty Glas, the maths department also plays the key role in the selection of testing and teaching materials

In the comparable American school in Maryland, teachers were more directly involved in aligning curriculum with the state tests and state standards. Teachers participated on the School Improvement Teams, whose membership included administrators, one parent and one school board member per team. Teachers worked with their departmental colleagues to recommend specific instructional changes for the following year to address weaknesses in student skills. Their recommendations were incorporated into the SIT reports. District administrators review progress made in subsequent years in the areas targeted for improvement.

In the absence of strong district control over curriculum in the Maine districts, subject departments offered teachers opportunities to explore new instructional approaches or organise curricula differently. In departments instituting such innovations, teachers worked in collaboration with their peers and shared similar pedagogical goals. In Farm Town, for example, a team of three 7th-grade teachers had successfully reorganised the subject-specific instruction into thematic units, which allowed students to investigate topics of interest to them, from an interdisciplinary perspective. Students still rotated between all three teachers during the day but teachers co-ordinated instruction so that students could engage in longer-term projects that incorporated skills and topics from more than one discipline. The team had received crucial support from their principal and superintendent to experiment with new forms of instruction and curriculum organisation in their school. The principal had also served as a buffer for parent concern over the instructional changes. He commented that one of his goals was 'allowing teachers to explore and take risks without fear of reprisal. Not to be afraid to make mistakes, but to try new things'.

As the 'Ty Glas' vignette and the Maryland data reveal, curriculum and assessment policy, pupil grouping policies, strategies to address new challenges in subject knowledge and pedagogy, generated by external agencies have differential impacts on a variety of elements or domains within the school. The American study suggests that where external monitoring was relaxed, teachers and departments had opportunities to innovate. The department has become a significant organisational and mediating influence on the relation between individual teachers' interpretations of, and responses to, external assessment programmes. Other studies have demonstrated the ways in which departmental cultures are important regulators of pedagogic change and innovation, notably, for example, in their acceptance, say, of the relevance and utility of information technology (Sisken 1997; Selwyn 1999)

Certainly, the American study demonstrated the extent to which teacher beliefs about effective maths, for example, also involved and were regulated by their beliefs that student capacity to do maths was largely the outcome of inmate ability. Thus, where the testing programmes in Maine and Maryland offered opportunities to do something new, nevertheless, across the whole sample, there was a reluctance to move away from drill-based instructions and tracking. The maths departments in our British study appeared to operate in much the same fashion.

Conclusion

At the beginning of this paper we argued that centrally generated policies distribute power and control across local agencies and actors. We also argued that central policy-makers set frameworks that locally-based institutions and agents selectively interpret and recontextualise. In this sense, we argue that educational leadership is spread across a variety of levels that compose systems of education. How then does this connect with and inform our comparative study?

In England and Wales, assessment policy has been driven primarily by a national political agenda concerned with standards and accountability. The relationship between the centre and the schools has been direct and overtly regulative. The post-1988 central arena features powerful, ministerially-appointed agencies responsible for the creation and monitoring of curriculum content and national testing. Leadership in this context includes no clear role for LEAs, who were seen as barriers to change. That was also the case with teachers' subject associations. In consequence, the responsibility for the interpretation and implementation of national policies had fallen primarily on the schools, according to our research.

The American scene is much more diffuse. In effect, there are fifty 'centres' in the federal system compared to a dominant national centre in the UK. We noted, though, that at the national level, subject associations have been given considerable latitude and support to devise curriculum content and pedagogical strategies in a de facto nationally applicable standards-driven reform strategy. In effect, then, professional educators have retained a top table place in the formulation of subject content and 'standards'.

Our comparison between Maine and Maryland, however, demonstrates the difficulties that federally supported reforms might face. These cases illustrate the considerable variation between states in their relationship to school districts and schools. Maryland is an example of a state strongly committed to an external agenda of standards-based reforms. In addition, it has the policy lever of 'reconstitution' with which to apply downward pressure on schools districts and schools to align school practice with state-determined preferences. One result has been the narrowing of curriculum and pedagogical options open to teachers of maths. In this sense, Maryland comes closest to the British model and in this context leadership involves a considerable degree of external pressure on local institutions.

Maine has a state-testing programme but does not have the corresponding policy instruments to convince its schools or school districts of the seriousness of the stakes. On the other hand, the relative independence of action enjoyed by Maine teachers has led to the development of collaborative, teacher-based strategies to improve the teaching of maths. There was more scope here for teachers to act as reflective and extended professionals.

Regulation in Britain, though, is not entirely administrative in character. For sure, KS3 and other national tests provide the centre with further means for it to identify and bring to bear pressure on schools deemed to be 'underachieving'. But part of central policy was the creation of markets in education, and schools are concerned about KS3 and other performance indicators in order to sustain or improve their market location. In this sense, the market is also a very powerful regulatory device. In the US study, the fear of market censure does not prevail to the same extent.

At the level of the local authority (that is school district, and the LEAs) there is an interesting contrast between the US and Britain. In Maryland, school district administrators emphasised to school principals the importance of taking state-testing programmes seriously. In Maine, in the absence of sanctions, relations were more muted. Unlike their US counterparts, in Cardiff and Bristol, where financial resources have been largely devolved to schools, LEAs could exert very little pressure on schools. They could offer advice but only when it was requested by the schools. Indeed, LEAs were only one, and not necessarily the main, source of advice from which schools drew upon to support their KS3 teaching and assessment strategies.

There are indications though that this situation is set to change. First, LEAs have now been given a strategic role in raising standards in schools. By April 1999, each LEA must develop an Education Development Plan (EDP). In the EDP, each LEA will set out targets agreed with schools and will identify its strategies for assisting schools in meeting the targets (DfEE 1999). Second, the introduction to the National Literacy Strategy in England (it is still in the pilot stage in Wales) and the planned introduction of a counterpart Numeracy Strategy, has been accompanied by increased LEA activity in supporting schools in meeting national requirements. Whether this signals an increasing trend for LEAs to move more uniformly from curriculum advisors to curriculum leaders remains to be seen. Although in these respects LEAs have been given a clearer leadership role in curriculum issues, the concurrent introduction of Education Action Zones, in which groups of schools are placed under the control of public/private partnerships, simultaneously threatens to diminish the capacity of some LEAs to influence the operation of schools in their administrative boundaries.

At the school level in the UK, heads and senior management teams have adopted, and emphasise, a strategic role. The emergence of new kinds of leadership, exercised by headteachers of self-managing schools located in local educational markets, has also been identified by Grace (1995) and by Whitty *et al.* (1998). The subject department has increasing become the locus of curriculum leadership and, to a considerable degree, curriculum and assessment matters have also been devolved to the subject departments. In our UK study, teachers have ubiquitously responded to national assessments by sorting their students by academic ability into class sets.

In the US study, the influence of teachers' prior understanding about maths and effective maths teaching, seem to be crucial factors which frustrate opportunities to change classroom practice. How different maths departments are from other subject departments is clearly an area for further investigation. However, our impression was that in our Bristol and Cardiff schools, other subject departments were less inclined to set their students so early in their secondary school career.

Our approach to leadership has emphasised the importance of the various domains within education systems and their relative capacities to enable or frustrate change. We have suggested, however, that these capacities are by no means unconstrained, rather there is top-down determination of who is empowered to do what. We also concluded that those central authorities with well-developed powers to take over or assume control of local institutions (Maryland and England–Wales), also demonstrate tighter alignment between central purposes and local practices.

Note

1   The research reported here was supported by a grant from the Spencer Foundation. The Foundation is not responsible for any of the opinions expressed.

References

Ball, S.J. (1990) *Politics and Policy-making in Education,* London: Routledge.

—— (1994) *Education Reform: A Critical and Post-structural Approach,* Buckingham, Open University Press.

Bernstein, B. (1996) *Pedagogy, Symbolic Control and Identity: Theory, Research and Critique,* London: Taylor and Francis.

Black, P. (1994) 'Performance, assessment and accountability: the experience in England', *Educational Evaluation and Policy Analysis* 16(2): 191–203.

Boyd, W. L. (1995) 'The loyal opposition and the future of British and American school reform', paper presented to the European Conference on Educational Research, University of Bath, September.

—— (1996) 'The times they are a-changing', *Times Educational Supplement,* 13 September.

Brown, M. and Rutherford, D. (1998) 'Changing roles and raising standards: new challenges for heads of department', *School Leadership and Management* 18(1): 75–88.

Chitty, C. (1989) *Towards a New Education System,* London: Falmer Press.

Daugherty, R. (1995) *National Curriculum Assessment: A Review of Policy 1987–94,* London: Falmer Press.

Dearing, R. (1993) *The National Curriculum and its Assessment: Final Report,* London: School Curriculum and Assessment Authority.

DfEE (1997) *Excellence in Schools,* London, Department for Education and Employment.

—— (1999) Department for Education and Employment, 'The Standards Site' @ http//: www.standards.dfee.gov.uk/library/publications/development.

Firestone, W.A. (1989) 'Educational policy as an ecology of games', *Educational Researcher* 18(7): 18–24.

—— (1997) 'Standards reform run amok: what the British experience can teach us', *Education Week,* 8 October, pp. 30–2.

Fitz, J., Fairman, J. and Davies, B. (1998) 'Implementation: how different levels of the education systems interpret testing policy', unpublished paper presented to the Annual Meeting of the American Educational Research Association, San Diego.

Fitz, J., Halpin, D. and Power, S. (1997) 'Between a rock and a hard place: diversity, institutional autonomy and grant maintained schools', *Oxford Review of Education* 23(1): 17–30.

Fuhrman, S., Clune, W. and Elmore, R.F. (1988) 'Research on educational reform: lessons on the implementation of policy', *Teachers College Record* 90(2), 237–57.

Grace, G. (1995) *School Leadership. Beyond Management: An Essay in Policy Scholarship,* London: Falmer Press.

Gipps, C., Brown, M., McCallum, B. and McAlister, S. (1995) *Intuition or Evidence:*

Teachers and the National Assessment of Seven Year Olds, Buckingham: Open University Press.

Jennings, J.F. (1998) *Why National Standards and Tests? Politics and the Quest for Better Schools*, Thousand Oaks, California: Sage

John, P. (1998) *Analysing Public Policy*, London & New York: Pinter.

Levacic, R. (1995) *Local Management of Schools: Analysis and Practice*, Buckingham: Open University Press

Maclure, S. (1988) *Education Re-formed*, London: Hodder and Stoughton.

Maclure, S. (1998) 'Through the revolution and out the other side', *Oxford Review of Education* 24(1): 5–24

Maw, J. (1993) 'The National Curriculum Council and the whole curriculum; the construction of a discourse *Curriculum Studies* 1(1): 55–74.

National Council of Teachers of Mathematics (1989) *Curriculum and Evaluation Standards for School Mathematics*, Reston, VA.

Pollard, A., Broadfoot, P., Croll, P., Osbourne, M. and Abbott, D.(1994) *Changing English Primary Schools? The Impact of English Reforms on Key Stage 1*, London: Cassell.

Rhodes, R.A.W, (1997) *Understanding Governance*, Buckingham: Open University Press.

Selwyn, N. (1999) 'Students' use of educational computing: the influence of subject sub-cultures' *Curriculum Journal* 10,1 (Forthcoming).

Siskin, L. (1997) 'The challenge of leadership in comprehensive high schools: school vision and departmental division', *Educational Administration Quarterly* 33 (supplement), Dec., pp. 604–23.

Steinmo, S., Thelen, S. and Longstreth, F (eds) (1993) *Structuring Politics*, Cambridge: Cambridge University Press.

Spillane, J. (1998) 'A cognitive perspective on the role of local educational agencies in implementing instructional policy; accounting for local variability', *Educational Administration Quarterly* 34(1), February, pp. 31–57.

Stearns, K. (1996) *School Reform: Lessons from England*, Princeton NJ: Carnegie Foundation.

Taylor, T. (1995) 'Movers and shakers: the high politics of the National Curriculum', *The Curriculum Journal* 6(2): 161–84.

Turner, D.K. (1996) 'The roles and tasks of the subject head of department in English and Welsh secondary schools: a neglected area of research?' *School Organization* 16(2): 203–17

Whitty, G., Power S. and Halpin, D. (1998) *Devolution and Choice in Education: The School, the State and the Market*, Buckingham: Open University Press.

Woods, P., Bagley, C. and Glatter, R. (1998) *School Choice: Markets in the Public Interest?*, London: Routledge.

Part 3

The leadership stage

New actors, new roles

Part 3

The leadership stage

New actors, new roles

9   Bringing teacher organisations back into the frame

John Bangs

In 1997 a new Labour government was elected in the UK, wresting control after some eighteen years from a succession of Conservative administrations, led most notably by Margaret Thatcher. Amongst many challenges, the new Labour administration has had to seek a new accord with trade unions and with teachers. The 1998 Labour Party Conference highlighted the uncertainty of the relationship between the teaching profession and the government. In his Conference speech, the Prime Minister, Tony Blair, proclaimed to the Conference 'There are too few good State Schools'. Yet, two days later, his Secretary of State, David Blunkett, felt able to assert 'Teachers are doing a first rate job'. The need of teachers, through their own organisations, to have a clear voice, and one which cuts through the spin of government, is well illustrated by this bewildering exchange.

What now is the role and function of the organisations that speak for teachers? In many countries in the world, particularly in Europe and in the United States, teacher organisations are asking the same questions. In America, the National Education Association and the American Federation of Teachers at local level have to negotiate new contracts regularly with employers, including Districts and Charter School companies. Nationally, both organisations provide professional help and pedagogical advice to their local affiliates. In Europe, teacher organisation negotiations are much more national government focused but the questions are the same. Are teacher organisations able to provide policies and ideas which balance the development of government-initiated education policies? Can teacher organisations act as an agent for the improvement of education services? Are teacher organisations marginal or at the centre of the education policy process? This chapter seeks to address those questions.

A brief mention of the past

I will not attempt a potted history of teacher organisations since 1970; others can attempt that. It is sufficient to mark that during the 1980s, teachers and their organisations were deprived by the then Conservative government of the right to negotiate on national pay and conditions; a national curriculum and its assessment was imposed on schools; the employment powers and flexibility of local education authorities (LEAs) to deploy teachers were removed; and the Schools' Council (a national quasi-independent body which had given a somewhat progressive lead on the curriculum) was closed down. These are just four examples of reforms which swept away the dispensation which had existed since the 1944 Education Act.

The shift in relationship between government and teachers is neatly summarised by Lawn:

> The teacher was responsible for the curriculum and the pedagogy in the school through a partnership in the local and central state via the teacher unions. Yet it is this discourse which was interrupted by the Conservative reforms of education in the late 1980s, so severely, it was the Union and the teacher who were deliberately excluded from the reforms. They were excluded from the deliberations about the reforms, the pace of their introduction and discussion about their operation and review. The success of the reforms was to be judged by other criteria than whether teachers took an enhanced responsibility for their success.
>
> (Lawn 1996)

It is tempting to believe that the rearguard actions of the teachers' organisations in the late 1980s to retain influence with government, particularly on pay, were complemented by a weakened ability by the National Union of Teachers to defend the individual interests of its members. In reality, the opposite was true. The NUT moved decisively to accommodate the changes in organisational circumstance brought about by local management of schools. With schools becoming responsible for their own budgets and for most of the employment functions previously held by LEAs, the NUT further developed its network of regional offices to negotiate not only with local education authorities but directly with the managements and governing bodies of schools.

Disagreement with the nature of reform did not prevent teacher organisations from accommodating to new circumstances. Indeed, the ability to accommodate pragmatically to changed circumstances is an essential criteria of effectiveness in any organisation. As Lawn has noted:

> Teacher unions in England have always changed following the reorganisation of the work (schooling), the new demands of members and the political and social context in which they operate. But what changes are to be observed in the 1990s? The first sign is an internal reorganisation to meet the demands of these conditions.
>
> (Lawn ibid.)

The issue for the 1980s was not whether the NUT, or any other teacher organisation for that matter, could accommodate government-determined change but whether teacher organisations could reassert their influence on government policy.

Despite the near severance between the government and the teachers' organisations during the 1980s, there are examples which show that even when governments are at their most intransigent, teachers' organisations such as the NUT can retain a level of influence in education policies and practice. Thus, the NUT was able to influence significantly, for example, the professional development model of appraisal (through the National Steering Group) and the development of the national qualification for 16-year-olds – the General Certificate for Education (GCSE). The balance of coursework assessment in the GCSE was also the product of NUT intervention. Similarly, the NUT had enormous influence in fighting racism by campaigning against the use of school premises by racist organisations.

Why even try?

Why was it important then, and why is it important now, for teachers' organisations to influence government education policy? For one thing, there is clear evidence that policies which have not been modified by argument and discussion with teachers and their organisations carry a far greater likelihood of having fundamental faults which need correcting later on.

There are two outstanding examples of government policies which fall into this description. By the year 2000, the National Curriculum in England and in Wales will have been subject to fundamental review no less than three times. A study, commissioned by the NUT from Coopers and Lybrand in 1991, forewarned the government of the consequences of it not costing the introduction of the National Curriculum. Neither the start-up nor the opportunity costs of its introduction were taken into account by government. The consequent additional workload on teachers was a well-recognised fact by 1993. The study was the first to recognise the effects on the curriculum of this uncosted introduction, a full two years before the events of 1993.

The National Curriculum's assessment and testing arrangements imposed on teachers culminated in an overwhelming boycott of the tests by the NUT, the National Association of Schoolmasters/Union of Women Teachers (NASUWT) and the Association of Teachers and Lecturers (ATL) in 1993. Less well recognised was the fact that the then government had received plenty of notice that a boycott was imminent through NUT evidence, through indicative surveys of teachers and, in particular, from teachers of English at Key Stage 3. This is well documented by Michael Barber in *The Learning Game* (Barber 1997) who was the NUT's Assistant Secretary of Education at the time and is currently a leading government adviser on Education. In addition, a 1991 Coopers and Lybrand report identified other effects of the imposition of an uncosted curriculum; effects which government has only just begun to recognise.

There is no doubt that the National Curriculum and present levels of resourcing have changed the balance of the primary curriculum away from reading, writing and number towards the other National Curriculum subjects . . .

(Coopers and Lybrand 1991)

There is also a further answer to the question, 'Why even try?' All governments appear either to resist auditing teacher perceptions of the effects of their policies on schools or to be very poor at gathering them. The present UK government has expressed, sporadically, concern about the low level of teacher morale but has, so far, failed to identify its causes.

Yet there is evidence that imposed changes which are not perceived as being supportive to teaching and learning, alienate and demotivate teachers, particularly those who are the most experienced. Prior to the 1997 General Election, the NUT commissioned a poll of teachers by ICM Research (NUT 1997). Findings from the poll indicated that teachers would vote overwhelmingly for the Labour Party, but also highlighted the causes of the pressures and stress which they faced. Constant changes, administration, disruptive pupils, government/political interference, lack of support and bureaucracy came top of the list; all issues which have been 'hot potatoes' for the Department for Education and Employment (DfEE) in the first two years of the Labour government.

It is worth comparing the findings of two studies commissioned by the NUT to detect the professional anxieties of primary teachers about the effects of the overloaded primary curriculum. The gap between the two studies is six years.

1991
There were now too many subject requirements to be met to allow pupils to influence the paths of educational enquiry to the extent they once did. Within lessons, the amount of time for pastoral care (social time) and time spent talking to children, had all decreased.

(Coopers and Lybrand 1991)

1997
Teachers complain there are now fewer opportunities to develop their relationships with pupils by pursuing a child's immediate interest, such as a precious object brought to school one morning or setting aside time for a child to tell a story about some event which has taken place at home.

(Galton and Fogelman 1997)

Both quotes illustrate the need for the Government to listen to teachers. The need for teachers to engage with children in a two-way dialogue in order to establish working relationships is rarely, if ever, recognised by

Government, OFSTED and government agencies. Learning, to most policy-makers, flows from instructional teaching; the importance of the chemistry of the teacher/pupil relationship does not often feature in government policy initiatives. That it does not is probably a key reason why teacher morale is still low and why governments should listen to teachers and their organisations.

We all have our audiences

'We all have our audiences' is a familiar refrain for anyone involved in politics. It was a phrase used by education ministers during the last Conservative government and an example of the current Government's 'spin' for different audiences, illustrated earlier in this chapter. In the context of the discussion about the role of trade unions in contributing to the education agenda, there is a further meaning to that phrase. To teachers' organisations its meaning is rooted in an awareness that membership is voluntary and freely entered into by teachers and is, therefore, just as freely withdrawn.

Teachers' organisations appear to exasperate commentators rather than draw from them clear analyses. For example, Barber (1997) attributes the 'weakness of the profession' to the malign influence of teacher organisations. Such criticism ignores the nature and purpose of teacher organisations. Again, to quote Lawn:

> A reform is not neutral and the Union must respond to it, not just on its own merits but on its effect on the cohesion and growth of the Union. This may appear opportunistic to the outsider but it is based on the same organisational imperatives as other kinds of work.
>
> (Lawn 1996)

In other words, the ability of teachers' organisations to grow depends on their ability to respond to their members' needs and views.

Most teachers join teachers' organisations for purely practical and pragmatic reasons. Providing protection against professional or contractual disasters is the main reason. There have been companies which have offered such protection in the same way as insurance companies but they have not thrived. Why? The main reason is that teacher organisations add value to the financial commitment made by teachers to membership. Financial and professional services are part of that added value, but only a part. At the centre of that added value is the reason why most teachers become teachers in the first place.

Perhaps it is a truism to say that people want to become teachers because of their perceptions that teaching is a force for change in children's lives. If that sounds a cliché, it is worth examining the findings of a recent NUT/Teacher Training Agency (TTA) survey on the attitudes of 16–19-year-olds to teaching as a career (NUT/TTA 1998). Although long holidays were a top attraction to teaching (beware those who argue for the removal of the long summer holiday!), 'liking children' and 'job satisfaction' also received top ratings. And, significantly, when asked to agree or disagree with a set of statements describing teaching as a career, school students gave the highest percentage of positive responses to the statement 'teaching changes children's lives', a statement closely followed in order of priority by 'teaching is a stressful job'. *A stressful job which changes children's lives* could not be a better description of teaching!

It is impossible for those involved in such work not to have opinions about the nature and direction of their work, even if those opinions are confined to the staff-room or to friends. Most teachers give little thought on a day in, day out basis to their membership of teacher organisations. Yet on occasions, they look to teacher organisations to express their thoughts and views. There is also an expectation from teachers that those views are expressed in the media and in the press. Indeed, the public expression by teacher organisations of their members' views is a regular confirmation that they have joined the right union; that the right union will protect them effectively and represent their opinions. If a teacher organisation fails to achieve that synergy with its members, then doubt is sown in members' minds about membership. When teachers find that their membership challenges instead of supports their professional lives, they consider resigning.

It is vital, therefore, for the NUT, as it is for other unions, to remain in touch with the opinions of its members. Those who criticise teacher organisations for being out-of-touch with their members could not be further from the truth in their criticisms.

Action, policies and influence

Remaining in touch with member opinion is one thing but can teacher organisations be effective in changing policies? For the purposes of this chapter, I do not want to explore the industrial action mechanisms available to unions or the conditions for their use. Other writers have examined teacher organisations and industrial relations. Explored in this chapter are examples of union activity which demonstrate that teachers' organisations continue to have a role in government policy-making.

Campaigning against excessive workload faced by teachers has been a feature of NUT activity in the last ten years. The boycott of the National Curriculum tests in 1993–4 is an example of such activity and is referred to earlier in this chapter. A further example concerns the effect of excessive bureaucracy and administration on teachers.

During the autumn of 1997, Government representatives, teacher organisations and representatives of LEAs met in a working group in order to produce recommendations on reducing the bureaucratic burdens on teachers. The report was informed by a study commissioned by the Government from

Coopers and Lybrand (Coopers and Lybrand 1997) on reducing bureaucratic burdens. In addition to listing specific bureaucratic burdens, Coopers and Lybrand came to the same conclusion that it had come to when costing the National Curriculum for the NUT six years previously. Governments, they observed, do not cost the start-up costs, the opportunity costs, nor the implementation costs of their education initiatives. They concluded naturally that it was vital for governments of whatever political complexion to estimate such costs. All members of the Working Party agreed to this recommendation being inserted in the final Working Party report.

The NUT and the NASUWT subsequently balloted their members on applying union guidelines, putting into practice the recommendations of the report. Immediately after the ballots, the Working Group wrote and agreed a government circular (DfEE 2/98), focusing on each school's responsibilities to reduce bureaucratic workloads. A circular in similar terms was published by the Welsh Office.

As a result of an initiative by the NUT, a joint letter from the Secretary of State and the Chair of Education of the Local Government Association was sent to all LEAs, outlining the action LEAs should take to reduce bureaucratic burdens. For example, as a result of the Working Group's decision, LEAs were limited to seeking with schools only those targets for improved pupil performance which are statutorily required. This position subsequently appeared in the Government's Education Development Planning guidance to LEAs (DfEE 1998). In addition, the National Employers' Organisation for School Teachers sent out advice to its members on implementing the government's circular, which was framed in the spirit of the joint work of the Working Group and couched in the following terms:

> it may be helpful to remind school management that the long-term relationships in schools would be assisted by avoiding hasty or unthought-out responses to particular reactions by teachers acting collectively.
>
> (LGMB 1998)

While no one could claim that the processes involved in achieving the circulars and advice have been anything but smooth, the whole episode led to new possibilities and potential emerging for teachers' organisations. Government policy was changed. Polices were developed jointly by government and the teacher organisations. LEAs, government and the teacher organisations agreed on action to be taken by the local education authorities. The representatives of the employers agreed to follow the initiative. All this was achieved with teacher organisations applying industrial action to implement the initiatives of government circulars. The 'bureaucracy' episode was an example of government intervention to tackle the problem identified by teachers through their organisations. It may do so again.

Excessive workload is only one area where the NUT has influenced government policy development. In the area of educational policy, the NUT has gained a significant number of successes. Probably the best example of such a success is the impact of the NUT's commissioned work on school self-evaluation. Professor John MacBeath's study *Schools Speak for Themselves* (MacBeath *et al.* 1996), recast and re-invigorated school self-evaluation, and not just for development planning purposes. The report's conclusion that 'self-evaluation should be central in any national approach to school improvement' and that 'school inspections should continue to be a feature of the drive towards school improvement but as part of a collaborative strategy with schools and local authorities' was extremely radical at the time. It says something for the Zeitgeist of the last years of the Conservative government that teachers asking questions about the functioning of their schools should have been considered so radical.

The NUT's purpose in commissioning the report was to apply the lessons of the Scottish Office Education Department and Scottish HMI model of evaluation to England and Wales in order to find out whether the balance between internal and external evaluation of schools could be reinstated. Such a model of school evaluation has self-evaluation at its core. The study restored to teachers the confidence that their own judgements and insights on the strengths and weaknesses of their schools are as valid as those of external evaluators such as OFSTED.

Few could have predicted the impact of *Schools Speak for Themselves*. For teachers who, between 1992 and 1996, had had their successes and failures determined exclusively by external evaluations and outcomes such as OFSTED inspections and National Curriculum test result rankings, the message that the mechanisms for evaluation were in their own hands was liberating. This message was liberating not only for schools. LEAs, anxious not to leave to OFSTED judgements about their own schools, understood the message: school improvement depends on school communities respecting and understanding the mechanisms by which they are evaluated.

Self-evaluation is important in the restoration of teachers' respect for assessment of school performance. It also has enormous potential for the systematic gathering of information about life and learning in the school. It has opened up possibilities for teachers finding out about pupils' attitudes to learning and to each other.

This sense of discovery about how the various parts of schools operate and the nature of their expectations and attitudes said, and still says, something much wider about the current paradigm of education in schools than self-evaluation itself. It is extraordinary that the idea of school communities being encouraged to evaluate themselves should have seemed so radical. The impact of *Schools Speak for Themselves* says as much about the low morale of teachers as it does about the high quality of the study itself.

As an educational document, *Schools Speak for Themselves* represents an enormously powerful partnership between a respected academic noted for his school improvement work in another educational system (Scotland) and a teachers' organisation which recognised that the top-down' model of school improvement gave it an opportunity to redress the balance. The study and its impact fairly and squarely demonstrated that the NUT, as a teachers' organisation, could influence policy and practice at all levels: in schools, at LEA level and at government level. *Schools Speak for Themselves* has influenced government policy. It is now part of the DfEE's Standards and Effectiveness Unit's school improvement database and is a school improvement priority in the DfEE's Education Development Plan guidance for England.

Internationally, the report has been tremendously influential. The NUT has promoted the findings and approach of the report for other teachers' organisations in Europe. The European Commission's 101 schools' pilot project on self-evaluation (MacBeath, Schratz and Meuret 1998) grew directly from *Schools Speak For Themselves,* a project with which ETUCE has become integrally involved.

If *Schools Speak for Themselves* represents an example of the NUT as a teachers' organisation influencing national policy-making, there are other examples. *Class Size and Pupil Achievement* (Galton *et al.* 1996), a study for the NUT, provided evidence that small class sizes in themselves are a critical factor in improving pupil achievement. The report provided a boost to the Labour Party's intention, prior to the General Election, to include reduction of class size as one of its 'credit card' election promises.

From the NUT's own experience, at least, the combination of its own collective knowledge of education can help it pinpoint issues which are at the leading edge of research and policy development. This is one of the reasons why the NUT campaigned alongside other teachers' organisations for the establishment of a General Teaching Council (GTC), a national professional body to oversee teaching. Some have argued that the GTC presents dangers and threats to the continuing existence of teacher organisations. In fact, the proposed English GTC, with its new responsibilities for advising the government and the Teacher Training Agency on the education and supply of teachers, also place new and important responsibilities on the shoulders of teacher organisations.

The GTC's advice to government and the TTA on professional development of teachers and initial teacher education will have its genesis from an organisation which will include representatives of teachers' organisations. The GTC's effectiveness will depend on how much commitment is invested in their existence by teachers and their organisations. Unlike the GTC in England, the Welsh GTC's credibility is in jeopardy. There is no automatic right for teachers' organisations, currently, at the time of writing, to be represented on the GTC in Wales, nor to a majority of independently elected teacher representatives.

There are other areas in which teacher organisations can and should be effective in promoting new policies. Local education authorities are on government probation. If they fail to play their part in delivering the targets set by government for literacy and numeracy, then the Labour Government, in its second term, will conduct a fundamental review of their future role. In *LEAs and Schools : A Social Partnership* (Bangs 1998), I argued that:

> The fate of the local education authority depends less on its capacity to meet government targets and more on whether it is perceived by teachers, parents and governors as essential to the provision of free, high quality education, accessible and accountable to the community it serves . . . it is for LEAs to make themselves relevant to schools and to classroom teachers as much as to headteachers and to school governing bodies, if they are to survive.

Prior to the publication of this pamphlet, the NUT had argued for LEAs to develop a social partnership model with schools. The NUT's pamphlet *Social Partnership in Education – A Challenge for the Government and for Local Authorities* highlighted the European Union's Maastricht Treaty requirement on member countries to promote:

> 'A dialogue between management and labour' and 'Information for the consultation of workers'.

The pamphlet emphasised that:

> Social partnership . . . enables LEAs to use and draw from the greatest available pool of ideas and to meet problems before they become crises . . . for teachers and their organisations, social partnership means knowing that their experience and ideas are valued.

The fact is that LEAs need the active involvement of teachers and their organisations for their continuing existence. The role of teacher organisations at local level is to use their unique organisational and political strength to develop social partnership approaches on behalf of all teachers including classroom teachers.

And finally

This chapter has set out to demonstrate that government and local education authorities ignore teacher organisations at their peril. For teacher organisations, the twin approaches of policy-making and protection of members are symbiotic in their relationship to each other. An organisation such as the NUT can speak to a significant part of the profession. It has active lay officers whose job is to maintain a large membership base. Its offer to teachers, therefore, has to be powerful and credible. And since that appears to be the case, and there is no evidence currently of NUT or other teacher organisation membership declining, at the very least, a government which is interested in a motivated teaching force should ask itself about what drives that credibility. Indeed, one lesson from the history of the last ten years must be that some of the worst mistakes made by government occur when they ignore teacher organisations.

There are those that have argued that the industrial model of a trade union sits uneasily with a model which prioritises teachers' professional interests. Such a dichotomy is unrecognisable to those who know teacher organisations. Those who would wish to pigeonhole teacher organisations into one model or another ignore not teacher organisations but teachers themselves. For children and young people, whose future depends on an effective and motivated teaching profession, bringing teachers and their organisations into the frame is a vital necessity.

References

Bangs, J. (1998) *LEAs and Schools: A Social Partnership,* London: The Education Network.

Barber, M. (1997) *The Learning Game,* London: Gollancz.

Coopers and Lybrand (1991) *Costs of the National Curriculum in Primary Schools,* London: NUT.

—— (1997) *Reducing the Burdens on Teachers,* London: DfEE.

DfEE Circular 2/98 'Reducing the Bureaucratic Burdens on Teachers', London: DfEE.

—— (1998) *Education Development Plans 1999–2002,* London: DfEE.

—— (1998) 'David Blunkett and Graham Lane – reducing the bureaucratic burden on teachers', a joint letter from David Blunkett and Graham Lane, London: DfEE.

Galton, M., Hargreaves, L. and Bell, A. (1996) *Class Size and Pupil Achievement,* Leicester University.

Galton, M. and Fogelman, K. (1997) *The Use of Discretionary Time in the Primary School,* Leicester University/NUT.

Lawn, M. (1996) *Modern Times? Work Professionalism and Citizenship in Teaching,* London: Falmer Press.

LGMB (1998) 'National Employers' Organisation for School Teachers Education Employers' Bulletin No. 384', London: Local Government Management Board.

MacBeath, J., Boyd, B., Rand, J. and Bell, S. (1996) *Schools Speak for Themselves,* London: National Union of Teachers.

MacBeath, J., Schratz, M. and Meuret, D. (1998) *European Pilot Project on Quality Evaluation in School Education,* European Commission.

NUT (1997) *Teacher Attitudes Survey* (conducted by ICM Research), London: NUT.

—— (1998) *Social Partnership in Education,* London: NUT.

NUT/TTA (1996) *Perceptions of the Teaching Profession,* a joint survey by the Teacher Training Agency and the National Union of Teachers, London: NUT/TTA.

10 The role of unions as leaders for school change

An analysis of the 'KEYS' programme in two US states

Karen Seashore Louis, Patricia Seppanen,
Mark A. Smylie, and Lisa M. Jones

It sounds like a humble dream . . ., that the advocacy that we provide for members and our legal responsibilities will extend to the quality of teaching and learning environments the folks of Minnesota expect for every kid in the state, that we disallow the petty bickering and finger pointing that seems to run rampant, and that the communities will come together and say 'enough of this already'. We all know what we want. . . . How can we go about it?

(An MEA UniServ Director)

Teachers unions, in both the United States and Europe, are typically portrayed as defenders of the status quo, as perpetuating a 'management–worker' model that emphasizes salary and working conditions rather than professional performance and outcomes (Bascia 1997). Union agendas are seen to conflict with recent education reforms. For example, proponents of charter schools in the United States and grant-maintained schools in the United Kingdom argue that current union practices must be altered to develop more flexible staffing and work procedures in 'break the mould' schools. Some reformers go so far as to advocate that teachers become 'owners' of schools or 'partners' with management rather than 'employees'. Unions counter by promoting reforms of their own, which emphasise more professional accountability for increased teacher autonomy and control over their work environments.

Kerchner, Koppich and Weere (1997) argue that unions are not irrelevant to school reform, but must re-orient themselves around the moral and academic ends of schooling. In the United States, both the National Education Association (NEA) and American Federation of Teachers (AFT) have recently accepted greater responsibility to improve the quality of schooling and have proposed to enhance the professional development and accountability of their members. Each has begun to move in the direction of what has been called 'new unionism'.

This chapter examines a large-scale initiative of the NEA to enhance its role in school improvement. This initiative, called 'Keys to Excellence in Your School' or KEYS, reflects many of the principles of new unionism. KEYS is instructive for several reasons. It illustrates an inventive strategy not only for school improvement but also union reform. And importantly, study of its early implementation illuminates complexities and barriers unions face, some within their own organisations, in moving toward new unionism.

We begin with a brief overview of new unionism. We then turn to an analysis of the early implementation of KEYS in two states – Minnesota and Illinois. This analysis draws on data collected as part of an NEA-supported national case study project of KEYS implementation in nine states. We conclude with a summary of lessons learned about the prospects and problems of using strategies such as KEYS to promote new unionism in teacher unions.[1]

'New unionism' and teachers unions

New unionism represents a significant departure from traditional models of unionism (Rankin 1990; US Department of Labor 1996). Where traditional unionism focuses primarily on the protection and well-being of the membership as ends themselves, new unionism sees membership protection and well-being as instrumental of broader organisational goals. Where traditional models are grounded in adversarial relations and confrontational techniques, new unionism proceeds from assumptions that collaboration and cooperation between labour and management can be mutually beneficial.

In the late 1970s, we began to see changes in private sector union–management relations that reflected the principles of new unionism. Changes occurred in (a) the source of impetus for improvement; (b) employee job design; (c) the focus of union–management activity; (d) incentive systems; and (e) decision-making processes at the work site. These areas of change provide a framework to examine the more recent movement of the NEA, the AFT, and its affiliates toward new unionism.

Impetus for improvement

A key feature of new union–management relationships involves the source of the impetus for improvement. Complex environmental and technological pressures, operating within a financially volatile atmosphere, have forced management and labour in the private sector to reconsider their traditional roles and relationships. In manufacturing and in the automotive industry in particular, we have seen shifts from traditional, adversarial union–management relationships to more collaborative ones. The push for more collaborative relations has come from management, rather than the unions. Companies have found they need to work with unions to adapt to changing conditions and avoid actions that might put themselves and their growth at risk (Mahoney and Watson 1993).

Myron Lieberman (1997), a staunch union critic, argues that public schools lack the competitive threats that exist within the private sector. He contends that lacking these threats, the NEA and AFT have little incentive to develop more collaborative relationships with school district management. Public education faces a small but increasingly visible alternative market, however, ranging from charter schools to home schooling. And public officials and concerned constituencies are exerting more political pressure on teachers and their unions to change. For example, Pennsylvania Education Secretary Hickok's recent push for school quality included a recommendation that college students who want to teach must maintain a 3.0 undergraduate grade point average, and that the best math and science student should be certified to teach without traditional college of education coursework (*Education Daily* 1998). The Illinois legislature passed a Chicago school reform package in 1995 that included an 18–month moratorium on teacher strikes and removed from collective bargaining several professional workforce issues such as class size. In 1998, the Illinois legislature considered reforms that would have tied re-certification of practising teachers to professional development and performance-based assessments. Because no public school district in Illinois can employ a non-certified teacher, these reforms would have, in effect, overridden locally bargained teacher tenure provisions.

Job design

Traditionally, industrial unions have gained their power from the division and assignment of work (Kerchner, Koppich and Weeres 1997). In traditional union–management relationships, union negotiations focus typically on shift assignments, work hours, job classifications and compensation. In contrast, new unionism focuses on activities that enhance workforce capability while ensuring the economic vitality of a company. It promotes the development of more flexible work systems and new models of employee training rather than a mass-production structure dependent upon specific job rules (Rankin 1990).

Recent initiatives of the Chicago Teachers' Union (CTU), an AFT affiliate, and the Milwaukee Teachers' Education Association (MTEA), an NEA affiliate, illustrate the expanded role of teachers unions to improve educational quality. While the CTU continues to argue that pursuing 'bread and butter' issues gives teachers the 'security and freedom to become better educators' (Lowe and Fuller 1998: 46), it has become increasingly involved in teacher professional development. It has begun to play a more active role with system administrators in selecting new teachers for the Chicago Public Schools and has helped to implement programmes for beginning teacher mentoring and induction. Similarly, the MTEA has sponsored professional development programmes for teachers, such as annual lectures, speakers, and continuing education courses in specific content areas to improve instructional quality (Lowe and Fuller 1998).

Focus of union–management activities

In traditional union–management relationships, quality and productivity are usually contentious issues. The US Department of Labor (1996) has portrayed traditional union activity as saving one-job-at-a-time rather than improving service. Management tends to view traditional labour unions as impediments to quality and productivity and threats to company profitability. But according to Rubenstein and his colleagues (1993), the new unionism alters this focus, fostering joint commitment by unions and management to improve quality and productivity. Rankin (1990) argues that workplaces founded on shared responsibility and teamwork adapt more readily to changing environmental conditions than do their more conventional counterparts.

NEA President Bob Chase recently called for local affiliates across the country to unite with school districts to improve low-achieving schools (Chase 1997). These schools, labelled 'F' schools by the NEA, are characterised by overcrowded classrooms, lack of educational materials, inadequate or deteriorating facilities, and high student absenteeism. At the time, Chase offered no concrete plan but he emphasised the importance of improving the quality and effectiveness of teachers (Gergen 1997). In some contrast to assumptions of the new unionism that workforce quality is now high, Chase's comments suggest a more reflective posture in the union that quality of the teacher workforce could be enhanced.

Incentive Systems

According to critics, the concept of teaching as 'labour' pervades the view of compensation and incentives under traditional unionism (Bascia 1997). The new unionism recognises that financial incentives have limited effectiveness in professional work. A more educated and skilled workforce seeks more meaningful work, individual responsibility and shared authority (Lawler 1990). According to Mahoney and Watson (1993), new unionism replaces traditional job-based policies with more knowledge-based and performance-based reward systems.

Local teacher unions vary in the extent to which they reflect this shift. Some locals have refused to allow teachers in individual schools to work outside the union contract even when the school staff has unanimously agreed to do so. Other locals have supported waivers to their contracts. Still others have worked with school boards and central administrators to completely reform compensations systems to better support professional work. For example, the local teachers union in Robbinsdale, Minnesota, has worked with district administration to create a new teacher incentive system. Unlike traditional merit pay plans, the district contract now requires teachers to submit skill portfolios every five years, which may result in significant bonuses (Bradley 1998). Similarly, the Minneapolis Federation of Teachers negotiated a contract that calls for increased oversight of new teachers and mandatory demonstration of competence prior to receiving tenure. The CTU supports school-initiated contract waivers allowing teachers to work beyond their 33–hour negotiated work week on school improvement and professional development activities. Also in Illinois, the Glenview Education Association worked with district administration to develop a compensation system that linked salary and stipends to teachers' roles and responsibilities rather than to hours worked.

Decision-making processes at the work-site

Traditional unionism maintains authority within a hierarchical management structure responsible for long-term strategic planning and floor supervision (US Department of Labor 1996). New unionism requires co-operation between labour and management to improve performance and productivity. This can extend the union's role into traditional areas of management prerogative such as determining suppliers, quality control, problem identification, and product and programme development. Such redistribution of authority is thought to increase innovation and performance (Rankin 1990). As applied to education, the new unionism requires teacher unions to provide forums in which educational goals and improvement agendas can be debated (Bascia 1997). It also demands union collaboration with school boards and central administrators in developing curriculum, selecting textbooks and instructional materials, and evaluating teaching.

Shared decision-making between local teachers unions and school districts is growing across the United States (Cooper 1998; 'NEA's "New Unionism" Takes Hold' 1988). Increased numbers of local affiliates are beginning to accept responsibility for school quality and improvement. In Dayton, Ohio, for example, teachers and administrators share the responsibility for decisions about funding programmes to improve student achievement. In Milwaukee and Topeka, Kansas, teacher evaluation and supervision procedures involve both administrative and peer review. The recently negotiated teacher contract in Minneapolis includes roles for teachers in monitoring student progress on state tests, in reviewing teacher professional development plans, and in other innovative efforts that focus on educational quality. Among the most significant initiatives of the national teacher unions to move toward new unionism is NEA's KEYS project which illustrates and promotes the principles of new unionism. Its initial implementation reveals important lessons about how effective such initiatives can be in enacting these principles at this time.

The KEYS initiative

In 1995, NEA made a commitment to an unconventional initiative – developing and implementing a data-driven local school improvement process known as KEYS. KEYS followed and built upon NEA's longest-running national school improvement project, the Mastery in Learning (MIL) project (see McClure 1995). Begun in 1985, MIL was guided by the conviction that the most important and lasting improvements in learning opportunities for students come from those closest to them – parents, teachers, and other members of school communities. Accordingly, people at the school level should take charge of their own improvement efforts.

Components of KEYS

KEYS was developed around four components. The first component consists of thirty-five research-based indicators of school quality. These indicators represent organisational characteristics of 'high-achieving' schools in which students are reported to perform well on standardised tests. They are grouped into five categories: (a) shared understanding and commitment to high goals; (b) open communication and collaborative problem-solving; (c) continuous assessment for teaching and learning; (d) personal and professional learning of school staff; and (e) resources to support teaching and learning.

The second component consists of a diagnostic survey instrument for local schools to collect their own data on the KEYS indicators. The KEYS survey is intended for teachers, but administrators, other professional and support personnel, parents and community representatives, are encouraged to complete it. When a school completes its surveys, they are sent to NEA's national headquarters in Washington DC for analysis. The findings are returned to the school to serve as a basis of school improvement planning.

The third KEYS component is a collaborative process to engage state and local associations with schools in school improvement activities. KEYS was designed to operate within the current structures of state and local union affiliates. Its implementation relies on existing staff, primarily UniServ Directors who are state staff members assigned to work in local districts. It was NEA's intention to use KEYS to develop the capacity of state and local affiliates to collaborate with administrators and support local school improvement.

The KEYS process begins with an agreement by a state affiliate to participate in the programme.[2] The state affiliate subsequently selects a 'cadre' of staff members to assume responsibility for the initiative. The cadre is trained by NEA staff to introduce KEYS to local schools and to help other state affiliate staff members become a 'pivotal resource' for successful implementation (NEA 1996). School involvement is elicited in different ways, depending on the state, but requires written support from the local union affiliate and the superintendent. The NEA office mails surveys to the school and subsequently produces a school report. When the results are returned from NEA to the school, a school-based improvement team presents them and begins a discussion to identify problems and plan to address them. The role of the UniServ Director is to work with the improvement team and the school as a whole to facilitate these activities.

The last KEYS component is a system of training and technical support. The NEA supports state and local participation in KEYS by training state-level cadres. It produces print materials that state and local affiliates may use to work with schools (see NEA 1996). It has also assembled a national consulting team to assist state cadres as well as individual schools.

KEYS functions

KEYS has three general functions related to new unionism. The first function is *technical*. KEYS aims to stimulate research-based local school improvement. A second function is *political and organisational*. NEA expects KEYS to increase the role of state and local associations in school improvement and increase collaboration between association representatives and school and district administrators by focusing on a concrete school improvement activity. A third function of KEYS is *symbolic*. As an initiative to improve schools and promote more collaboration between the union and district and school administrators, KEYS may help reshape public perceptions of the NEA and its affiliates in the image of the new unionism.

In the rest of this chapter, we examine the prospects that KEYS may fulfil these three functions. Our analysis is preliminary. It is based on relevant theoretical and empirical literature and on initial findings from case studies of KEYS in Minnesota and Illinois. Our data sources include (a) state and local school district documents related to KEYS; (b) interviews of key informants associated with KEYS, including state and local association officials, UniServ Directors, state education agency officials, and district and school administrators; and (c) visits to two KEYS schools. The two state associations we refer to are the Minnesota Education Association (MEA) and the Illinois Education Association (IEA).

School improvement function of KEYS

The potential of KEYS to promote local school improvement is influenced by a number of factors. Many who have studied school improvement since the early 1970s have noted that planning, decision-making strategies, and leadership can affect significantly the implementation and outcomes of any innovation (Crandall, Eiseman and Louis 1986; Gross, Giacquinta and Bernstein 1971). Even for innovations not driven by rational management models, 'minding the store' and attending to details are important to any major change effort. While rational management may not ensure the success of an innovation, the absence of attention to basics can lead to a host of problems. Programme credibility, that is, its perceived validity, practicality and relationship to organisational needs; adequacy of resources; and consistency of effort are other factors that can affect significantly the implementation of innovations, large or small (see Fullan 1991).

The Rand Change Agent Study was one of the first studies to support the programme implementation adage, 'nothing ventured, nothing gained' (Berman and McLaughlin 1977). But demanding that a school stretch beyond its capacity will not accomplish very much (Huberman and Miles 1984). In his analysis of school culture and the problem of change, Seymour Sarason (1972) observed that a primary issue in implementing innovations is not necessarily the adequacy of financial resources but the availability of time and energy to support change. Equally important was his observation that schools are buffeted by multiple goals and are typically host to many programmes and change initiatives, all of which compete for the limited time and attention available. In a recent revision of this work, Sarason (1996) argued that sustaining the active participation of teachers is fundamental to change. Yet, we know from many descriptions of school change that sustaining attention to a particular initiative is difficult given the complex, chaotic, and political environments of schools. We know that teachers may lack the knowledge and skills to understand and implement innovations well. And, there may be no imperative for them to do so. The importance of these factors in the early implementation of KEYS is examined below.

Programme credibility

In general, the KEYS indicators can be said to have legitimacy and merit. They reflect much of what the literature on effective schools indicates are organisational conditions that support teaching and student achievement. Among the people we interviewed in Minnesota and Illinois, all saw the KEYS indicators as appropriate and useful targets for school improvement. The basic KEYS process also has face validity. There is growing attention in the literature on fostering improvement through self-study, reflective discussion, and planning from data (Louis and Kruse 1999). There is also long-standing recognition in the literature that change is most effective when it emerges from those who are experiencing problems and who will bear responsibility for the implementation of programmes and policies aimed to solve them (Crandall, Eiseman and Louis 1986). KEYS embodies these basic principles of local change processes; however, what KEYS fails to include may be problematic.

The KEYS indicators focus primarily on general elements of effective school organisation. KEYS is intentionally silent on matters of students and classroom instruction. NEA believes that KEYS should apply to all local pedagogical preferences and should not appear to endorse any curriculum or method. Thus, the indicators provide no clear vision of student outcomes or effective teaching, and little guidance for how to improve curriculum and instruction.

Our case study schools in Illinois and Minnesota were consumed with making changes in areas on which KEYS is largely silent. At our Illinois elementary school, for example, concerns about curriculum, bilingual education, and the educational needs of a student population rapidly becoming more ethnically diverse and language minority had greater salience for school improvement than the general characteristics of school organisation represented in KEYS. Our Minnesota elementary school, like other Minnesota schools, was consumed by the pedagogic implications of new state learning goals and standards.

Further, the KEYS indicators of effective school organisation are essentially 'content-free'. For example, indicators point to the need for 'high quality' and 'state-of-the-art' teacher professional development, but do not define attributes that are associated with these qualities. Again, this was assumed to be the stuff for local planning and decision-making. KEYS relies heavily on state union staff and local actors to flesh out the meaning of the indicators in schools with different needs, concerns and interests. NEA provides printed materials and consultants to help, but as we argue below, these resources have some shortcomings.

School capacity and commitment

While KEYS seeks to build school capacity and commitment for improvement, NEA acknowledges that initial levels of 'will and skill' for collaborative change are crucial to KEYS' success (NEA 1996: 1–12). NEA encourages state association staffs to look first to develop the capacities of existing school improvement teams before creating new ones.

The importance of initial school capacity and commitment to KEYS implementation is illustrated in both the Minnesota and Illinois cases. MEA staff members who were interviewed observed that lack of preparation and commitment at the school and district levels made the introduction of KEYS difficult. One UniServ Director remarked that it is a 'waste of time' to pursue KEYS 'unless there's a commitment to using it as a basis for dialogue about change'. The same director noted that it was very difficult to find schools with such commitment that would be 'viable candidates' for KEYS participation.

In Illinois, commitment to KEYS may have been moderated by its representation by IEA officials as one of many 'tools' that schools and school districts could use to pursue more substantive programmatic interests. This pragmatism may have made it more difficult to generate sustained interest in KEYS, particularly as schools' needs for change are driven by other pressing concerns. In the Illinois elementary school we studied, KEYS was overwhelmed by issues related to increasing student diversity, staff instability, and the need for curricular reform.

Momentum and lassitude

At the heart of the KEYS process is collecting of school-level survey data and reporting findings back to schools. These two steps have taken up to nine months to complete in some cases. Getting the data analysed and the findings back to schools has been delayed by summer vacations, competing activities, and, in Minnesota, long stretches of inclement weather. It is difficult to sustain initial commitment to KEYS during such delays, particularly when other matters compete for priority. Initial momentum, so important for implementation, may quickly dissipate as teachers and administrators fail to see tangible outcomes of their initial efforts.

Several UniServ Directors considered loss of momentum a problem in Minnesota. One commented, 'To me, that's been the biggest frustration, not moving fast enough'. Another reported that a middle school began to complete the KEYS survey in late May, but the principal did not return all the surveys until the end of June. Sending the surveys to the NEA for analysis was delayed at the MEA and, of course, 'Summer vacation is always bad'. By fall, the school had not yet received its findings. In Illinois, similar delays were noted. At our case study school, initial momentum was lost. The time between data collection and receipt of the findings was long enough for KEYS to be displaced by other concerns.

Alignment with other initiatives

Because KEYS indicators and processes address basic aspects of school organisation, they have potential to serve as a foundation for most local improvement initiatives. However, the general nature of KEYS was not necessarily helpful in Illinois and Minnesota. To some school districts, KEYS was less salient than more substantive initiatives that addressed specific goals and immediate needs of schools. KEYS can be pursued independently from such initiatives, but if it is, it is unlikely to help align them. Instead, KEYS is likely to compete with other initiatives for a school's time and attention, as it did unsuccessfully in our Illinois case.

In Minnesota, KEYS faces stiff competition from other state and local reforms and has yet to be linked to them. A good example is Minnesota's new state graduation standards and testing programme. According to several UniServ Directors, the new state standards and tests take precedence over local efforts to implement KEYS. One commented 'They'll be lucky if they can handle all of that'. Most directors believed that KEYS could help schools meet the demands of new state reforms. At the same time, they predicted that KEYS could easily be overcome by them.

Resources and follow-through

The UniServ Directors we interviewed understand that the survey and reports of findings are only the beginning of the KEYS process. Teachers and administrators at the school site must come together to study and make decisions about what to do in light of the findings. Helping schools work with their findings and develop an agenda for improvement lies at the heart of the role that UniServ Directors play in KEYS. Their preparation for this role is crucial.

While some UniServ Directors feel confident in their KEYS role, others express concern about their lack of preparation and effectiveness. One Minnesota UniServ Director, who received KEYS training, described the work required in schools as 'a potential bottomless pit'. Commenting on his preparation, he claimed, 'I really don't have a clue what to do with the [survey results] other than to say 'Here's the stuff and do what you can with it'.

The issue of alignment, earlier discussed in terms of programmes and policies, also applies to roles and responsibilities of state association staff and their ability to support KEYS at the school and district levels. The UniServ Directors we spoke with are well aware that in order to be successful KEYS requires attention and nurturing. Said one Minnesota director, 'You have to have somebody out there beating the bushes and making sure that they keep on track and that it just doesn't dissipate'. At the same time, MEA and IEA staff members are keenly aware that KEYS is only one of many responsibilities they have. Ironically, traditional union responsibilities may interfere with KEYS work. According to one UniServ Director, 'There's too much to do. . . I get bogged down in grievances and putting out little fires that shouldn't have started in the first place.'

For classroom teachers, KEYS may come on top of daily classroom responsibilities and school improvement initiatives to which they and their schools are already committed. One building-level union representative with whom we spoke observed, 'When it comes to our teacher members, I think the general response to [KEYS] is this is great, but where are we going to find the time?'

Finally, a number of district and school-level people we interviewed noted the importance, but also the lack of sufficient direction and support from the state associations. KEYS is only one of many initiatives that state associations present to their memberships for consideration. As such, the MEA and IEA have not pressed hard for KEYS implementation. Nor have they provided much support for KEYS implementation beyond what UniServ Directors can provide.

Profile and imperative

At this stage, KEYS is being implemented as a pilot initiative. It has not received much sustained attention by either the MEA or IEA. These state associations have not promoted the programme widely nor developed much constituent support for it. This gives KEYS a relatively low profile and a weak identity. According to one Minnesota UniServ Director, 'I don't think we've done anything to maximise PR [for KEYS]. . . . Of the 1,800 [teachers] with whom I have interaction professionally, less than 100 would even recognise the name of KEYS'. In Illinois, KEYS is represented as 'one tool among many' and subsumed within broader leadership training programmes that are promoted with much greater intensity. KEYS is seen as potentially useful, but the message to schools and school districts is clear that 'It is OK not to participate'.

The imperative to participate in KEYS has also been affected by the way it was introduced to schools and school districts. In Illinois, KEYS was introduced through an existing school improvement network of district administrators and local union leaders. This created some early joint interest among administrators and union leaders for local participation, but because it was also introduced as one of many tools and as part of larger leadership training programmes, that interest was hard to sustain. In Minnesota, securing local school participation before involving district administrators and union leaders engendered little commitment at the district level.

Political and organisational functions of KEYS

KEYS can serve at least two important political and organisational functions associated with new unionism. It can focus state and local associations more directly on supporting school improvement. It can also promote more cooperative and collaborative working relationships between associations and school administrators, with a common focus on school improvement.

A political perspective of organisational change focuses attention on how self-interests, domains of influence, coalition building, bargaining, and decision-making processes affect the success of innovations (Bolman and Deal 1997; Boyd and Slater 1999). An important element of this perspective concerns the politics of non-rational behaviour (March and Olsen 1976). When thinking about organisational behaviour as non-rational, problems, people who are available to solve them, and solutions are independent streams and coalesce in particular situations where there are 'decision opportunities'. Accordingly, the outcome of a decision opportunity is less a function of rational consideration of options than of self-interests and immediate exigencies. In examining why an innovation might succeed or fail, it would be important to consider whether the 'right' people were involved and whether 'the solution' was applicable to 'real' problems, defined as most pressing by participants' self-interests. Often included in such an analysis is whether there are zealots or 'idea champions' who muster support during decision-making and implementation (Wahlstrom and Louis 1993).

A political perspective also directs our attention to the internal dynamics of organisations in which changes are being sought (Ball 1987). There is ample evidence that advocacy of new unionism by national union leaders is not always met with enthusiasm within the ranks of their own organisations. In teacher unions, resistance may come from teachers who are afraid of losing union protection and from staff employees and mid-level leaders who have defined their professional careers according to more traditional, adversarial models of unionism (Bradley 1997). The literature on the new unionism points out that the most successful efforts to change relations between management and employees in the private sector have been driven by management concerns about productivity not by unions' efforts to professionalise their memberships or organisations (Rubenstein *et al.* 1993).

This discussion suggests several factors that may influence the ability of KEYS to influence state and local associations and the national organisation to play a more active role in school improvement and promote more collaborative working relations between those associations and school administrators. These factors include goal shifts within the union, current relations between union and management, and the presence of 'idea champions'.

Goal shifts within the union

KEYS was introduced at a time when the concept of new unionism had not achieved a common meaning or widespread acceptance within the NEA. Several persons we interviewed at NEA's national headquarters told us that not everyone at the national level shared a common understanding of the new unionism or agreed about its implications. Similarly, one of the UniServ Directors we interviewed observed that 'Bob Chase [president of the NEA] has the stamina and an opportunity to change the direction of the juggernaut'. 'But,' he continued, 'I'm willing to bet that there are blockers all over the place who are trying to slow it down, stop it, or do whatever they can to stick with the status quo.' Another state association staff member made a similar observation: 'I just came back from a week of new unionism at the national level an they're all over the place, both in experience and in philosophy. And I think that is reflecting where our members are at, I think that is reflecting where the leadership is at . . .'

Our cases point to similar issues in the state associations. The IEA has generally supported collaborative labour relations at the local level, in its rhetoric and in assigning staff to support local initiatives. It has also supported efforts to bring school system administrators and local association leaders together to promote school improvement. Still, not all members of IEA's leadership and staff have been supportive. In one documented instance, an IEA staff member created notable tension in a school district to which he was assigned by his strong opposition to the efforts of that district's local association to bargain collaboratively with the district's central administration (Smylie 1993). Similarly, it is not at all clear that new unionism is understood or has taken hold among MEA members. According to a Minnesota respondent, 'If you went to [a school] today and talked to the teachers, "What does new unionism mean to you?" it is possible they would not recognise the term.'

This lack of understanding is manifest in how member teachers think about the role of the union in their professional lives. Many teachers do not see the union as an active agent in school improvement. They continue to see it primarily as an advocate of their individual and collective interests and as an agent to resolve their grievances. For association leaders and staff members, the shift to new unionism is made difficult when members' expectations are aligned with more traditional unionism. In addition, standard operating procedures that govern work roles and working relationships in state and local associations may constrain efforts to alter beliefs and practices embedded in traditional unionism. These procedures have yet to be aligned systematically with new unionism. A Minnesota UniServ Director observed:

> Local leaders are often pretty traditional. Part of the dilemma is they become accustomed to working a certain way, they become good at whatever it is they do and they know the actions from the other side. If they're bargaining, over the years they developed a relationship, they know how to bargain. . . . Something like KEYS, they don't have the foggiest clue what that might be.

With such sources of persistence at work in the union, KEYS appears to be a weak stimulus for change in the orientations and behaviour of union staff and leadership. Our data, while limited, point to long-standing patterns of belief, self-interest, and practice grounded in more traditional views of unions that persist in the presence of new unionism. As organisational theory makes clear, such institutionalised patterns are extremely difficult to alter (March and Olsen 1984). Much organisational behaviour is grounded in embedded, taken-for-granted assumptions. It is less intentional and purposive than consistent with routines or 'scripts' (Zucker 1987). As pressures for change increase, organisations try to maintain a sense of order and stability and protect their deepest 'technical activities' (Meyer and Rowan 1977; Thompson 1967).

It is not surprising, then, to find in our two cases that KEYS has been received with some reluctance, and perhaps suspicion, and that union leaders and staff are slow to get on board. The principles of new unionism that KEYS reflects, and the new roles and responsibilities it implies, challenge national, state, and local union leaders and staff to depart from more conventional ways of defining the union and doing its business.

Relations between union and management

KEYS also holds the prospect of promoting more collaborative working relationships between the union, its members and school administrators. The KEYS indicators promote collaborative relations as a goal for school improvement. Its processes of studying survey results and planning school improvement call for collaboration. Yet, the ability of KEYS to promote collaborative working relationships may depend on the nature of working relationships at the time it is introduced into a school district. As the KEYS programme itself acknowledges, its prospects for success may depend upon this 'base state'.

In Minnesota, KEYS was introduced into a context where relationships between the union and school administrations were characterised by a disconnect between 'what we want' and 'what we are willing to do'. Local associations and district administrators both lament their poor relationships and lack of joint commitment to improve school quality and student learning. By implication, they both value better relationships and joint commitment to school improvement. This does not mean, however, that they agree on what to do about it. Furthermore, there are indications that the lack of a common agenda is rooted in local histories of conflict and distrust.

Who initiates change may also be an important issue. At all levels in Minnesota, KEYS has been a union initiative. There is little evidence of coalition-building with state-level policy-makers, leadership in the state education agency, professional associations, or local school officials. The push to implement KEYS in Minnesota has come primarily from the six UniServ Directors who introduced KEYS to principals and teachers in individual schools. KEYS was then introduced 'up the line' for what was, generally, pro forma support from the district office and the school board. Not surprisingly, we found little evidence that KEYS has been a catalyst for joint union–management dialogue or activity in Minnesota.

In Illinois, KEYS was introduced through a school improvement network that was founded by a regional IEA staff member to promote collaboration between local associations and district administrators for school improvement. This context presented a more fertile collaborative field for KEYS to take root. Furthermore, KEYS was presented as option to both local associations and district administrators to be discussed and entered into jointly. As such, the complicating dynamic in Minnesota of union initiation and lack of management buy-in seems to have been avoided.

Idea champions

KEYS was introduced at a time of tremendous change within the NEA, including the possibility of a merger with the AFT. At the same time, KEYS was introduced into states and school districts beset by a myriad of programmes and policies for school reform. These programmes and policies often pursue different goals, are highly politicised, and compete for educators' time and attention. Some initiatives are troubling to teachers and the union. In the Illinois, for example, recurrent legislative proposals for school vouchers, choice, new standards and accountability systems for teacher licensure and certification, and the elimination of teacher tenure create a political context in which the IEA must defend the interests of its membership. This context makes it difficult for the IEA to focus on school improvement and promote collaborative labour relations.

In Minnesota, preoccupation within the MEA with the merger and with state education reform agendas left little room for KEYS. A UniServ Director we interviewed observed, 'I think [the MEA has] become so preoccupied with the merger that they've lost sight, at least temporarily, of some of this stuff.' Another MEA staff member observed, 'I see us locked in an ongoing struggle with the policy-makers and the legislature and the governor. . . . I don't think [KEYS] fits in the political agenda of our leaders'.

In these contexts, the prospects that KEYS will be implemented with the intensity required to promote change within state and local associations and promote more collaborative association–administrator relationships may depend on the presence of idea champions. By idea champion, we mean an individual who believes in KEYS, who actively promotes it, and who takes personal responsibility for its success. Overall, we found few champions for KEYS. There is little indication that the NEA, once launching KEYS, has been available to advocate for it intensively or nurture its implementation at the state and local levels. Said one Minnesota UniServ Director, 'I have not had an official communication from the NEA that I haven't initiated since our KEYS training over a year ago'. With the exception of a particularly active UniServ Director in Minnesota, the regional IEA staff member who founded the school improvement network through which KEYS was introduced in Illinois and who now is Director of IEA's statewide Center for Educational Innovation, and a few of their colleagues, we found few advocates for KEYS at the state and local levels. In the field of competing and potentially overwhelming reforms, it is likely that KEYS will be overwhelmed without its own champions.

The symbolic function of KEYS

In addition to promoting school improvement and political and organisational change, KEYS has the potential of serving an important symbolic function. Along with other union initiatives, it may help reshape public perceptions of the NEA as a more professional labour organisation, concerned about school improvement as well as the well-being of its members. By reshaping public perceptions, KEYS may also enhance NEA's political legitimacy at a time when teacher unions have come under increasing criticism, particularly from elected public officials.

The symbolic function of programmes and policies has been recognised in the literature for some time. According to Edelman (1977), policy language and symbols evoke most of the political 'realities' people experience. They portray policy problems and solutions and shape how people think about them. They may also create perceptions of the beliefs and values of policy-makers. Majone (1989) argues that the most important function of policy making is defining norms that determine when latent problems require political attention. Thus, policy-making is more than the pursuit of solutions to particular problems; it involves 'pushing out the boundaries of the possible' (Majone 1989: 36).

Institutional theory also speaks to the symbolic function of programmes and policies. Meyer and Rowan (1977) observe that organisational structures are largely determined by the expectations and norms of external environments. In order to achieve legitimacy and promote survival and success, organisations incorporate elements that have been socially sanctioned. In other words, organisations tend to transform themselves to reflect the expectations and myths held for them in their environments. Meyer and Rowan note, however, that such transformation may not occur at the core of organisational activity. Organisations may create symbols and rituals of conformity and seek to manage their public image rather than embark on any systemic change.

Symbolism is central to the concept of compensatory legitimation. Weiler (1983) argues that when the legitimacy of political systems (and organisations) is challenged, programme developers and policy-makers are likely to become concerned not only with instrumental outcomes (e.g. performance and productivity), but also with programmes and policies that might re-establish legitimacy. Weiler (1990) notes that there is a wide array of policy strategies with strong symbolic value that could serve as putative sources of legitimation, including the use of expertise and research and the development of new programmes and processes that are consistent with external norms and expectations. Malen (1994) reminds us that such symbolic strategies have limitations. While they may reinforce legitimacy, they do not eliminate external pressures for evidence of organisational performance. Symbolic associations may ease, but not erase, the need for reasonable correspondence among policy premises, policy provisions, actual practice, and outcomes. At some point, the same policies that symbolically support an organisation may later compromise it if the policies are not reflected in what the organisation does and what it achieves.

At least three symbolic aspects of KEYS may help reshape perceptions of NEA as a more professional organisation and, in turn, enhance its public and political legitimacy. First, KEYS represents an important extension of the union's role in school improvement. Second, the KEYS indicators present a 'neutral', 'externally-valid' agenda for school improvement that transcends any self-interested agendas that might be held by the national organisation and its affiliates. Third, the KEYS process represents and reinforces the NEA's position on the importance of localised, professional determinism. Each of these symbolic aspects of KEYS is consistent with principles of new unionism. They are also responsive to external criticism of the national teacher unions that allege that they are large, self-interested bureaucracies that have little interest in and accept little responsibility for the quality of schools. As such, the potential of KEYS to fulfil its symbolic function is enhanced because it 'fits' with existing perceptions of what a teachers union should be and do.

Role in school improvement

KEYS is an important symbol of NEA's commitment to school improvement. It signals recognition by the union that its members and the schools in which they work can and should be improved. It demonstrates concern and acceptance of some responsibility for the quality of schools and student learning beyond protection of its members.

The state and local actors we interviewed uniformly pointed to KEYS as a symbol of the union's efforts to become more involved with school improvement. One state association official in Illinois told us that KEYS was clearly seen as an effort by NEA to 'get its oar in the water' of school reform. Similarly, UniServ Directors in Minnesota viewed KEYS as a vehicle for and symbol of union partnership with management in school reform. According to one director, KEYS really has to do with 'being responsible for what's happening in the schools and being accountable to it'. 'It symbolises,' he continued, 'that we are going to be full partners in this with the community, with the school district administration, and all the players in the school.' To several directors, KEYS symbolises a return to 'the old days', before collective bargaining, when the NEA's mission focused more specifically on school reform and quality. Said one director, 'Actually, we're going back to our roots, when . . . we were a professional association'.

Beyond bureaucracy and self-interest

To some local and state association officials, KEYS is a concrete symbol to the public and to policy-makers that the union is focused on more than 'bread and butter' issues of its members. The content of KEYS – research-based indicators for school improvement – links the union with best practices in education that make a difference in student learning. Involvement with KEYS at the state and local levels may be strategic in this regard. According to one Minnesota UniServ Director, 'My own personal perception is that [MEA became involved with KEYS because it was] really trying to work into other areas outside of bargaining and teacher rights. Number one, to improve its image. Number two, to be of service or better service to teachers and to school districts.'

Similarly, KEYS offers evidence to teachers that the NEA is becoming a more professional organisation. The foundation of the KEYS process – local, professional determinism and collaboration – stands in stark contrast to the image perpetuated by union critics of NEA as a large, monolithic, unresponsive and recalcitrant bureaucracy. KEYS symbolises that the NEA is responsive to and supportive of local initiative for school improvement, for empowering local associations and teacher members, and for joining school district administration in partnership for change. As said by a Minnesota UniServ Director, 'It gives us an opportunity to let our members know that the NEA is something other than a bureaucratic organisation in Washington DC'.

Conclusions

In this chapter, we reviewed principles of new unionism and analysed the prospects that a recent NEA initiative – KEYS – might fulfil three functions consistent with those principles. Drawing on relevant literature and findings of case studies of early KEYS implementation in Minnesota and Illinois, we suggested that while KEYS' content and processes are consistent with research on effective schools and change processes, the ability of KEYS to promote school improvement may be hampered by a number of factors. Our analysis raised questions about the way in which the initiative makes use of existing staff and the organisational structures of state and local associations as delivery systems, the adequacy of preparation and support, role alignment, and follow-through. Further, our analysis suggested that implementation may be made more difficult by the general nature of the KEYS indicators and goals for improvement they imply. While worthwhile and important to support change generally, KEYS risks being pushed aside by more well-defined initiatives related more specifically to the substantive needs and interests of schools, particularly those needs that schools find pressing.

We also argued that KEYS has the potential to promote political and organisational change within the NEA and its affiliate associations and in working relationships between associations and state and local and school administrators. We suggested, however, that the ability of KEYS to promote such changes might be frustrated by several factors. Those factors include forces of persistence within the union and the absence of champions for the initiative. They also include 'base state' levels of trust, mutual interest, and collaboration that define relationships between associations and school administrations. These base states are the fields in which KEYS is sown. Our cases showed variation in the fertility of these fields and suggested that problematic relationships pose significant challenges for KEYS to overcome.

Finally, we argued that KEYS could serve a symbolic function to reshape perceptions and enhance the legitimacy of the NEA inside and outside the union. We described how KEYS is a potentially potent symbol of NEA's commitment to and responsibility for school improvement, of transcendence beyond its own self-interests, and of an emphasis on local, professional determinism. At the same time, we cautioned that the symbolic value of KEYS may depend over time on NEA's ability to make good on the initiative's goals of school improvement and political and organisational change. In other words, the symbolic value of KEYS may depend on the union's ability to 'walk the talk'.

Our analysis suggests that while KEYS has many noteworthy features and has potential to help NEA move in the direction of new unionism, its ability to surmount these obstacles will depend on the political and financial support it receives from the national organisation and its state affiliates. This may involve revision of some of the substantive elements of KEYS to make it more relevant to schools and school districts that struggle with immediate, specific, substantive concerns.

Currently, KEYS maintains the status of a pilot project within the NEA and a low-profile option at the state and local levels. It has not been embraced (nor perhaps widely understood) throughout the national organisation nor within state associations. Its long-term political and financial support within the union is unpredictable and there appears no firm base of constituent support outside the union to advocate for it. At this point, KEYS remains on the margin. Our examination of KEYS in Minnesota and Illinois strongly suggests that until it becomes better integrated into and supported by the NEA, and until the NEA can develop a constituent base for it, KEYS' potential to promote principles of the new unionism through school improvement will not likely be realised.

New unionism requires fundamental changes in assumptions, values, work roles, and working relationships of union leaders and of members. And, while not explored in this chapter, it requires fundamental changes in school management. By examining the early implementation of KEYS we are able to understand better some of the complexities and barriers to new unionism in the teacher unions. Some of these complexities and barriers are structural. Others are normative and political. We learn much about an organisation when we examine efforts to try to change it. It is naïve to think that one programme alone can turn an organisation as large, complex, and as 'loosely-coupled' among its national, state, and local units as the NEA. Still, KEYS holds prospects of making a difference. As our analysis of KEYS suggests, those prospects could be enhanced as new unionism is pressed through other initiatives at the national, state, and local levels.

Perhaps one of the most important lessons to be learned from the KEYS experience so far is that moving toward new unionism in teacher unions requires a systemic effort. It requires resources, individual advocates, and leadership. It also requires efforts to encourage and reward locally-initiated change, develop leadership at the state and district levels, and re-educate the membership. It will also require patience and time if we are to see the benefits of new unionism in improved schools and learning opportunities for students.

Notes

1 The contents and conclusions of this chapter reflect the views of the authors and not necessarily those of the NEA or any of its employees.

2 To date, twenty-two state affiliates have volunteered to participate. They include Arizona, California, Colorado, Delaware, Florida, Illinois, Indiana, Iowa, Maine, Maryland, Minnesota, Mississippi, Montana, New Hampshire, North Carolina, North Dakota, Ohio, Tennessee, Texas, Utah, Virginia, and Washington.

References

Ball, S. J. (1987) *The Micro-Politics of the School: Toward a Theory of School Organization*, New York: Methuen.

Bascia, N. (1997), 'Invisible leadership: teachers' union activity in schools'. *Alberta Journal of Educational Research* 43(2–3),: 69–85.

Berman, P. and McLaughlin, M. W. (1977) *Federal Programs Supporting Educational Change: Vol. II. Factors Affecting Implementation and Continuation*, Santa Monica, CA: Rand Corporation.

Bolman, L. S. and Deal, T. E. (1997) *Reframing Organizations: Artistry, Choice, and Leadership* (2nd ed.), San Francisco: Jossey-Bass.

Boyd, W. and Slater, R. (1999) 'Schools as polities', in J. Murphy and K.S. Louis (eds), *Handbook of Research on Educational Administration* (2nd ed.), San Francisco: Jossey-Bass, 323–36.

Bradley, A. (1997) 'Teacher's pact deters achievement, study says', *Education Week*, October 1, pp. 1–13.

Bradley, A. (1998) 'A better way to pay: project studies innovations in teacher compensation and seeks to spur more people to try new models', *Education Week*, February 25, pp. 29–31.

Chase, B. (1997) 'The new NEA: reinventing teacher unions for a new era', speech delivered to the National Press Club, Washington, DC, February 5.

Cooper, B. S. (1998) 'Merging the teachers unions: opportunity amid complexity', *Education Week*, March 11, pp. 52–4.

Crandall, D., Eiseman, J. and Louis, K.S. (1986) 'Strategic planning issues that bear on the success of school improvement efforts', *Educational Administration Quarterly* 22: 21–53.

Edelman, M. (1977) *Political Language: Words That Succeed and Policies That Fail*, New York: Academic Press.

Fullan, M. (1991) *The New Meaning of Educational Change* (2nd ed.), New York: Teachers College Press.

Gergen, D. (1997) 'Chasing better schools: surprising but true: a union president serious about reform', *U.S. News & World Report*, December 8, p. 100.

Gross, N., Giacquinta, J. and Bernstein, M. (1971) *Implementing Organizational Innovation: A Sociological Analysis of Planned Educational Change*, New York: Basic Books.

Huberman, A. M. and Miles, M. B. (1984) *Innovation Up Close*, New York: Plenum.

Kerchner, C. T., Koppich, J. E. and Weeres, J. G. (1997) *United Mind Workers: Unions and Teaching in the Knowledge Society.* Jossey-Bass: San Francisco.

Lawler, J. J. (1990) *Unionization and Deunionization: Strategy, Tactics and Outcomes*, Columbia: University of South Carolina Press.

Lieberman, M. (1997). *The Teacher Unions: How the NEA and AFT Sabotage Reform and Hold Students, Parents, Teachers, and Taxpayers Hostage to Democracy*, New York: Free Press.

Louis, K. S. and Kruse, S. (1999) 'Creating community in reform: images of organizational learning in inner city schools', in K. Leithwood and K.S. Louis (eds), *Organizational Learning in Schools*, Lisse, The Netherlands: Swets & Zeitlinger.

Lowe, R. and Fuller, H. (1998). 'The new unionism and the very old: what history can tell Bob Chase and his critics', *Education Week*, April 1, pp. 46–50.

Mahoney, T. A. and Watson, M. R. (1993) 'Evolving modes of work force governance: an evaluation', in B. E. Kaufman and M. M. Kleiner (eds), *Employee Representation: Alternatives and Future Directions*, Madison, WI: Industrial Relations Research Association, pp. 135–68.

Majone, G. (1989) *Evidence, Argument, and Persuasion in the Policy Process*, New Haven, CT: Yale University Press.

Malen, B. (1994) 'Enacting site-based management: a political utilities analysis', *Educational Evaluation and Policy Analysis* 16: 249–67.

March, J. G. and Olsen, J. (1976). *Ambiguity and Choice in Organizations*, Olso, Norway: Universitetsforlaget.

March, J. G. and Olsen, J. P. (1984) 'The new institutionalism: organizational factors in political life', *American Political Science Review* 78: 734–49.

McClure, R. M. (1995) 'Mastery in learning, 1985–1995: sharing a decade's lessons', *Doubts & Uncertainties* 9(5): 1–5.

Meyer, J. W. and Rowan, B. (1977) 'Institutionalized organizations: Formal structure as myth and ceremony'. *American Journal of Sociology* 83: 340–63.

'NEA's "new unionism" takes hold' (1998) *Education Daily* 31(29): 1–3.

National Education Association (1996) *KEYS Training for Governance and Staff*, Washington, DC: Author.

Rankin, T. (1990) *New Forms of Work Organization: The Challenge for North American Unions*, Toronto, Canada: University of Toronto Press.

Rubenstein, S., Bennett, M. and Kochan, T. (1993) 'The Saturn partnership: co-management and the reinvention of the local union', in B. E. Kaufman and M. M. Kleiner (eds) *Employee Representation: Alternatives and Future Directions*, Madison, WI: Industrial Relations Research Association, pp. 135–68.

Sarason, S. B. (1972) *The Culture of the School and the Problem of Change* (2nd ed.), Boston: Allyn & Bacon.

Sarason, S. B. (1996) *Revisiting 'The culture of the school and the problem of change'*, New York: Teachers College Press.

Smylie, M. A. (1993) 'Glenview, Illinois: From contract to constitution', in C. T. Kerchner and J. E. Koppich (eds), *A Union of Professionals: Labor Relations and Educational Reform*, New York: Teachers College Press, pp. 98–115.

Thompson, J. D. (1967) *Organizations in Action*, New York: McGraw-Hill.

Upgrading teacher quality outranks smaller classes (1998) *Education Daily* 31(4): 1–3.

US Department of Labor (1996) *Working together for public service* [On-line], available: www.ilr.cornell.edu/lib/bookshelf/e_archive/LaborExcellence/Working Together.

Wahlstrom, K. and Louis, K.S. (1993) 'Adoption revisited: decision-making and school district policy', in S. Bachrach and R. Ogawa (eds), *Advances in Research and Theories of School Management and Educational Policy*, vol 1, Greenwich, CT: JAI, pp. 61–119.

Weiler, H. (1990) 'Comparative perspectives on educational decentralization: an exercise in contradiction?' *Educational Evaluation and Policy Analysis* 12: 433–48.

Zucker, L. G. (1987) 'Institutional theories of organization', *Annual Review of Sociology* 13: 443–64.

11 Creating a school culture from the ground up
The case of Celebration School

Kathryn M. Borman with Edward Glickman and Allyson Haag

Background

Celebration School enrols students from the ages of 5 through 18 in a comprehensive public (i.e. state) school programme. The school, in operation since fall, 1996, in close proximity to Orlando (See Figure 11.1), is located in Osceola County in a small central Florida community recently created by the Walt Disney Company's development group, the Celebration Company. What makes the school's development interesting, apart from the cachet associated with anything Disney in US and British culture, is both the particular care that was taken to construct a school from ground zero and the intent on the part of the early visionaries to provide a case example for replication. The location of the school in a setting of contrasting and often conflicting interests – developers on one side, county government on the other; wealthy Celebration residents in contrast to less affluent county residents – placed the enterprise at risk from the beginning.

In a Fall, 1997, conversation with the new principal Dot Davis, curriculum co-ordinator, Donna Leinsing, Kathy Borman and others, Don Rollie, a consultant to the National Education Association involved in Celebration's Teaching Academy, reflected on why a chronicle of the school's development was inherently important:

> [It is important because it addresses the question of] . . . How do you build a school from zero, ground zero, into an effective, functioning, cutting-edge educational institution? Now the fact that it's also being created in a brand new community is interesting, but in some respects sort of incidental. You can't separate them probably. But one of the features this school purports to be aiming at is replicability. In your own chartering language you say that this school should be replicable anywhere.

While Celebration's developers held the ideal of replicatility, it is difficult to imagine many school districts investing similar resources in the creation of a school. It is also the case – and Celebration School presents a good example

– that early visionaries are often succeeded by practical realists whose concerns focus on the bottom line of the enterprise, e.g., student discipline, achievements, enrolment and parent satisfaction. Nonetheless, documenting Celebration School's development and first two years as a fully implemented school provides a road map or, more accurately, a cautionary tale for those considering such an undertaking.

Celebration was designed over a period of ten years through a unique private/public collaboration involving the Walt Disney Company, Stetson University and the Osceola County School District. In addition, a leading national professional organisation representing teachers, the National Education Association (NEA), as well as elite universities, notably Johns Hopkins, Brown and Harvard in addition to Auburn University, were also instrumental in creating a school culture from the ground up with such features as electronic portfolio assessment; multi-grade teaching and learning in a comprehensive Kindergarten through 12th grade arrangement (i.e. primary grades through high school in one setting); and a strong emphasis on equity and access to academic learning for all students through work on projects cutting across traditional school subjects. Learning at Celebration School was envisioned as a life-long endeavour carried out in a community of learners with teachers as 'learning leaders'.

This chapter chronicles the development of the concept of the school from its earliest incarnation as a component of Walt Disney's dream of a community of the future to its present 'neotraditional' emphasis on community, place, technology, and a healthy lifestyle, the cornerstones of the built community of Celebration. Important issues throughout the school's development include the extent to which business and education work as partners in creating a school, how a school culture was put in place during the school's initial years of operation, and how problems of school leadership were addressed by a principal whose backing by a vocal and articulate group of home owners and developers gave her the leverage she needed to 'take charge'.

The planning phase – mid-1980s to early 1992

The Disney Development Company (DDC) now part of Walt Disney's Imagineering, was the seed-bed for the creation of the town of Celebration including its school. The Imagineering people are Disney employees in the development side of the business. Formed to manage the development of the town, The Celebration Company is a division of Walt Disney Imagineering. According to Terry Wick, the Education Liaison for the Celebration Company from 1996 to August 1998, Michael Eisner, the Walt Disney Company's CEO, agreed to support the project when the Imagineering people 'came up with five cornerstones . . . education, health, technology, community and place . . . place meaning the physical space – the architecture and . . . community being that kind of spiritual piece that pulls people together and gives them that sense of here's where we're gonna go.' In his recent autobiography, Eisner discusses the town of Celebration and especially its school. His appraisal of the school and its approach proved to be prophetic:

> We knew that an experimental approach would be controversial. My children attended a similar school, the Center for Early Education in Los Angeles. When Breck [Eisner's son] was eight years old, my parents asked what grade he was in. 'Continuum purple', Breck blithely replied. A simple 'second grade' would have been far easier to explain to my mother. Jane [Eisner's wife] and I were relieved when the school adopted a more standard language . . . Despite some early complaints about the Celebration school, applications [from county parents] far exceeded openings, and standardized test scores for students at all levels significantly exceeded state averages.
>
> (Eisner 1998: 408)

Eisner's children's progressive, student-centred school in southern California was inherent in the model at the centre of Celebration School's original plan. The model was also in keeping with schools such as Dalton or Allen-Stevenson, the small private school Eisner attended in the 1950s on Manhattan's upper East Side.

Walt Disney's original vision in the 1960s was of a utopian community sheltered by a dome where Disney employees and their families could find homes, safe neighbourhoods, and a feeling of community. However, the plan 'pretty much sat on the shelf' according to Charles Adams, a Director of Community Development for Disney during the construction of the town, until Peter Rummel was hired by the Disney Development Company in the mid-1980s to plan additional theme parks including the recently-opened Animal Kingdom as well as the Celebration community (see Figure 11.1). In Adams' words,

> He [Peter Rummel, now Chairman of the Jacksonville-based St. Joe Paper Company] came aboard with the Disney Development Company in the mid 80s. They had done an analysis of the land then and determined that they would put all the theme parks and resorts . . . north of Highway 192. [This] was the northernmost 20,000 acres, leaving us 10,000 acres site down here [south of 192] kind of as excess land. The company asked him to consider the highest and best use for it. It was for a mixed community like this, housing, offices, retail, schools, golf courses, and all those kind of things. [Since he had] developed planned communities, particularly in the Southeast and in Florida . . . he clearly had the background to take off on an endeavour like this. He just played with it for three or four years and then finally decided to hire people with residential background and community development.
>
> (Charles Adams, personal communication, 10 March 1998)

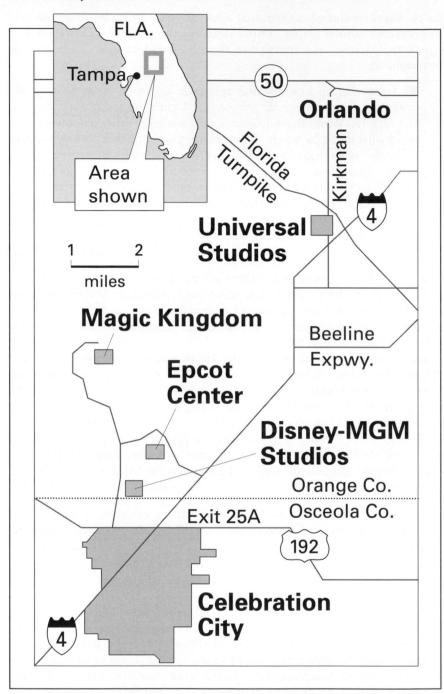

© The St Petersburg Times.

Figure 11.1 Map of Celebration City and surrounding area.

Celebration's distinctive architecture, including a post-office designed by Michael Graves, is influenced by what Adams and others refer to as 'neo-traditionalism'. The goal was to create an environment with a maximal fit between its inhabitants, their needs, and the city's infrastructure, services and appearance. Criticisms of the community have appeared (Pollan 1997: 58), arguing rather convincingly that the founding ideology is bound up with consumerist principles underscoring residents' paramount concern with 'corporate sensitivity' to their needs. After all, the land that was purchased by Disney in the mid-1960s for less that $250 an acre is now being sold in quarter-acre parcels for more than $85,000 each.

Few, however, criticise the architectural features of individual buildings and homes or the overall ambience. Celebration's streets are lined with mature trees (brought in by Disney) and porch-fronted homes; garages have been relegated to alleyways that connect blocks of homes that vary in cost. Garages are topped with small mother-in-law apartments that have turned out to be critical in creating communal links with the school. Today, many interns from Auburn, Johns Hopkins, the University of Central Florida and Stetson doing their student teaching live in these apartments, paying next to nothing in rent to the families who own them.

Planning for the school was begun in 1989. The Disney designers believed that a public school was the best choice, taking into account such factors as affordability, competing models, and impact on the greater community. In Terry Wick's view:

> Education was the piece that brought the school district, the State of Florida, Stetson University and the Celebration Company together. The district kept saying 'You're just not gonna have a school out there.' Disney kept saying that residents won't move in unless there is a school. it was a long, long, long negotiation process with the school district.
>
> (Terry Wick, interview, 10 March 1998)

The image of the 10,000-acre site south of Highway 192 as excess or 'left-over' property has haunted the development of both the community and the school. On the school district side, from the perspective of Osceola County, taking a cautious position with anything 'Disney' seemed a reasonable thing to do. Residents in the county have seen themselves as less privileged than those residing in Orange County (Orlando), enviously noting that Disney paid 65 million dollars a year (in 1997) in taxes to Orange County while contributing only 10 million dollars in taxes to Osceola County. Indeed, the district eventually agreed to finance a new school, funding up to 15.5 million dollars for its construction. The remainder, including the land, valued, according to Wick, at 7 million dollars, was underwritten by the Walt Disney Company. Fearing that its development would not sell, Disney became an active agent in the establishment of the school:

> Disney knew that this could not just be another Osceola school . . .
> What Disney decided it would do is use its name under the Celebration
> Company and go out and leverage colleges and universities and other
> educational experts . . . To work with a cadre of teachers from the
> county as well as some teachers from the state of Florida who had been
> former teachers of the year to say 'If you could start all over from
> scratch and build a building, what would that be?' . . . We . . . [Disney]
> have a vested interest in the school's success . . . we're kind of like a
> business partner on steroids.
>
> (Terry Wick, Interview, 10 March 1998)

In 1992, as an example of Disney's business partner resolve, 5 million
dollars was put aside for two purposes. First, this sum was to help fund the
development of the school design – what eventually became the DNA model
– by educators. The second, and from Disney's perspective, more critical
concern, was to augment the district's per pupil allotment of $3,200 – a figure
far less than the national average of approximately $7,000 in 1997. According
to Wick this ($5 million) 'enhancement' fund contributes approximately $300
for each enrolled student to augment the per pupil allocation provided by the
county. This $5 million fund is controlled by the district and the school.

Describing herself as a person 'who was not hit as hard with the pixie
dust' as some of her colleagues in the district, a long-term resident of the
county, member of the School Board, and until it was dissolved in late
spring 1998, member of Celebration School's Board of Trustees, Donna
Hart is quick to note the scepticism with which Disney is regarded by
county residents, many of whom are low-paid service workers at the Disney
attractions or in the businesses that support them.

> There was a lot of distrust on the part of our people that lived in our
> county They worked for Disney; they were not especially enamoured
> . . . A lot of them felt like they didn't get a fair shake . . . didn't make
> enough money, or whatever the case may be. They were not that
> excited about going into partnership with them to build a school. Some
> of it was equity issues. People complained. They said you're going to
> have this super school out here, and we're from the county, and we're
> never going to get this kind of stuff. We [on the school board] were
> trying to explain that we were looking to use this as kind of a pilot, and
> spread it out throughout the district. I think people in the county think
> Disney's got plenty of money to do whatever they want to do . . . [but]
> what Disney brings to us more than their own checkbook is the
> resources of other people . . . We've got 29 schools in the district, so I
> guess spreading the wealth is going to take time.
>
> (Donna Hart, interview, 9 March 1998)

Not surprisingly, the Disney interests were regarded with more than a
measure of caution on the part of many county officials and residents

outside the Community of Celebration who believed that the profit motive was pre-eminent in Disney's hierarchy of values. In Donna Hart's interview, the Celebration Company people were taken aback by the process of developing a school in the public sector:

> They just were so used to being autonomous. 'We're going to do this, and talk to the head of a company' and the head of a company says 'yes', and they spend money on it or whatever. When you're working in a public forum, it's totally different. You don't sit behind closed doors with your board of directors. You're out there in the public talking about all of this. Which I think was part of the problem. One thing that made contract negotiations so difficult, was that Disney had closed doors. They could sit behind closed doors and talk about the contract. Dealing with stockholders is one thing, but dealing with the public in general in a public forum, that's something very different.
>
> (Donna Hart, interview, 9 March 1998)

One solution to the problem of reconciling Disney corporate interests with those of the county became obvious fairly early on – turning over the development of the school programme to a team of teachers and their expert advisors who bore Disney's stamp of approval.

This process began when members of the Disney Development Company (DDC) travelled to Auburn University in Alabama in 1992 to consult Rich Kunkel. Larry Rosen, a professor of education at Stetson University in Florida, had come to Disney's attention as a person respected in the district for his work in faculty development, in demand throughout Osceola County. Kunkel had been Rosen's major advisor in the graduate school at St Louis University, a Midwestern Jesuit college. As Dean of the School of Education at Auburn with an active, far-flung and influential network, Kunkel was regarded as knowledgeable about Professional Development School (PDS) research and development, especially partnering relationships between public schools and universities. Professional Development Schools have been the focus of considerable interest in both reforming US schools and changing teacher preparation programmes in colleges and universities. Typically, a PDS incorporates faculty from the university who reside part time at the school site where they engage in collaborative faculty development, research and teaching, and supervise undergraduate students in teacher education.

Kunkel was also experienced in making alliances with businesses, having developed a working partnership with Pepperell, the textile corporation, and funding from RJR Nabisco's 21st Century Schools. Kunkel helped the DDC establish an advisory board for the creation of the school, with the development of a PDS for Celebration. This board was eventually comprised of the 'big names' that Disney desired, including Howard Gardner, the Harvard University psychologist credited with developing the theory of 'multiple intelligences'. In addition to his assistance in framing the PDS plan and forming a board of advisors, Kunkel also takes credit for convincing the Disney interests that the school should be inclusive, serving a diversity of students: 'The last thing the world needs is another white suburban school, no matter how excellent.' Rich Kunkel, Larry Rosen and the teachers from the county who worked on early plans of the DNA2 model for the school held no illusions about the importance of stressing diversity and were fortunate to have an ally in Charles Adams, the developer, who remained committed to constructing housing available to renters as well as buyers at affordable costs.

Schools as organisations

Schools, regardless of their settings and structures, communicate a sense of values held by members of the school organisation. There is an observable relationship between organisational values and internal and external environments; further, the actions of organisational members reflect learned patters of thought and activity that powerfully shape people's organisational experiences (Deal 1985). These experiences reflect the culture of the school. Schools have interrelated qualities that inform constituents about the implicit or explicit agreement among teachers, administrators, and others on how to solve problems and how to behave; constituents understand that it's the way things are done in the organisation. At Celebration School, sets of core values, ways of viewing the curriculum as organised into domains for the active, constructivist teaching and learning of integrated sets of ideas, were embodied in the school's key documents, specifically the DNA2 (See Appendix 1). The DNA2, so named for its obvious connection to the double helix, was designed by the visionaries to describe the 'diverse domains' (curricular frameworks), 'nurturing neighbourhoods' (classroom organis-ation to include cross-age/grade groupings of students), and 'authentic applications' (alternative assessment practices such as electronic portfolios to assess student project work) that formed the central framework for teaching and learning in the school

The culture of an individual school is a subset of the culture of the larger organisation and its community (Lutz and Merz 1992). In the case of Osceola County and the community of Celebration itself, major alter-ations in the assessed valuation of property, population demographics and patterns of student attendance and performance occurred by dint of the creation of the school itself, leaving the school and district vulnerable to community dissatisfaction, a problem for the school and the district as events unfolded during the first year. Parents and other residents in the newly developed community of Celebration were well aware of the contrast between the value of homes in the county, worth $60,000 on average, compared to their homes which ranged in cost from $160,000 to close to a million dollars.

Organisation culture has more to do with relationships and assumptions that people hold regarding a complex interweave of lived experience, expectations, ideals and future plans; schools do not exist in a vacuum. Assumptions about the organisation develop over time and rely on shared philosophies, ideologies, values, beliefs, expectations, attitudes and norms that knit a community together (Kilmann, Saxton and Serpa 1985). They are usually passed down from one generation to the next; teachers, parents and administrators learn about the school's culture from those who have lived in the culture. These established individuals share with newcomers a stable collection of common assumptions, beliefs, artefacts, and language patterns that operate beneath the surface and exert a powerful influence on behaviour in the organisation (Deal and Bolman 1991). The history that contributes to a school culture also serves to distinguish it from other schools within the larger school district organisation.

But, what occurs if there are few mutually agreed-upon cultural assumptions to invoke in the process of initiating new members into the school culture? What happens if instead there are deeply conflicting beliefs held by various constituencies? Of interest in our account of Celebration School is its creation *de novo* as a school Disney developers assured buyers would be 'world class', a phrase that became equated with student achievement measured by performance on the SAT. This image was in stark contrast to the emphasis placed by the visionaries on an interdisciplinary approach to teaching and learning carefully constructed on 'best practices'. Finally, in the summer of 1998 both these images were at odds with the views of Celebration residents in a newly constituted committee of 'concerned parents'. Along with the principal, committee members saw the school as 'chaotic', lacking structure, paying far too little attention both to teaching basic skills, and to enforcing student discipline.

People, particularly administrators vested with authority, may have considerable influence on school culture. Administrators, for example, exercise a strong influence on how a school operates on a day-to-day basis. During her first year as principal, Dot Davis hired an assistant principal whose tasks from January 1998 onward were to create procedures for addressing absenteeism and tardiness, accounting for student course credits and GPAs, and arranging for tutoring older students in preparation for taking the SAT exam – all vital concerns of vocal Celebration parents. Nonetheless, organisational newcomers must contend with the history of the organisation as well as the norms and shared beliefs that influence accepted rules of behaviour – in this case the visionaries', teaching and learning plan. Clearly, those with formal powers can insist on compliance with procedures and policies that govern formal behaviour within a school or district. In fact, vocal parents expected Dot as the principal to actively rein in the visionaries who came to be regarded as 'the clique' during the summer of 1998. In a town where customer satisfaction is paramount, where many building lots were as yet unsold and property values still shaky, it was simply good business for the person in charge – the principal – to respond to community pressure to take control of the situation.

Not all elements of the culture are readily controllable even by the person in charge. Components of the culture include: (1) shared values, which influence day-to-day life in an organisation; (2) heroes and heroines, the people who embody the values of the organisation – often visionary heroes who provide role models that represent what an organisation stands for; and (3) rituals and ceremonies – manifestations of the values and beliefs, that influence everyday social interactions, work rituals, management rituals, and rituals that reinforce values (Deal and Bolman 1991). Because cultures evolve to meet the needs of their environment, their strength and influence may vary among organisations. In the case of Celebration School, the first two years saw a number of elements working to both construct and unhinge an embryonic school culture from its moorings in the original vision as articulated most forcefully in the design for teaching and learning, the so-called DNA2 model. Leaders may possess either formal or informal power, but over time they have the potential to influence an organisation's culture. The critical variable is time, whether it is to influence an existing school organisation or to establish a culture for a new school organisation. Cultures support different behaviours that are consistent with distinctive patterns of values; those in leadership positions have the opportunity to influence those behaviours. Dot Davis, Celebration's principal during the school's first year in its new building (1997–8), came with a more conservative approach than that of the visionaries, one more responsive, as it turned out, to the local community of Celebration's own views.

The case of Celebration School

The development of Celebration School occurred in phases. Marking each of the phases is a fairly distinctive leadership regime. Each phase witnessed the leadership of a set of individuals who were supplanted in the phases of development that followed. Louis and her colleagues (see for example, Louis and King 1993: 217) argue that while the development of new or radically redesigned schools may 'constitute a relatively straightforward solution to systemic school improvement', such a notion ignores the legion of problems that beset visionaries who would undertake such a task. Several themes that Louis and King derive from their case studies of such schools have direct relevance to the case of Celebration School. The most important here are related to the construction of a professional culture based on trust and stability of relationships.

Closely related to the formation of trust and collegiality is the lack of precedent for new teacher and administrator roles coupled with the press of demanding workday schedules, allowing little opportunity for the cultivation of trust, norms, rituals and solidarity based upon collective reflection on the ebb and flow of organisational life (Louis and King 1993). In addition, the

Celebration School case highlights the problematic nature of building an innovative school programme in collaboration with a number of organisational, business and individual policy entrepreneurs, each seeking recognition, influence and authority. The school may be new, but the external constituents bring their sets of beliefs and assumptions about what this school should do and how it should look. These may (and in the case of Celebration School did) conflict with those held by internal constituents, especially those who developed the guiding principles of the curriculum. Finally, as summer planning for the second year came to an end in July 1998, the intrusion of the local community with its agenda catapulted the school's administration into crisis. We are getting ahead of our story, and so will turn now to a chronology of the major phases of the planning and implementation of design for Celebration School to illustrate the problematic nature of creating a public school in partnership with business interests.

Building a school and constructing a curriculum, 1992–1997

The next phase of Celebration School's development was orchestrated through negotiations that were often extremely delicate between the Celebration Company and the district. According to developer Charles Adam,

> We [Disney] were all fired up and ready to work with the public schools and guess what, they weren't ready to work with the Walt Disney Company. There was a lot of baggage. Disney had been here in Orlando for 25 plus years and nothing had ever been done in Osceola County, except getting a lot of the lower-end housing development. All of the theme parks . . . [are in] Orange County. Until Celebration came along nothing at Disney had been developed in Osceola County.
>
> (Charles Adams, interview, 10 March 1998)

To reduce the level of mistrust and scepticism, the developers 'begged' school district people to attend a retreat referred to as the Visioning Workshop with delegates from the National Education Association (NEA), the representative body for teachers in the county; representatives from the school administration; principals; and state department of education representatives. Larry Rosen was asked to work as group facilitator for the retreat. The Visioning Workshop was held January 7–8, 1993. Participants included representatives from the Florida Department of Education, DDC, Osceola School District, and Stetson, with Kunkel as facilitator. Early on, he requested participants from each delegation place the organisational mission statement on the wall, pull the embedded values from the documents, and post them below the statement. Charles Adams went on with his story:

> Then we said, 'Whoa. Backup'. When you reduce it to just the core values, look how much overlap there is among all those various groups.

And all we did on that retreat . . . was agree upon the values in which the education delivery system would be based. That was invaluable, because later on we clearly ran into obstacles during the public processes. We could always refer back to them and ask, 'Have we changed our minds?' 'Are these values still important to each of us individually or as a group?' The answer was always 'Yes'.

(Charles Adams, interview, 10 March 1998)

One of the sticking points early on was the creation of the Teaching Academy (later renamed the Institute for Teaching and Learning). An important goal during this period was to target best practices in education with an eye to their successful implementation in the school. Both parties also desired to have a forum – the Teaching Academy – for institutionalising them. Rich Kunkel, Larry Rosen, participants from the NEA, especially Don Rollie and others, identified key national initiatives they considered most promising. 'Best practices' quickly became equated with current reform agendas including the 'integrated curriculum' associated with Theodore Sizer's Essential Schools and the 'multiple intelligences' concepts developed by Howard Gardner in Harvard's Project Zero, in addition to a number of other ideas such as 'authentic assessment', utilising electronic portfolios, a particular favourite of Larry Rosen. Strands of the educational reform nexus were examined over the next several months by school district people responsible for drafting the preliminary curriculum who read widely and visited schools throughout the US identified as successful in implementing systemic reform initiatives.

The developers, however, never lost sight of the larger political and economic motives for designing a 'world-class school'. According to Adams, 'we wanted a place where you could bring legislators and leaders and others to se how it could be done.' In addition, the developers were well aware of the importance home buyers attached to sending their children to excellent public schools. The district envisioned more practical uses for the Teaching Academy as a site for best practices. This idea found its way to Tallahassee and to the attention of then Commissioner of Education, Betty Castor. Because a showcase for best teaching practices was in line with her priorities, a line item of $4 million was added to the budget to cover construction costs. However, just as the Governor's budget was to be finalised, members of the legislature removed the Teaching Academy item, substituting moneys for reform schools in its place, an irony that did not escape many.

Following the Visionary Workshop, a curriculum planning team was formed to design the important components of the school, draft a mission statement, create a curriculum, plan the physical space, and develop designs for technology. In addition, staffing patterns, hiring plans and evaluation criteria, as well as governance structure and student body management, were also addressed. The team included teachers and specialists from the county schools. This team worked very closely with the Osceola District

School Board over the next few years while being paid through the district-controlled 'Enhancement Fund' Disney had set up. They decided to take on a K-12 school design, although in retrospect, now believe that a K-8 plan would have made implementation easier. Nonetheless, the planners intended to create a full inclusion school; children with severe handicaps were to be accommodated by facilities within the county.

Perhaps the most important accomplishment during the first year that the school was in session (1996–7) was the establishment of the Professional Development School (PDS). Representatives from Hopkins, Auburn, Stetson, and the University of Central Florida spent time at the school not only co-ordinating the activities of the interns sent from the various university teacher education programmes, but also meeting with Celebration School teachers and conducting staff development on an *ad hoc* and also more formal basis.

From planning to practice: fall 1997–July 1998

As the school year began in 1997, the doors opened on Celebration School's new elegantly designed campus. In keeping with the planners' vision of the school and other public buildings commanding central locations in the community, the lovely brick buildings constituting the school campus, punctuated by green Caribbean shuttered windows, grace a large centrally situated location steps away from the town's business and commercial centre, itself an interweave of palm trees and post-modern architecture.

Before the second school year began, a series of two meetings were held to allow community members – primarily parents – to become familiar with the school design. Two meetings were held at a hotel less than a mile from the town. According to Donna Leinsing, those attending were enthusiastically supportive with the exception of a few 'chronic complainers':

> We had two meetings at the Hyatt and filled up the ballroom twice on each date . . . [W]e introduced new staff, talked about the neighbourhood space and how we could use it to create schools within the school. We explained our reasons for deciding that K-5 would be good for the children. The audience was positive and excited about moving into the new school. We had a few chronic complainers . . . left over from the first year, but in general everyone was excited about learning more about how the school would operate.
>
> (Donna Leinsing, E-mail communication, September 1998)

While Donna points to the enthusiasm of the parents, it is clear that a number were sceptical about how well the school would work. The multi-age arrangement of students, inclusion of high school aged students, and other aspects of the school – especially the use of student portfolios in place of tests to gauge the students' progress – were questioned by parents. An additional meeting addressed some of these concerns:

> The second meeting featured a principal and a team of teachers from a K-8 multi-age school in Indiana (New Augusta). They did a very nice presentation focusing on the similarities between Celebration School and their school. They answered questions and emphasised their successes.

Nonetheless, some parents remained sceptical, questioning the balance between teaching basic skills and enhancing students' self-esteem. Their scepticism was apparent in an evaluation carried out by Auburn University in the summer of 1997.

Institutionalising the school structure

The school opened in the fall of 1997 with just over 800 students, in grades Kindergarten through 12, including students aged 5–18. Approximately 200 students lived with their families in the new community of Celebration itself while the majority of students were bussed in from around Osceola County. County students had been selected through a highly competitive lottery system to attend the school. Three to four core teachers worked with 65 to 100 students in each of the school's neighbourhoods. The neighbourhood was the key organisational structure for academic learning and team-building among teaching staff. As Donna Leinsing, the school's curriculum co-ordinator during the first and second years described it,

> A neighbourhood is a space which should not be confused with a classroom space because it's really 6,000 square feet. And we hope it resembles more of a house plan. But there's open space, there's closed space, the rest-rooms are here, the planning room is here, conference rooms, and each neighbourhood has a refrigerator, a microwave . . .

In other words, neighbourhoods constitute the locations in school where teaching and learning are formally enacted. Unlike a 'pod', each neighbourhood has some open space and some closed space in the form of rather traditional classrooms and science labs, for example, in the upper grades. Each neighbourhood determines its schedule, makes decisions as a team, and evaluates student performance in this context. In our observations at Celebration School over a six-month period, however, we saw few instances of team instruction. Rather, at least in the upper grades, teachers alternated teaching responsibilities according to curricular units with one social studies teacher, for example, teaching a unit on the Holocaust while another followed with a unit on post-World War II economic development in the US. The multi-aged nature of the neighbourhoods, which were organised to include students from grades K – 5, 6–9, and 10–12, fostered cross-age instruction and informal mentoring. At the primary level, approximately 100 children were divided among four teachers, the goal to have each student settle into a neighbourhood as a young child and move in a continuous progress model while remaining in a familiar setting with teachers and classmates with whom long-term relationships could be built. Continuous progress provides a model for teaching, learning and curriculum that shifts instructional planning from the group to the individual child while utilising flexible grouping procedures and team teaching. In a continuous progress arrangement, there is less emphasis on grade levels and tracking and more cross-age, cross-ability grouping, promoting a problem-solving, constructivist, hands-on approach to instruction and student learning (Goodlad and Anderson 1987).

Borrowing from established but progressive approaches including continuous progress, multi-aged arrangements that trace back to Maria Montessori and newer innovative practices, Celebration School's founders worked with the architects who designed the arrestingly beautiful building. As a result, the school's built structure was designed to accommodate the DNA2 design for teaching and learning. Response to the school's physical space was almost uniformly positive among the students and teachers. A primary grade teacher pointed out: 'It [the physical space] is so very different. We are not all off on a single hallway, in little rooms with our doors closed teaching a class. We really depend on one another to do what we do.' A senior remarked: 'Most of the schools I had been in, it was "these are my kids, my classroom, my books and I need my special area". And here it's not that way.' Because space is configured to allow students from different grade levels to interact in and outside class meeting times, boundaries between grade levels are blurred. Another student, also a senior, observed:

> [T]hat's the thing, the neighbourhood, I don't even think of it as me being a senior here and everybody else sophomores and juniors – it's, you don't even really think about it. I mean most of my friends are sophomores. That's who I play basketball with; that's who I hang out with. At other schools seniors don't hang out with sophomores or freshmen.

We observed many informal student interactions that indicated a strongly nurturing and caring relationship among those involved.

Creating a professional culture

In their analysis of the difficulties and rewards attached to creating a professional culture in the context of school reform, Louis and King (1993: 217) debunk the assumption that developing a new school culture, particularly one at odds with current district norms, is a simplistic endeavour. Rather, they argue, 'School reform through the initiation of new schools is no cure-all but instead creates its own set of challenges'. In the context of Celebration School, the construction of a school organisation based on multi-age neighbourhoods and professional collaboration among teachers across traditional subject-matter areas, while embraced as fundamental to the workings of the school by its planners, was at odds with both the training and experience of most teachers, and, as it turned out, with the belief systems of many Celebration parents and community members. Unfortunately, a professional culture based on trust and collegiality never developed during the course of the first two years.

At the start of the second year, hiring decisions were still being made. In addition, a new principal, Dot Davis, had been offered her position during the summer from a pool of over 1,000 applicants. Although the unanimous choice of the search committee, it was apparent to many that her approach was cautious and reserved as though she were taking stock of the enterprise for which she was now responsible. As we noted earlier, schools and the professional culture of teaching within the school are constructed over time to include symbols, rituals, traditions, myths and language that are transmitted from one organisational generation to the next to channel behaviours (Barth 1990). In new schools, building a culture begins long before the children, teachers, or parents arrive. In the case of Celebration School, the activities of a number of individuals who were deeply invested in creating a culture in line with the vision established in the earliest planning days had been ongoing for several years and had been implemented during the school's very first year, in 1996–7 before our chronicle begins. The newly hired principal, embraced by Disney, the school district and 'old' teachers, appeared determined to follow her own vision. Dot left Alabama where she had been successful in implementing an imaginative public magnet school serving very poor children. She also had the advantage at Celebration School in being the candidate all participants in the hiring decision agreed upon.

Hiring new teachers had proven more difficult than many had anticipated. In one of the key school design documents framed as a memo to the Celebration School staff in early 1997 outlining the features of the Celebration Professional Development School, then Principal Bobbi Vogel wrote:

> Since Celebration is a new school, it provides a unique opportunity to hire school staff based on their 'fit' to the school and its shared vision as designed by educators and parents. This 'new beginning' provides a school staff chosen for their excellence as educators and their agreement with the concept of a PDS as described herein.
>
> (Memo to staff, dated 6 March 1997)

While the nationally advertised teaching positions at the school drew a large number of applicants, the relatively low salaries paid to teachers in Florida compared to salaries earned by teachers nationally dampened the enthusiasm of many applicants who responded to the nationally advertised search. Those who were hired were for the most part young and inexperienced or at least new to teaching. In the end, youth, inexperience, and a traditional pre-service education proved a disastrous mix. One of the experienced team leaders remarked,

> I am old enough to be the mother of three people that are on my team. I just turned 50 this year. The rest of my team-mates haven't hit 30. The average age among the three of them is probably 26, if we are lucky. We have a brand new teacher and then two teachers, one who has taught for four years and one who has taught for five.

In a similar vein, Donna Leinsing, the curriculum co-ordinator, saw creating a well-integrated faculty, on-board with a cross-disciplinary, project-based curriculum as a major challenge:

> The only challenging piece at this point is that very good, strong, individual teachers are probably the ones who are experiencing the most change. Children are fine. Children are resilient, flexible, enjoying every minute of it. But the teachers need to stop and rethink everything they do. Which is something we did last year. We rethought everything we did. But now this is another dimension. There are forceful personalities here. We did one thing very well last summer. We spent the whole summer together which was very important to me. It was good time spent together. We did bond, as a core faculty. But we also had time to decide which people would be most comfortable working together as a team. And I think that's why we're still here right now. Because those teams really are so strongly bonded, and have similar styles, person-alities, very supportive of each other, they take turns being up or down individually, but collectively they hold each other up.
>
> (Donna Leinsing, interview, May 1998)

While Donna may have been correct in her perceptions about teachers, from the perspective of vocal parents in the town of Celebration, what was being created was not so much a tightly bonded group of teachers as a clique that saw itself as knowing what was best for the community's children but who were unwilling to listen to parents whose concerns about their children learning basic skills, having structure and being prepared for the SAT and college, not in constructing portfolios of their work that state universities would be reluctant to consider in making admission s decisions. Nonethe-less, during the course of the school's first two years, teachers and students embraced the notions of project work and teaming. A teacher in the upper grades remarked,

> The atmosphere is certainly more collaborative and less competitive. If one of us in neighborhood K-12 has an idea of something that we think

would make work easier or documenting easier, or planning easier; it's an idea for a unit that can be, no matter what. The entire group is very quick to say, 'You know, let me show you what we are doing and it works really well for us.' And you don't tend to find that in other environments. That shared collaboration really has produced some really creative things.

(Suzanne Snow, interview, 30 January 1998)

At Celebration School, collaboration was socially and culturally constructed at multiple levels among students and teachers. The planners had designed this school to look different, feel different, and produce different results from those in traditionally arranged schools. A top-down hierarchical arrangement typical of most schools, including those in the district, was replaced by co-operation and collaboration to enhance each person's unique skills and qualities. Student project work at all levels was designed to be cross-disciplinary and problem-based in nature. For teachers, this meant focusing within neighbourhoods on ways to integrate traditional subject-matter content into an interdisciplinary and applied framework. One elementary teacher observed:

> In my neighbourhood it's very team oriented. I work in a team with three other [elementary teachers] which creates for a very collaborative environment. So, whereas we're responsible for separate things we all meet together to make sure that we're all focusing on the same topics – same goal which is the learner so that's very beneficial for us.

The PDS plan outlined in her memo to the Celebration teaching staff by Bobbi Vogel in the early spring of 1997 had called for the involvement in the implementation of the PDS of the university partners, Auburn, Johns Hopkins, Stetson and the University of Central Florida to support, among other activities, the mentoring of future teachers who carried out internships at Celebration School. During the first and second years, each of the university partners sent several interns (future teachers) to the school. Clinical supervision was provided by teams representing the four universities; during the second year a course in clinical supervision for Celebration staff and other teachers from the county was offered by an experienced consultant. By and large, the interns were extremely competent and therefore well received by teachers working with them. In fact, the Johns Hopkins interns, all of whom had returned to school to earn teaching credentials after pursuing successful careers in other fields, were judged to be exceedingly gifted teachers and in two cases were offered teaching positions for the 1998–9 school year. Similarly, several of the Auburn interns have been offered and have accepted teaching positions. According to Rich Kunkel, the PDS concept is an extremely important aspect of the school and one that is becoming established in an increasingly more mature role at Celebration School. While collaborative research agendas and university appointments for key teachers at the school have yet to be arranged, Kunkel sees important gains through the introduction of technologies, teaching strategies, and business and university partnerships in support of the PDS at Celebration.

Three of the original planning group for the school, Donna Leinsing, Paul Kraft and Carolyn Hopp remained at the school in leadership positions among the faculty until mid-July 1998, when Leinsing received notice that she had been 'reassigned to In School Suspension' for the 1998–9 academic year. Hopp along with Suzanne Snow received notices the same day that Leinsing had received her reassignment advising them that they would not be recommended for appointment in the 1999–2000 academic year. While a number of the remaining teachers were disturbed by what some saw as a high-handed approach taken toward these early 'visionaries', many gave their tacit support by remaining silent and still others saw their departures as an important signal that the new principal was in charge, and an arrogant, 'know-it-all' regiment was over.

Developing a student culture

During its first year of full implementation, Celebration School drew most of its students from outside the immediate town of Celebration. Of the 800 students who enrolled in grades K-12, approximately 500 were drawn from the county by lottery, with 300 attending from the town. Although there are notable differences in socio-economic status between Celebration residents and Osceola residents in general, we found it difficult to distinguish between students based on residency.

In attempting to understand the student culture, we drew upon both observations and interviews of students. Our experiential sampling survey, for example, revealed that fully half the time that students were working in an instructional mode, they carried out their activities in self-selected groups. The interactions students experience in these arrangements contributed to their enjoyment of school-related tasks, and also contributed to the involvement in students who differed in age, fostering collaborative efforts in groups of varying sizes and kinds. There may be drawbacks to an emphasis on group work, however. Some students apparently struggled with the independence they were given. Absenteeism, so far as parents were concerned at least, became an issue in the upper grades toward the end of the year. Although some students and local town parents saw absenteeism as a problem, the school as compared with other district schools had an exemplary attendance record. Among the county schools, Celebration ranked first among central Florida schools in a four county area (Lake, Orange, Osceola, Seminole and Volusia). When we asked what made Celebration different from other schools they had attended, a female senior student replied,

Um, the set-up of it, like, the project atmosphere. You don't have, like, tests that you have to take. You show your work by actually doing it, and showing it by a project you may do. However you want to present it, you can present your project. Um, the classes aren't set up the same. They're kind of like an open-atmosphere class, and not like a sit down and do work. You know you have, like, more discussions I think, and more time to sit in class and talk with the teachers about things . . . I think it's pretty well structured. I mean that's my point of view. And the teachers have a class and it's all set up and, you know, we go over the notes that we need to go over, we do everything we need to do. And then we have project time. if we have projects to work on, or class time discussion and whatever – we just learn.

Seniors we observed during the course of the year seemed especially mature. Although they uniformly held clear and focused academic and career goals, most planned to attend either the nearby community college or state university. Further, students seemed enthusiastic about how and what they were learning at all levels. One of us observed the school student leadership elections early in the year and recorded in his field notes:

I observed elections for student offices, not just president. The candidates made presentations for a specific position. What I found to be most interesting, was how each of them assimilated the team concept present in the school. In each presentation, the candidate referred to the importance of working as part of a governance team. They did not talk about what they could do as an individual, rather they emphasised their role as a team member. Celebration seems to have a real sense of team and working together both among the professional staff and its students. I thought the student candidates demonstrated their commitment to that 'team spirit' in their presentations to the student body.

Throughout the year, students from outside the gates of the community mingled easily with those whose parents had purchased more expensive Celebration properties. In fact, these county students held elected student governance offices, were active in the fledgling sports activities of the school and generally did well academically.

Trouble in paradise, summer 1998

By the conclusion of the 1997–8 school year, several issues seemed ready to percolate or, conversely, appeared to be settled at last. One of the latter such issues was the matter of the Teaching and Learning Institute (formerly the Teaching Academy) leased during the year by the Disney Cruise Line to train its new children's programming staff. Separate agreements were reached with the Celebration Company interests and the county on the one hand, and between the Celebration Company and Stetson on the other. Terms reached with the county were in line with those that had been discussed from the outset: the county would use the Institute facilities at a nominal cost to carry out staff development attended by Osceola teachers and staff. Stetson, on the other hand, agreed to pay close to $80,000 to lease space in the Institute to conduct courses, workshops and in-service programmes aimed at Celebration faculty and, with their NEA partners, to host 2–3-day institutes providing training in areas such as national certification for teachers.

A new generation of development for the Celebration enterprise seemed imminent at the outset of the new 1998–9 school year. Brent Harrington, the Community Services Manager (*ad hoc* 'mayor') – after declaring at a concerned parents' meeting that the school was no longer in the hands of the founders ('This is no longer Bobbi Vogel's school') announced his intention to move back to the Phoenix area where he had accepted a new position with DMB, a national developer of master planned communities. Terry Wick, the education liaison, was offered and accepted a promotion within Disney to develop corporate education initiatives including an updating of the American Teacher Awards, requiring her to move to Los Angeles. The Osceola County School District Superintendent who had also come from Arizona and who had generously supported the work of the visionaries reached an amicable decision with his board to step down. Even Charles Adams and his family made the decision to move to a site his company was developing in North Carolina. Finally, Larry Rosen withdrew his son from the school, put his house up for sale (although Disney interests frowned upon the sale of a home before a three-year time period had passed) and moved back to DeLand Florida, where Stetson is located.

Meantime, the teaching staff at Celebration School undertook its summer staff development work during the months of June and July. Teresa Field of Johns Hopkins University agreed to facilitate workshops during the summer involving all members of the teaching staff. Teachers' time during the six-week session was paid through the district's 'Enhancement Fund' set up by Disney. The summer began with a resolve to continue to build a strong professional community among teachers; task groups for the summer workshops were organised to focus on specific issues including curriculum, assessment, safe environment and technology with the addition of a governance task group.

For the second year, the School Advisory Council sent out a survey to parents during the spring of 1998. As it had been during the previous year, response was light. Fewer than 10 per cent of those surveyed responded. The responses indicated a bipolar distribution with parents split almost evenly in their estimate of how well things were going. As a way of reaching out to the community of parents, Dot the principal, scheduled parent information nights. The first focused on the Professional Development School notion while subsequent seminars touched upon integrated learning, co-operative learning and assessment. Groups of teachers were present and actively participated, sharing information with those who attended. These meetings may or may not have been the springboard that launched the Concerned Parents Committee, a group of individuals who lived in the town and whose children were in the upper grades.

An hour into the meeting, as the general discussion got underway, in the back of the room a parent stood with his Franklin Planner open, an outline of his points written on a piece of paper. He began:

> As far back as PD [pre-Dot] there has been a paradigm that has been projected that borders on educational fundamentalism – that you either agree or disagree; you are either for it or agin it – you're a stakeholder or not. If a person expresses concern – and I have seen it a lot over the past three years – that person is a 90s version of tarred and feathered. If I am a concerned parent, do you think I'm going to express my views easily?
>
> I am pro-Dot. My concern is that there is a faculty who don't understand their own administration and principal's desires. Why do they have that much weight?
>
> [Audience members murmur 'Yeah' and 'Right']
>
> There is an element of distrust – this is a town issue – this is everybody's issue. As one who deals with language, let me say that typically an organisation will resort to highly technical language when it is distances from its audience. What's a neighbourhood? What's a level? Let's call a class a class.
>
> [Audience members murmur their agreement]
>
> I just got back from New York. I went to the Disney Store in Times Square . . . It looks like every Disney store in the US. 'Consistency'. When every neighbourhood develops its own curriculum there is no consistency . . . The old way worked for me. It is not the best but it worked. This town is about new ways. It's both – the best practices of yesterday *and* today. *This* [the current situation at the school] is not progressive. If the Disney Corporation changes every year, it will lose customers . . . consistency.

This plea for 'consistency' and a return to the way things were when these 'concerned parents' were themselves in school appeared to galvanise those present at the meeting that July evening. The discussion that followed moved to a general agreement that, although there might be some small differences in opinion among those present, there was enough consensus to move forward. A future meeting date was established to address concerns to Dot and the meeting was adjourned.

Conclusion

Staff and community members who were close to the school have always believed that Disney would do whatever was necessary to guarantee the success of the school. According to Donna Leinsing, Disney interests held a concept of success that had

> something to do with keeping grumpy residents happy at all costs. Real estate is the name of the game in Celebration and we know it's overpriced. Some parents think textbooks teach children; I'm sure some people want more technology and technology that works.

Interpreted this way, Disney's guiding motive was to make sure that residents remain appeased and happy; keeping property values secure and rising over-rode any concern with the pedagogical mission of the school.

What important lessons can be learned from the Celebration case to guide organisations and individuals who ally themselves and their organis-ations with efforts to build a school from the ground up? First, as one example, the NEA's approach, as interested participant/observer, allowed the organisation to keep tabs on important developments, especially with respect to the establishment and development of the Professional Diploma School. As a consequence of a position as disinterested observer, the NEA was, remarkably, able to navigate among competing visions and desires for Celebration's development and also remained a trusted partner in the school's ongoing work. Third, because the NEA's stance was somewhat distanced, as an organisation it was not in a position to either guide or evaluate the day-to-day operations of the school.

As we have argued here, the development of a school culture from the ground up is always a difficult proposition. In the Celebration case, com-peting pedagogical visions, monied developers, planners more interested in the social and moral development of the child than in the inculcation of basic skills and high marks on the SATs, clashed with vocal parents who valued academic achievement-related outcomes for their children. According to a report on a series of focus groups conducted by Kunkel and colleagues in the summer of 1997, teachers saw their role as carrying forward the 'burden' of a good public education and the creation of the best learning settings for each child (Richard Kunkel, personal com-munication, August 1998). While teachers shouldered these responsibil-ities, they unfortunately lacked the capacity to see the bigger picture all too apparent to an influential group whose children attended this school and who ultimately found support for their position with the current school administrative staff.

Appendix 1: Timeline

1993	Planners take blueprints of Celebration School to the Osceola School Board.
1993–1995	Osceola School Board suggests architectural and other changes to Celebration School plans, throughout their negotiation process.
1996	Celebration receives 4,500 resumes for fifty teaching positions.
1996	August – Celebration School building is officially under construction. Meanwhile, 200 resident students begin taking classes at the Teaching Academy, since renamed.
1996–1997	Administration holds a lottery for Osceola County student enrolment; over 500 students were selected.
1997 August	Celebration school opens its new doors to nearly 800 students.
1997–1998	Our research team chronicles the development of Celebration School, its culture and professional comunity.

Appendix 2: Those involved in creating Celebration School

Charles Adams:	Director of Community Development of DDC during the time of Celebration's construction.
The Celebration Company:	A division of the Walt Disney Company
Disney Development Corporation (DDC):	A former division of the Walt Disney Company
Diverse Domains, Nurturing Neighbourhoods, and Authentic Applications (DNA):	The Celebration School Curricular Documentation. Designed to be replicable, like DNA.
Michael Eisner:	Chief Executive Officer of the Walt Disney Company
Donna Hart:	Osceola County School Board member since 1992. During planning phase, acted as the liaison between designers of Celebration School and School Board, working closely with Disney and the public in the process.
Carolyn Hopp:	Now former teacher and founder of Celebration School, currently pursuing a doctoral degree. One of the five planners on the payroll before ground was broken on the campus.

Walt Disney Imagineering:	A division of the Walt Disney Company
Paul Kraft:	One of the five planners on the payroll before the campus was constructed, and main wirter for the DNA2. Since then, has served as media specialist at Celebration School.
Rich Kunkel:	Professor at Auburn University, Alabama. Played key role in developing a board of experts on the development of the school, and worked as consultant to the DDC.
Donna Leinsing:	A founder of Celebration School. One of the five planners on the payroll before they broke ground on the campus and formerly (until the summer of 1998) curriculum co-ordinator for the school.
Professional Development School (PDS):	Usually refers to a public school, and the agreement between a school and a university. Generally considered to be a symbiotic relationship, it allows for research to enter into classroom practice, facilitates internships for students in Education and combines resources. Most professional development schools involve just one university; Celebration involves four; Auburn University, Alabama; University of Central Florida; Stetson University of Florida; and Johns Hopkins University of Maryland.
Peter Rummel:	Worked for the DDC, now chairman of the St Joe paper company.
Larry Rosen:	Former graduate student of Rich Kunkel at Auburn, and consultant to the DDC especially in connection with Celebration School's computer technology.
Suzanne Snow:	One of the original teachers at Celebration, but not one of the five planners. She taught classes at Celebration during the year before the school building opened.
Terry Wick:	Education Liaison for the Celebration Company, during the planning and building phases.

References

Barth, Roland S. (1990) *Improving Schools from within San Fransisco*, CA: Jossey-Bass.

Deal, Terrence E. (1985) 'Cultural change: opportunity, silent killer or metamorphosis?' in Ralph H. Kilmann, Mary J. Saxton, Roy Serpa and associates (eds), *Gaining Control of the Corporate Culture*, San Fransisco, CA: Jossey-Bass, pp. 301.

Deal, Terrence E. and Bolman, Lee G. (1991) *Reframing Organizations: Artistry, Choice, and Leadership*, San Fransisco, CA: Jossey-Bass.

Eisner, Michael (1998) *Work in Progress*, New York, NY: Random House, Inc.

Goodlad, John I. and Anderson, Robert H. (1987) *The Nongraded Elementary School*, New York: Teachers College Press.

Kilmann, Ralph, Saxton, Marjy and Serpa, Roy (1985) 'Five keys to understanding and changing culture', in Ralph H. Kilmann, Mary J. Saxton, Roy Serpa and associates (eds), *Gaining Control of the Corporate Culture*, San Fransisco, CA: Jossey-Bass, pp. 301.

Louis, K. S. and King, J. (1993) 'Professional cultures and reforming schools: does the myth of Sisyphus apply?' in J. Murphy and P. Hallinger (eds) *Restructuring Schooling: Learning from Ongoing Efforts*, Newbury Park, CA: Corwin Press.

Lutz, Frank W. and Merz, Carol (1992) *The Politics of School/Community Relations*, New York: Teachers College Press/ National Education Association.

Pollan, M. (1997) 'Town building is no Mickey Mouse operation', *New York Times Magazine*, December 14, pp. 56–63, 76–81, 88.

Saffir, Barbara J. (1998) 'Too many schoolkids play hooky too often', *The Osceola Sentinel*, A1, A2, August 30.

Part 4
Summary thoughts

Part 4
Summary thoughts

12 Leading towards improvement

Kathryn A. Riley and Karen Seashore Louis

If there ever was a time in which schools could operate in isolation, that time has long since vanished. There are now many actors and players who want their say in shaping what is taught, to whom, and how, and who want to take a lead on the education stage. Some will have greater legitimacy than others, but none will be able to lead on their own. As the contributors to this book demonstrate, the leadership tapestry is complex, rich and ever changing.

The conceptualisation of leadership which we have presented in this book is a broad one. Leadership, we argued earlier, is more than a role-based function assigned to, or acquired by one person in an organisation who uses his or her power to influence the actions of others. It extends beyond the immediate school community, embracing those many actors on the wider leadership stage – governments, trade unions, school districts and businesses – acknowledging the diverse roles which they play. The notion of leadership as a network of relationships among people, structures and cultures, both within, and across organisational boundaries has been re-affirmed by the contributions to this book.

The many actors are drawn together in pursuit of the education reform agenda: an agenda that has focused to a large degree on schools. Increasingly, governments of different persuasions have shared the belief that the macro-problems of the state and society can be addressed through improving the micro-efficiency of the school. As a consequence, schools have been assigned the task of righting a range of social and economic ills – a role which many would argue is beyond the capacity of schools to achieve. Rising national expectations about schools have been accompanied by reduced teacher autonomy and increasing demands for higher performance – of teachers, as well as of pupils (MacBeath, Moos and Riley 1996).

Despite common concerns, state or national government approaches to reform have differed significantly. Some governments have pursued the path of decentralisation, giving greater autonomy to schools, although often, as in the case of the UK, retaining significant degrees of central control. Others have embraced privatisation, deregulation and choice. Others still have placed greater emphasis on quality control, evaluation and testing, as part of a general accountability thrust (Riley 2000).

How the reform 'problem' is identified and characterised, together with the political possibilities and policy options, and the final choices and priorities, is a product of national circumstances and historical arrangements. Key local individual and organisational actors also shape this national framework. Businesses are taking a larger role: the Disney Corporation was a major player in creating Celebration School (Chapter 11). Trade Unions are seeking to influence both the nature of educational reform, and how it is implemented on the ground (Chapters 8 and 9). Whilst the national context is critical, local contexts influence how reforms are interpreted and implemented. At the school level, a school's history, leadership and community context will effect how a national reform initiative is perceived. The local actors will have different views and perceptions about the nature of the reform or change initiative, about priorities, and about how the local and national agendas come together.

Contributors to the book demonstrate the specific ways in which leadership is circumscribed by the national political climate. The cultural context and legislative framework create, cumulatively, the expectations and boundaries about what can and should be achieved, and how. In Chapter 6, Lejf Moos describes the ways in which national differences can shape the structure and management of schools. The hierarchical school traditions which characterise many English schools are in marked contrast to the flatter structures and participatory culture of most Danish schools. Both reflect legislative requirements, as well as cultural values.

The national climate not only sets the boundaries and context for schools but the parameters within which other organisations, such as intermediary authorities and teacher organisations, can operate. John Fitz, William Firestone and Janet Fairman (Chapter 8), highlight the ways in which expectations at national and state level can influence the scope and direction of decision-making – and the capacity to govern – in school districts in the US, and local education authorities in England and Wales. And yet, despite the common national framework, as Kathryn Riley, Jim Docking and David Rowles indicate in Chapter 7, English local education authorities both interpret and carry out their role in the change process in very different ways, with varying levels of success and with different consequences. The national or state context may constrain but there is much scope for local interpretation.

The contributors to the book come to the issue of leadership from different perspectives and vantage points, and whilst they do not present one unified model of leadership – leadership is too bound in culture and context for that – a leadership paradigm is, nevertheless, emerging which incorporates a number of core conceptual themes. The first is to do with the *mobility and fragility of leadership, the shifting sands, the need to manage conflict as well as competing expectations.* These elements of the leadership paradigm are demonstrated in the findings from the international study of school leaders reported in Chapters 2 and 6 and elsewhere (Riley and MacBeath 1998; MacBeath 1998; Riley 1998a). The study has highlighted the ways in which school leaders need to be adept at responding to the complex and fluid inner life of the school, as well as to the demanding and ever changing external context. Schools have to serve internal and external constituencies which are often in uneasy coexistence with each other and, as a consequence, school leaders have to manage contested notions about achievement, as well as multiple interests and demands and complex ethical dilemmas.

The dynamics of the education reform and change agenda have led to the present focus on the leadership of schools, and on the role of individual schools leaders. Yet the second conceptual theme is that a more *dispersed, values driven* model of leadership is emerging which, according to Mel West, David Jackson, Alma Harris and David Hopkins (Chapter 3), will provide opportunities for teachers to study, to lean and to share leadership. Linked to this is the recognition that leadership is beyond the heroic undertakings of one individual in a school – the headteacher or school principal. School principals and headteachers are only one source, albeit a critical source, of school leadership. There are many within the school communities who also contribute to the leadership of the school – teachers, school governors and pupils themselves – a much more distributed notion of leadership.

In Chapter 4, Kenneth Leithwood and Doris Jantzi present evidence to suggest that teacher leadership has an equal (albeit small) impact on student engagement as has principal leadership: a finding which has led them to question the decision of many governments to allocate leadership resources primarily to school principals. Nevertheless, they also strike a note of caution, arguing against a view that 'everyone is a leader' and suggesting instead that schools may benefit most from the leadership of a small number of easily identified sources.

A third element of the paradigm which is emerging is the notion of leadership as an *organic* activity, dependent on *interrelations and connections.* Successful local education authorities, as Kathryn Riley and colleagues argue in Chapter 7, based on research from the UK but also reinforced by findings from the US, are those which have a strong and vibrant partnership with schools. Their sense of purpose is characterised by a relentless focus on teaching and learning. They manage competing demands and expectations and contribute to a local climate of rising aspirations and expectations in which schools feel valued, and also to the promotion of professional debate and exchange. In many ways, successful leadership at the school and local level are mirror images of each other and have the potential to feed off each other.

Successful school leaders model professional values and aspirations, supporting teachers in meeting professional challenges and have clear goals about student learning. Embedded within this is the fourth element of our paradigm: the notion of *leading and learning.* As Mel West and his colleagues argue in Chapter 3, many schools are structured in ways that are antithetical to teacher learning, and which constrain student learning. The solution, they argue, is not just to find new ways of working but also to unlearn the old ones. For the school principal, the aspiration is towards self-knowledge. The difference between good and successful leaders and those who are less so, John MacBeath and Gus MacDonald argue, may depend to some degree upon their awareness of the state of their own knowledge and their willingness to explore new avenues and approaches (Chapter 2). School leaders, as other leaders, need the opportunity to enhance their capabilities to be more collaborative leaders and effective learners.

Whilst this book is not designed as a professional development manual, nevertheless, contributors offer a number of useful tools which can be used to develop the capacity of education leaders to be learners. Slightly tongue-in-cheek, Gus MacDonald has his own 'Medieval Management Matrix' (Chapter 2). Other helpful analytical tools have been described elsewhere (Riley and MacBeath, op. cit.). Kathryn Riley and colleagues provide a template intended to capture the core features which characterise effective intermediary authorities (Chapter 7). In Chapter 5, we are reminded of other conceptual tools, such as the Mintzberg notion of *strategic thinking,* the ability to see behind, beyond, through, in a process of continuous activity and reflection. Within this, there is the notion of *strategic conversation,* a conversation driven by rigorous thinking but which is as freewheeling as possible. According to Brian Caldwell, school leaders need to perfect the art of strategic conversation, taking opportunities in a variety of circumstances, to use discussions to move forward the boundaries of thinking within the school community. The notion of strategic intent and the art of strategic conversation are as important for intermediary authorities and teacher organisations, as for schools.

Within the notion of leading and learning is the *aspiration* to manage change in a *purposeful and planned way.* This does not negate our criticisms in Chapter 1 of traditional approaches to planned change with their over-confidence on linear improvement and on the 'manageability' of organis-ations. What we would argues is that *school development is a process that occurs as a result of the interacting influences of three sources of change – that which is deliberately planned; that which is naturally occurring in the life-cycle of organisations; and that which is unforeseen or unknowable in advance.* Change is not linear. It is unpredictable and difficult to embed.

School leaders need to recognise this, but also focus on the educational goals which they are trying to achieve, and how they are trying to achieve them. The direct link between school-based management and improved learning outcomes is weak, but the indirect links are strong, as Brian Caldwell argues in Chapter 5. Changes in school-management practices (such as the better use of resources, or a clearer sense of direction) can improve the professional climate of a school which, in its turn, has a direct impact on learning outcomes. School leaders have choices. In decentralised school settings headteachers, or school principals, have the autonomy to develop two very different leadership models: a more hierarchical and directive model, or a more inclusive more inclusive model which brings teachers in particular, and the local school community into the frame.

The complexities and unpredictability of change are demonstrated in Chapter 11. Logic might well suggest that in the case of Celebration School, a new well-resourced school, planned over a period of time, and drawing on the knowledge and expertise of leading experts in the field would be an unqualified success. The Celebration story (detailed by Kathryn Borman, Edward Glickman and Allyson Haag) illuminates not only the complexity of the change process but the different and often competing sets of realities within which schools operate:

- the community location: the social needs and the neighbourhood context;
- the policy context: set at the national and state level; and
- the internal workings: how the school perceives and acts upon its re-sponsibilities (Silver 1994).

The policy context and community location are all too frequently ignored (Riley and MacBeath, op. cit.), even when there is evidence that national policies have had a detrimental impact on schools (Riley and Rowles 1996; Riley 1998b). Assumed certainties about the internal workings of the school are challenged not only by extreme events but by more regular events, changes in the school's dynamics: new staff, the arrival of a particular cohort of students, the election of certain representatives to the school board.

The Celebration story also highlights the central issue of '*voice*'. Different stakeholders have different views about what counts as a good school, and even within stakeholder groups there is rarely uniformity. As we argued in the introductory chapter, notions of what constitutes a good school are contested, bound in culture and context, and change over time. Notions of what count as 'good' leadership are similarly contested and bound in con-text. Lejf Moos demonstrates the ways in which stakeholders from different countries (parents, teachers and pupils) give different weight to particular 'headship' qualities (Chapter 6). English parents, for example, associate 'assertive or strong leadership' with effective management of a school, whilst Danish parents value 'co-operative and collaborative' leadership.

There is the issue of *pupil voice* which comes out in a number of the contributions (Chapters 3, 4, 6 and 11): their voice in relation to school reform, and their voice as potential leaders within their own school com-munity. Whilst some students at Celebration School apparently struggled with their newly found status as independent learners – a key feature of the school's aspirations – the majority welcomed the challenging experiences opened to them, and chose to emphasise their role as team members, rather than individual players within the school. Given the opportunity, students appear willing to take a leadership role within their school. The evidence presented in this book suggests that students from the UK and Denmark commonly value an inclusive model of school leadership which involves them in decision-making (Chapter 6). At Sharnbrook Upper School (described in Chapter 3) the notion of learning and leadership was extended not only to teachers but students who become involved as active participants in the implementation of improvement activities, and as leaders within their own school.

And there is the issue of the *professional and teacher voice,* and within this, the role and function of teacher organisations – usually cast in the role of defender of the status quo. The pressing question is: can teacher unions balance their twin aspirations to be agents for improvement, as well as protectors of the rights and conditions of their members? In Chapter 9, John Bangs, a trade union official himself, describes the attempts of the National Union of Teachers to shape the direction of the UK reform agenda and to influence teachers' practices. The potential and the aspirations exist, the reality is perhaps harder to achieve as Karen Seashore Louis, Patricia Seppanen, Mark Smylie and Lisa Jones indicate in Chapter 11, in their review of the American National Education Association's school-reform initiative: the KEYS programme.

As we suggested in Chapter 1, our intention in writing this book was to be heretical, integrative and international. We also hoped to demonstrate the rich tapestry of relational leadership for change, and to highlight the limitations of focusing on the school as the sole unit of analysis and change. The analysis of leadership for change presented by our contributors recognises the complexity of the task, as well as the range of variables involved. The chapters incorporate an expanded view of school change, challenging the view that designated leaders have the sole responsibility for, and influence, on change. There are many organisations and actors seeking to shape the direction of education and they carry with them different perceptions about what can be achieved and how. This book is only a beginning. Nevertheless, we hope that it offers insights into the ways in which leadership can be conceptualised, constructed and acted out.

References

MacBeath, J. (1998) (ed.) *Effective School Leadership: Responding to Change,* London: Paul Chapman.

MacBeath, J., Moos, L. and Riley, K.A. (1996) 'Leadership in a changing world', in K.A. Leithwood, K. Chapman, C. Corson, P. Hallinger and A. Hart (eds) *International Handbook for Educational Leadership and Administration,* The Netherlands: Kluwer Academic Publishers, pp. 223–50.

Riley, K.A. (1998a) 'Creating the leadership climate', *International Journal of Leadership in Education* 1(2): 137–53.

—— (1998b) *Whose School is it Anyway?* London: Falmer Press.

—— (2000) 'Leadership, learning and systemic reform', *Journal of Education Change.*

Riley, K.A. and MacBeath, J. (1998) 'Effective leaders and effective schools', in J. MacBeath (ed.) *Effective School Leadership: Responding to Change,* London: Paul Chapman.

Riley, K.A. and Rowles, D. (1996) *Learning from Failure,* London Borough of Haringey.

Silver, H. (1994) *Good Schools, Effective Schools,* London: Cassell.

Index